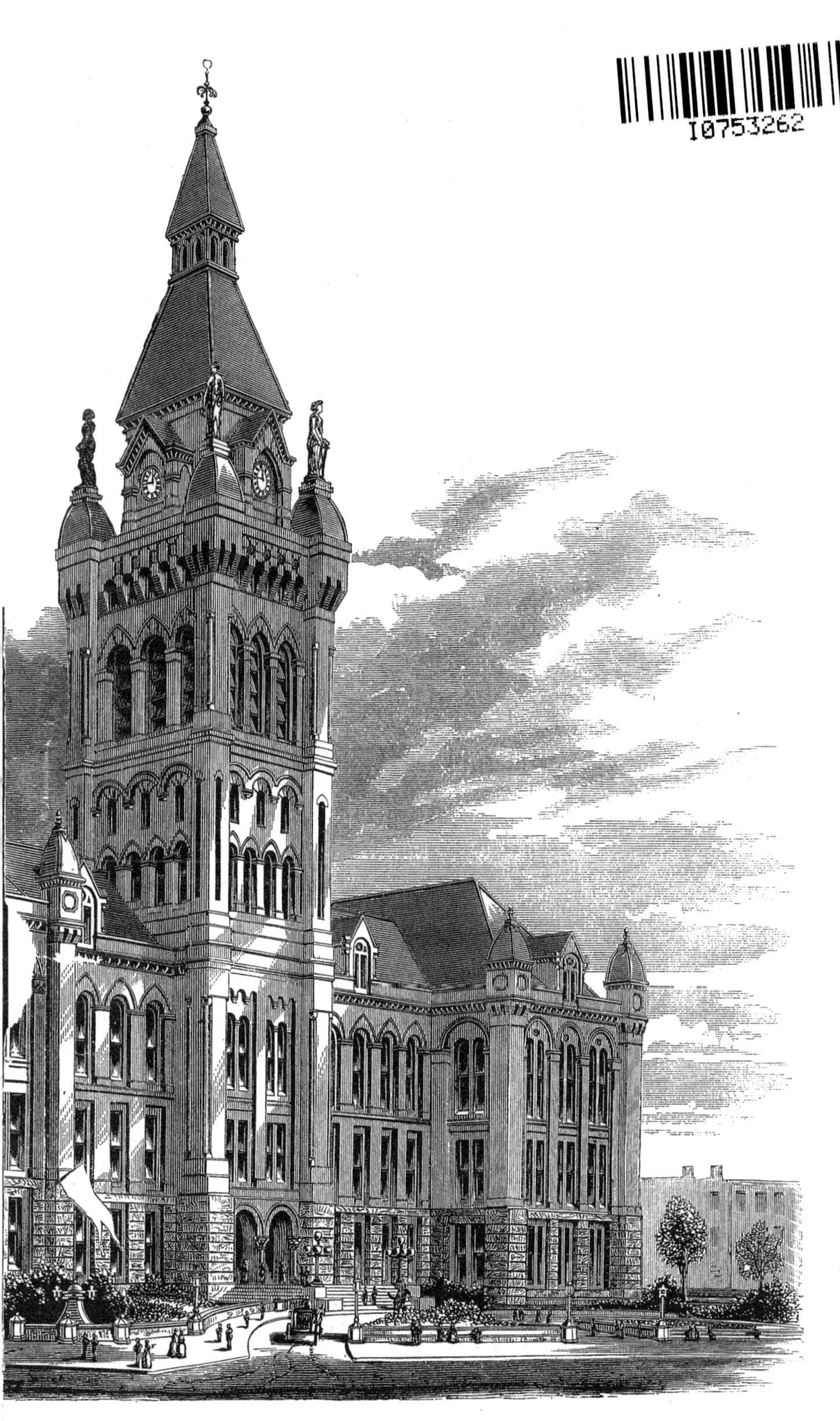

MEMORIAL

OF THE

CITY AND COUNTY HALL

OPENING CEREMONIES,

BUFFALO, N. Y.

EDITED AND PUBLISHED BY F. F. FARGO.

BUFFALO, N. Y.:
THE COURIER COMPANY, PRINTERS.
1876.

TO

JAMES M. SMITH,	GEORGE S. WARDWELL,
PHILIP BECKER,	DENNIS BOWEN,
JAMES ADAMS,	GEORGE W. HAYWARD,
ALLEN POTTER,	ALBERT P. LANING,
JOHN NICE,	JASPER B. YOUNGS,

BOARD OF COMMISSIONERS FOR THE CONSTRUCTION OF THE

CITY AND COUNTY HALL,

BUFFALO, N. Y.,

THROUGH WHOSE GOOD JUDGMENT, PRACTICAL KNOWLEDGE, AND ECONOMICAL MANAGEMENT, AS WELL AS BY WHOSE UNTIRING EFFORT AND UNSELFISH DEVOTION TO THE PUBLIC INTEREST, THE PEOPLE—AS IS CONFIDENTLY BELIEVED—HAVE SECURED A BUILDING AT LESS COST THAN HAS BEEN EXPENDED FOR ANY SIMILAR STRUCTURE IN THIS COUNTRY, THIS WORK IS MOST RESPECTFULLY INSCRIBED BY

THE PUBLISHER.

PREFATORY.

USAGE has sanctioned the well established custom of commemorating important events, whether occurring in the life of individuals, or the history of nations. The completion of the City and County Hall of Buffalo, is no ordinary occurrence for the people of Erie County. The object of this volume is to present to the public a compilation, arranged in convenient form, for reference and preservation, of such facts and papers as were developed on the occasion of the completion of the building. They consist of an elaborate description of the Hall, a history of its construction, an authentic account of the ceremonies observed in its formal opening and the valuable and highly interesting historical papers which were suggested and prepared in connection with its dedication and occupancy, by distinguished citizens, and old residents of Buffalo. The work also contains an impressive sermon by Rev. Dr. Heacock, especially addressed to the legal profession. An appendix is added, containing the civil list of the City of Buffalo, and the County of Erie, from their organization to the present time, together with other historical and statistical data of great value and interest to all who are concerned in the local affairs of the City and County. A beautiful and truthful engraving of the Hall, covering two pages, adds largely to the value of the work, and the diagrams of the several stories convey a correct knowledge of the internal arrangement of the structure.

Trusting that these pages will, in some measure, subserve the purpose of their design, in placing within the reach of every resident of the City and County, a record of an important local event in this the Nation's Centennial Year, they are submitted to the judgment of the public. F. F. F.

BUFFALO, *April*, 1876.

CONTENTS.

INTRODUCTORY.

One hundred years ago, Western New York was an unbroken wilderness. Dense forests grew, and ferocious wild beasts roamed unmolested, where now are cultivated fields, thriving towns and populous cities. The busy streets, broad avenues, and beautiful parkways of to-day, were then but rugged Indian trails, leading from the wigwams to the hunting-grounds, and fishing resorts of the red man.

In 1772, one hundred and four years ago, the Provincial Assembly of New York, organized the county of Tryon, which embraced all that portion of the State lying west of the city and county of Albany. In 1784, the name of the county was changed by legislative enactment, from Tryon to Montgomery, but the boundaries remained unaltered. Five years thereafter, or in 1789, Montgomery county was divided, by creating the county of Ontario, which embraced all that portion of the State lying west of Syracuse. Thirteen years later, or in 1802, the county of Genesee was organized, embracing all, or nearly all, the territory of the State west of Genesee river. Another subdivision was made in 1808, when Niagara county was formed and became the most westerly county of the State.

In 1821, the southern portion of Niagara county was set off and organized as Erie county, with boundaries substantially as they exist at present. Although Erie county had no legal existence until 1821, yet, practically, its history reaches back to 1808, at which time Niagara county was created, with the village of Buffalo, as the county seat. As a matter of course, official documents and records affecting that portion of Niagara, embraced in the new county of Erie, were left and still remain in the Buffalo office.

An association known as The Holland Land Company, being the owners of a large portion of the territory of Western New York, took the first step in 1801, towards founding a town on the present site of Buffalo, in causing a survey to be made, and a plat to be prepared, and gave to the proposed settlement the name of New

Amsterdam. Canandaigua and Batavia were the two principal settlements in Western New York at that time. Rochester was unknown—even the "blazed trail" through the forest from Canandaigua to Batavia did not take the Flour City in its course.

About this time an unusual inclination to "Go West" was developed in New England. The tide of emigration spread over the State, and Western New York was ultimately occupied by the sturdy yeomanry from the Atlantic seaboard whose decendants now constitute the intelligent population of a greater portion of the Empire State. Buffalo gained its full share of the new comers from eastern settlements, and grew apace. At the breaking out of the war of 1812, its population was about 1,500.

Its prosperity was somewhat impeded by an untimely visit from the British soldiery in December, 1813, who crossed the Niagara river at Black Rock, and destroyed the entire town by fire, with the exception of two dwellings. This check to the growth of the place was only temporary. The village was soon rebuilt, its dimensions enlarged, and its stability and future prosperity fully assured. The raid and fire brands of the British reduced its population to less than 1,000, but it soon retrieved its losses, and in 1820, numbered over 2,000. In 1825, it counted over 5,000 residents, and, in 1830, it boasted of nearly 8,000.

In 1813, New Amsterdam was incorporated by act of the legislature as the "Village of Buffaloe." The trustees named in the act, neglecting to organize, the law became void, and a new act was passed for a similar purpose the following year. The same fate attended this second effort to incorporate the village, and a third act was passed in 1816, from which period dates the corporate existence of the "Queen City of the Lakes."

In 1832, the place had grown to that importance which justified further promotion, and it was incorporated as a city, with a mayor, common council, and other necessary city offices. The charter has frequently been amended to meet the demands of increasing population and growing wealth, which have signally marked the history of the city. Its population has increased since its first incorporation as follows: 1832, 10,000; 1835, 15,000; 1840, 18,000; 1845, 30,000; 1850, 42,000; 1855, 74,000; 1860, 81,000; 1865, 94,000; 1870, 118,000; 1875, 140,000; and in 1876, probably 150,000. The same ratio of increase until the close of the present century, or until 1901, the centennial of the founding of Buffalo, will give the city a population of more than 500,000.

THE

CITY AND COUNTY HALL.

A DETAILED STATEMENT OF ITS INCEPTION, CONSTRUCTION AND COST, WITH A BRIEF DESCRIPTION OF THE STRUCTURE.

ITS INCEPTION.

It cannot be truthfully said that, hitherto, the city of Buffalo has been extravagant in its public buildings. With a population of more than one hundred thousand, and a wealth equal to that of most any city of its size, it has for several years continued in the occupancy of indifferent structures, until a suitable building—one commensurate not only with the present wants of the people, but for many years in the future—could be provided. The question of erecting such an edifice had often been discussed, and various plans had been submitted to attain the object, yet nothing positive was accomplished in the matter until the year 1870, when the project took definite shape by the introduction in the Common Council, on the twenty-first day of November, by Alderman John Pierce, of the following resolution:

"*Resolved,* That the Mayor, Comptroller, City Clerk, Gibson T. Williams, Esq., and James M. Smith, Esq., be and are hereby appointed a committee to take into consideration the project of building a new City Hall, and the expediency of including in the estimates for the next year the sum of fifty thousand dollars, enabling the city to commence the erection of the City Hall."

This resolution, on the motion of Ald. Evans, was referred to the Committee on Finance. On the twelfth of December, 1870, the Finance Committee reported in favor of its adoption, and it was adopted without division.

At a meeting of the Common Council, held on the twenty-fourth of December, 1870, the Finance Committee submitted a report, signed by all the members thereof, recommending the construction of a building to accommodate city and county officers, and recommending legislative action authorizing the appointment of a commission to procure a site, and construct such building. This report was also adopted by the Council without division.

THE COMMISSION.

On the twenty-first of April, 1871, the Legislature passed an act entitled "An act in relation to the location and erection of public buildings for the use of Erie county and the city of Buffalo." Messrs. James M. Smith, Dennis Bowen, Albert P. Laning, Jasper B. Youngs, and Allen Potter, were appointed by the governor a Board of Commissioners to select a site for, and erect such buildings, and on the twenty-second of May, 1871, the commissioners reported to the Common Council that they had selected Franklin square, bounded by Franklin, Eagle, Delaware and Church streets, as the site. On September 18, 1871, the Council adopted an ordinance setting apart the square named. In May, 1872, the following gentlemen were added to the Commission, in pursuance of an act of the Legislature, viz.: James Adams, Philip Becker, John Nice, and George S. Wardwell.

On the ninth of May, 1873, Mr. James M. Smith, Chairman of the Board of Commissioners, sent in his resignation as a member thereof, and Mr. George S. Wardwell was elected chairman in his stead, Mr. Geo. W. Hayward being elected commissioner in place of Mr. Smith.

At a meeting of the Common Council, held October 16, 1871, the Board of Commissioners, in compliance with a resolution previously passed by the Common Council, submitted a communication estimating the cost of the proposed public buildings at $772,000.

On the twenty-second of October, 1873, the commissioners sent a communication to the Council, giving the "original estimate" in detail, the amount footing up $799,734. To this was added an "amended estimate," as follows:

Additional for granite in place of local stone.............	$222,500
Additional for granite setting..........................	26,000
Additional for hard wood floors in place of white pine....	5,000
Additional for wainscoting of black walnut in place of pine base..	14,000

Additional for veneered doors in place of solid	$10,000
Additional for hard wood casings in place of pine	45,000
Additional for washbasins in rooms	5,000
Additional for heating	25,000
Additional for finishing hard wood throughout	10,000
Additional for anchors	5,000
Additional for laying and additional cost of brick	25,000
Additional for principal iron stair-case	3,000
Additional for gas fixtures	5,000
Additional for Superintendent's salary	7,000
Total	$407,500

This would make the total cost, as finally agreed upon, $1,207,234. On the twelfth of April, 1875, the legislature passed an act amending "An act in relation to the location and erection of public buildings for the use of Erie county and the city of Buffalo," by which it was provided that one-half the expense incurred in erecting said Hall, and completing and furnishing the same ready for use, should be borne and paid by the city of Buffalo, and the other half by the county of Erie, and all expenses to be incurred after the erection and completion thereof, for repairing, warming, lighting, and care thereof, should be borne and paid by the city and county in the same proportions.

This act also provided that the whole amount to be expended by the commissioners should not exceed one million four hundred and fifty thousand dollars. Also, that the commissioners should complete all the duties assigned them within six years from the time of their first meeting.

THE ARCHITECT.

The Board of Commissioners met on the second of May, 1871, and organized by electing James M. Smith, Esq., chairman. On the nineteenth of June Mr. Bowen moved that a committee of two be appointed to prepare and report plans, and procure the services of a capable architect to assist them. Messrs. Bowen and Laning were appointed such committee.

On the twenty-fifth of April, 1872, it was reported that Mr. A. J. Warner, of Rochester, had been selected as architect, that his plan had been accepted, and a contract entered into with him, which contract had been signed by all the commissioners. By the terms of the contract Mr. Warner was to receive $24,000 for furnishing the plans, specifications, working-drawings, &c.

MISCELLANEOUS.

From a report made by the Building Commission, the following general information is gleaned :

JULY 18, 1871.—The chairman was authorized to enter into a contract with S. H. Fields, for his services as Superintendent of the City and County Hall, at a salary not exceeding $2,500 per annum. Notices were also directed to be published requesting samples of stone to be furnished by the first of September, and inviting tenders for stone for the foundation walls.

Proposals for foundation stone were received from Lewis F. Allen and Nicholas Uebelhoer. The proposition of Mr. Uebelhoer was accepted at $6.50 per cord, delivered.

A proposition was received from the Akron Cement Company, to furnish cement at $1.00 per barrel, which was accepted.

AUGUST 17th.—The chairman was authorized to contract with Mr. J. Gallagher to excavate and remove the earth for the basement and foundation walls, at a sum not exceeding twenty-seven cents per cubic yard.

OCTOBER 7th.—On motion of Mr. Laning, the superintendent was authorized to contract for the quick lime for this season at ninety cents per barrel. This contract price was afterwards reduced to 88 cents.

OCTOBER 18th.—On motion of Mr. Bowen, the chairman was authorized to advertise for proposals for furnishing stone to be used in the construction of the building.

NOVEMBER 17th.—The following propositions for stone accompanied with samples were received:

Clough Stone Company, North Amherst, Ohio, one dollar per cubic foot, unwrought.

Worthington & Son, Amherst stone, ninety-five cents per cubic foot, unwrought.

Conieff & Dee, Onondaga gray marble, one dollar per cubic foot, unwrought; wrought, one dollar and fifty cents; wrought and set in wall at one dollar and seventy-three cents; wrought and set in wall in gross for $250,000. They would also furnish the Oswego brown stone, wrought and set in the walls in gross for $225,000.

Lyman Baker, Berea Stone Company, Ohio; Berea stone, wrought and set in wall in gross for $278,000.

Bodwell Granite Company, Hallowell, Maine; unwrought granite, $3.25 per cubic foot; wrought and set in wall, $3.65; unwrought, in gross, $149,500; wrought, in gross, $422,500; wrought and set in the wall, in gross, $474,500.

M. H. St. John and George Mark, Clark's Island granite, wrought, $3.10 per cubic foot; unwrought, $1.00 per cubic foot; unwrought, in gross, $130,000; wrought, in gross, $403,000.

DECEMBER 19, 1871.—On motion of Mr. Bowen, the chairman was authorized to contract with J. S. & F. H. Youngs for quick lime, at eighty-seven and one-half cents per barrel. Also that the exterior of the City and County Hall be constructed of granite.

On motion of Mr. Laning, the chairman, Mr. Bowen, and the architect were appointed a committee to contract with Messrs. Mark and St. John, to furnish and deliver granite from their quarry at Clark' Island, cut in accordance with the plans and specifications, under the direction of the architect, upon the basis of 130,000 cubic feet for $360,000, the price to be increased or diminished in proportion to the quantity required. The chairman and Mr. Bowen were also authorized to contract with Brush Bros. for all the brick required, on such terms as to quantity and price as they might deem expedient.

MARCH 27, 1872.—The chairman reported that a contract had been executed with Brush Bros. for all the brick required—2,000,000 to be delivered at six dollars per thousand, and the balance at the market price at the time of delivery, but the price not to exceed at any time $7.25 per thousand.

On motion of Mr. Bowen, the chairman was authorized to contract for the iron columns at a price not exceeding seven cents per pound.

APRIL 25, 1872.—The chairman also reported that he had executed a contract with Dunbar & Howell for the iron columns—those in the basement to be delivered at six cents per pound, and those in the upper stories at six and one-half cents per pound.

OCTOBER 11, 1872.—Mr. Cooley S. Chapin was appointed superintendent in place of S. H. Fields, and Addison P. Mason, clerk, in place of Frederick Masten.

OCTOBER 21st.—On motion of Mr. Adams, a committee consisting of the chairman, and Messrs. Wardwell and Bowen was appointed to procure models of the statues to be placed on the tower.

DECEMBER 31, 1872.—The chairman reported that a contract had been executed with Mr. Berger, of New York, to furnish the models for the statues.

On motion of Mr. Bowen, the chairman and Messrs. Becker and Youngs were appointed a committee with authority to purchase or contract for the purchase of the lumber required in the construction of the Hall, and provide a place for storing it, and cause it to be insured.

MARCH 12, 1873.—The chairman reported that a contract had been executed with Scatcherd & Belton to furnish the lumber required in the erection of the building.

On motion of Mr. Bowen, a committee consisting of the chairman and Messrs. Wardwell and Laning was appointed, with authority to contract for the construction of the statues to be placed on the tower. An estimate of the cost of constructing these statues was invited from Messrs. Batterson & Co., of Hartford, Conn. The price fixed by them for executing them was $22,000. The committee executed a contract with Messrs. Mark & St. John, the contractors, for furnishing the granite of the building.

APRIL 8, 1873.—Mr. Adams offered a resolution that the plan of the City and County Hall be so modified and changed that the exterior surface of the stone above the first story, which, according to the plan heretofore adopted should have a rock-finish, shall be dressed in the style known as six-steel-cut work, provided the contractors for furnishing such stone shall assent to such change, and contract to furnish such stone in the last-mentioned style, at a rate and price not to exceed two dollars per square foot on the surface, for the additional cutting of the stones to be caused by such change, and exclusive of openings. The resolution was adopted, and the chairman was authorized to execute a contract with Mark & St. John in accordance therewith.

SEPTEMBER 2, 1873.—On motion of Mr. Bowen, a resolution was adopted directing that the frames of the roof be constructed of the best kind of pine timber, and that the chairman and superintendent be authorized to purchase such timber at the best rate procurable.

The chairman and Messrs. Adams and Bowen were appointed a committee to examine into and report upon the best manner of heating and ventilating the building.

DECEMBER 19th.—The chairman and Messrs. Bowen and Hayward were appointed a committee to procure estimates of the cost of doors, sash and stairs.

The following is a summary of the prices paid for materials:

Brick, $6@7 per thousand.
Cement, $1.00 per barrel.
Excavating foundation. 27 cents per cubic yard.
Foundation stone, $6.50 per cord.
Granite prepared for setting, $2.77 per cubic foot.
Granite, dressed surface for all above first story, and not included in former contract, $2.00 per sup. foot, exclusive of openings.
Iron beams, 5 to 7½ cents per pound.
Iron columns, 6 to 6½ cents per pound.
Lumber, basswood plank, $18.00 to $20.00 per thousand feet.
Roof timber, Norway pine, $23.00 per thousand feet.

Flooring, Georgia pine, $45.00 per thousand feet.
Black walnut lumber, $66.25 per thousand feet.
Quick lime, 87½ cents per barrel.
Sand and gravel, $1.50 per yard.

Ground was first broken for the foundation of the building on the twenty-first of August, 1871.

THE GENERAL PLAN

is in the form of a double Roman cross, with the bases adjoining, and extending longitudinally north and south; the body of the cross covering a space of 114 × 255 feet; the arms and heads having each 20 feet projection and 52 feet front. The building thus has a total length of 295 feet, and a total width of 158 feet. The principal facade is on Franklin street, and in the center of the same is the clock and bell-tower, projecting 12 feet from the main building. The tower is 40 feet square at the base, and rises to a height of 268 feet. In the center of the Delaware street front is also a projection of 5 feet in depth and 45 feet in length.

THE EXTERIOR.

The first or principal story is finished with rock-face or pointed work, with heavy chamfers and tooled margins, and heavy projecting water-table. The second and third stories are finished with pilasters between the openings, with molded or carved capitals, receiving the arches and lintels of the windows. The jambs of all the windows have deep reveals, with heavy imposts and mullions. The pilasters between the windows in the second and third stories. in the pavilions at each end of the building, extend the full height of both stories. At each external angle of the pavilions there is a turret six feet square, with a pointed curved roof.

The cornice of the building is finished with plain modillions, and surmounted with a parapet 74 feet above the ground. The roofs are steep, covered with slate, and rise to a height of 105 feet from the ground. There is a turret, eight feet square, at each of the four corners of the large central tower, extending to a height of 166 feet from the ground, and surmounted with a pedestal. Upon these turrets stand the statues.

The main cornice of the tower is on a line with the base of the pedestals, and is finished with projecting parapets, supported by corbels. Next above the cornice, and between the statues, are the pediments containing the clock faces, nine feet in diameter, one on each side of the tower. The clock section has a curved slate roof, 27 feet in height, and next above is the lantern, or observatory, 200 feet above the ground. Upon the observatory is a pointed, curved roof of slate, similar to that on the turrets at the corners of the pavilions.

The bell section of the tower is 120 feet above the ground, and has three openings on each side, five feet wide and eighteen feet high, finished with heavy molded louvres.

In the first story, in the center of the building, both on the Franklin and Delaware street fronts, are the entrances, consisting of double-arched openings, enriched by detached columns with carved capitals. Each opening is nine feet wide and seventeen feet high. In front of each entrance is a fine flight of stone steps, rising six feet from the ground to the principal floor. The steps are flanked on either side with abutments and pedestals for lamps, and at the top of the steps, just outside of the building, is a stone platform 16 x 25 feet.

THE INTERIOR.

Entering the Franklin street front, the visitor is admitted to the lobby, which consists of the first story of the tower, and is 28 x 30 feet, entirely of stone. From the lobby he passes, through sash doors, to the main corridor, 24 feet wide and 150 feet long, running longitudinally in the building. The second and third stories also each have a corridor of the same dimensions, extending in the same direction; and with these corridors all of the rooms and offices communicate directly.

THE BASEMENT

of the building is intended chiefly for the storage of fuel and the apparatus for ventilating and heating, the latter being done by steam. There are rooms for the temporary detention of criminals awaiting trial. The basement is eleven feet high, dry, and well lighted. In the hall or entrance-way from Delaware street in the first story, is the grand stairway, occupying a space 36 x 40 feet, starting on either side, and passing two-thirds of the way up, towards the west, to a landing 10 x 36 feet, and returning thence, in the center, towards the main corridor. There are two intermediate landings in the stairs, each nine feet high. The stairs continue to the third story on the same plan, and are constructed of iron.

FIRST FLOOR.

The offices with which the public have the most to do are located on the first floor, as a matter of convenience. As will be seen by the diagram on page 18, the county offices of Sheriff, Clerk, Treasurer and Surrogate, are grouped in the northern end of the building on this floor, while the City Treasurer, Comptroller, Clerk, Street and Water Commissioners, occupy a corresponding position at the other end. The number and designation of the offices are given upon the tablet in the vestibule, or lobby, as follows:

No.	Office	Size
No. 1.	Water Commissioners	19 x 38
" 2.	City Treasurer	43 x 49
" 3.	City Comptroller	43 x 63
" 4.	City Clerk	43 x 49
" 5.	Street Commissioner	19 x 38
" 6.	Witnesses	19 x 38
" 7.	Grand Jury	19 x 38
" 8.	Sheriff	19 x 38
" 9.	County Clerk	43 x 94
" 10.	Surrogate	43 x 49
" 11.	County Treasurer	38 x 38

SECOND FLOOR.

The second floor is chiefly given up to the courts and court officers. There are no less than five large and commodious court rooms, most elegantly furnished with all the modern improvements and conveniences of halls of justice. Connecting with these are private apartments for judges' chambers, while the Clerk of the Superior Court, and the City and District Attorneys are conveniently by, as well as the necessary jury rooms and the Law Library. The Mayor, City Assessors and City Engineer are also upon this floor.

The diagram on page 19 will show the location of the several offices on this floor, which are in size and numbered as follows:

No.	Office	Size
No. 12.	Mayor's Office	38 x 38
" 13.	City Engineer	43 x 49
" 14.	Superior Court	43 x 63
" 15.	Assessors' Office	43 x 49
" 16.	District Attorney	19 x 38
" 18.	City Attorney	19 x 38
" 21.	County Court	43 x 49
" 22.	Supreme Court	43 x 49
" 23.	Law Library	43 x 63
" 26.	Superior Court	19 x 38
" 27.	Clerk Superior Court	28 x 28

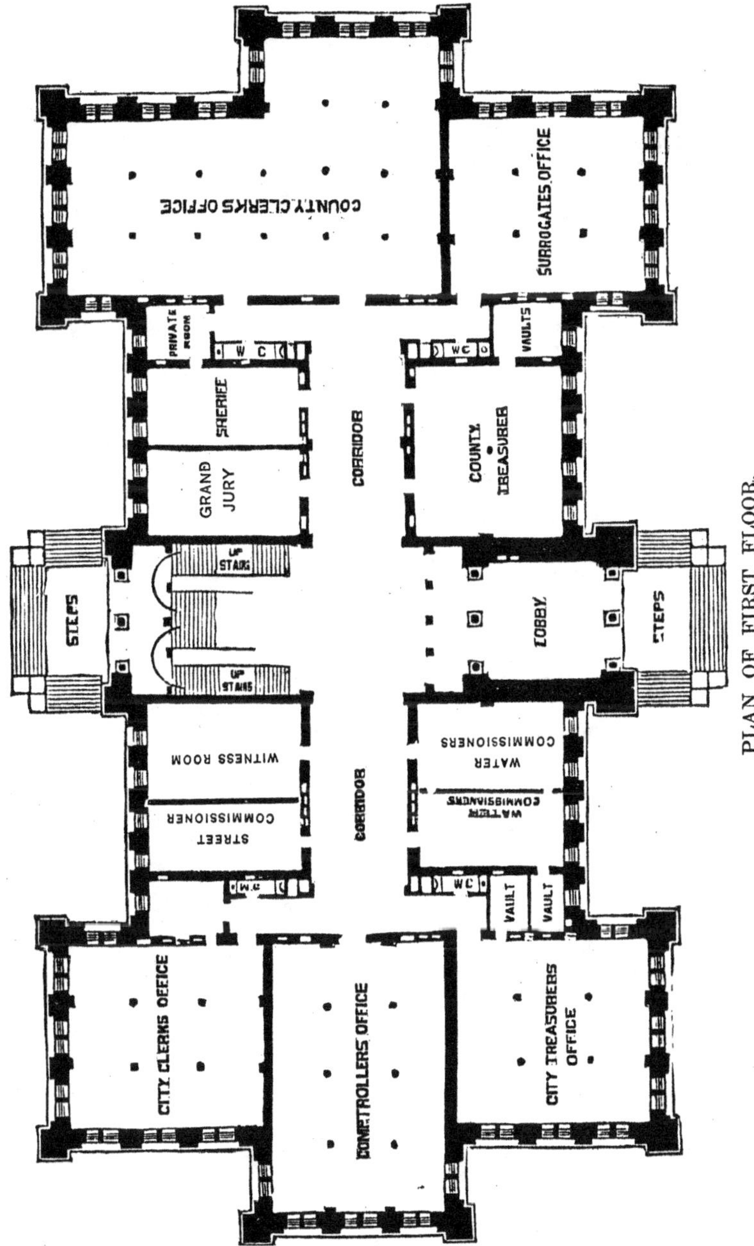

PLAN OF FIRST FLOOR.

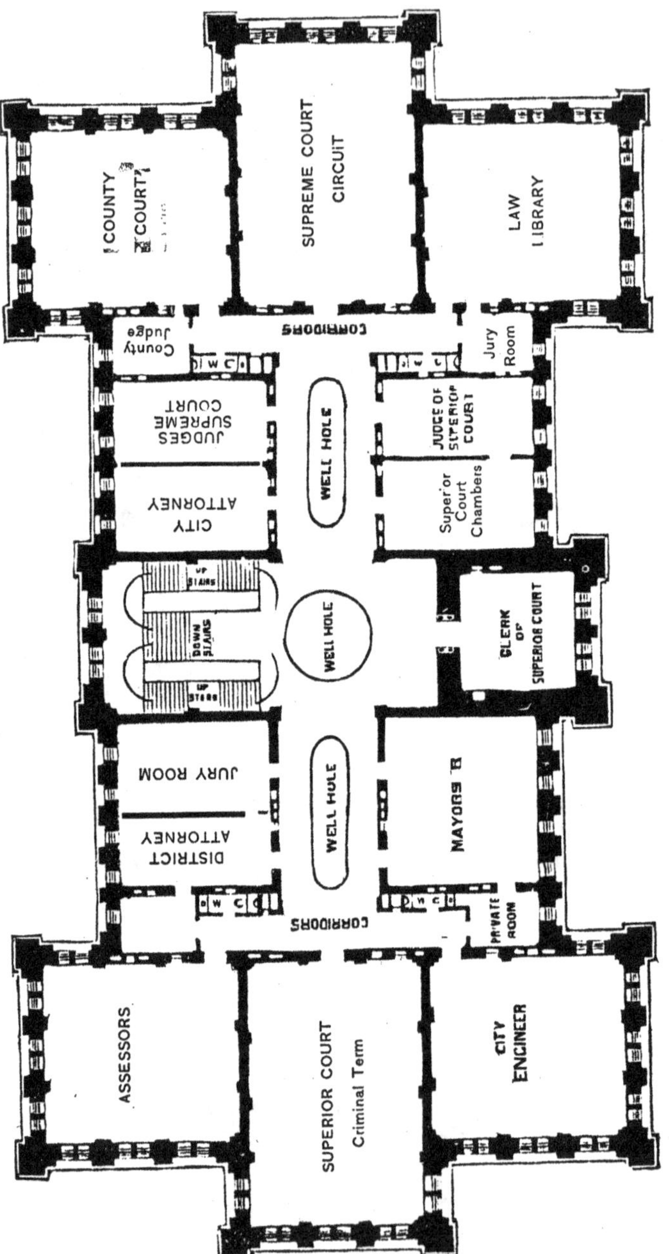

PLAN OF SECOND FLOOR.

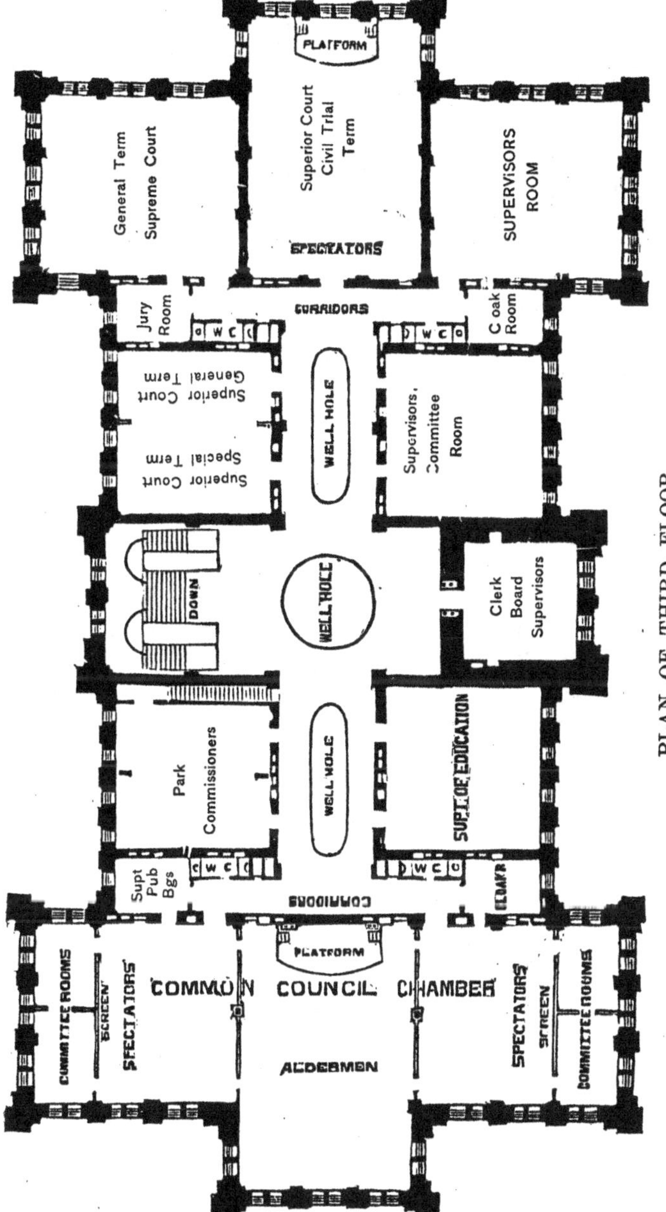

PLAN OF THIRD FLOOR.

THIRD FLOOR.

Upon the third floor are found the Common Council Chamber, which for elegance, beauty and elaborate finish, is not excelled, if equaled, by any similar room in the country, and the Board of Supervisors' Chamber, together with two large court rooms, and the office of the Superintendent of Education, the Park Commissioners, and Clerk of Board of Supervisors. The diagram on page 20 will show their location. They are numbered as follows:

No. 28.	Superintendent of Education	38 × 38
" 29.	Common Council	43 × 145
" 30.	Superintendent of Buildings	11 × 17
" 31.	Park Commissioners	38 × 38
" 32.	Superior Court, General Term	38 × 38
" 33.	Supreme Court, " "	43 × 49
" 34.	Superior Court, Civil Trial "	43 × 63
" 35.	Supervisors	43 × 49
" 36.	Supervisors' Committees	38 × 38
" 37.	Clerk of Board of Supervisors	28 × 28

COURT RECORD.

A fourth tablet on the wall in the vestibule gives the following information for those having business with the several courts:

SUPREME COURT.

Circuit	No. 22, second story.
Special Term	" 32, third story.
General Term	" 33, third story.

SUPERIOR COURT.

Judges' Chambers	No. 26, second story.
Criminal Term	" 14, " "
Civil Trial Term	" 34, third story.
General Term	" 32, " "

COUNTY COURT.

Court Room	No. 21, second story.

SURROGATE.

Room	No. 10, first story.

THE BOARD.

A marble tablet similar to those in the vestibule is placed upon the wall at the second intermediate landing of the grand stairway, and bears the following inscription:

CITY AND COUNTY HALL.

Commenced, 1871..........................Completed, 1876.

BUILDING COMMISSIONERS.

JAMES M. SMITH, *Chairman* (resigned).
GEORGE S. WARDWELL, *Chairman.*

JAMES ADAMS,	PHILIP BECKER,
DENNIS BOWEN,	GEORGE W. HAYWARD,
A. P. LANING,	JOHN NICE,
ALLEN POTTER,	J. B. YOUNGS.

A. J. WARNER, *Architect.*
S. H. FIELDS, *Superintendent* (resigned).
C. S. CHAPIN, *Superintendent.*
J. DRUAR, *Assistant. Superintendent.*

The floors of the corridors, and parts of rooms intended for public use are paved with marble tiles. In the floor of the main corridor, in the second and third stories, is an octagon well-hole, 20 feet in diameter, in the center of the building, and one 8×36 feet on each side of the same, affording light to the space below from large sky-lights, placed above them in the roof. The first story is plastered on the brick arches of the floor above, with plaster moldings run on the trains. The second and third stories have plaster cornices in all the rooms, with molded panels in the ceilings.

LAYING THE CORNER-STONE.

The corner-stone of the new building was laid on the afternoon of June 24, 1872, with appropriate ceremonies, on which occasion there was a grand turn-out. A procession, consisting of the Military, Masonic lodges, the Building Commissioners, Judges of the Courts, members of the Common Council and Board of Supervisors, City and County officials, &c., formed at three o'clock, and marched along Franklin street to the Terrace, across the Terrace to Main, up Main to Tupper, down Tupper to Delaware, and down Delaware to the scene of the ceremonies.

THE CORNER-STONE,

which is located in the south-east corner of the tower, is of granite, two feet eight inches by five feet, and two feet deep. It bears the following inscription:

A. L.	MASONIC	A. D.
5872.	EMBLEMS.	1872.

JUNE 24.

The ceremonies commenced with prayer by the Rev. Dr. Lord. The band then played "Hail Columbia," after which came an eloquent and appropriate oration by the Hon. Geo. W. Clinton.

ORATION BY THE HON. GEORGE W. CLINTON.

This mighty concourse of people of our city and county marks an epoch in our history; and the solemn ceremony which it is about to witness will be long remembered with pride and pleasure. The laying of this corner-stone and the completion of this Hall can afford no aliment to vanity, and must redound but incidentally to individual honor. The people of our county and city have decreed the performance of this most necessary and creditable work, and to them collectively are due the glory and the praise. The voice of an indignant people, jealous of its reputation, and incensed by long delay, has burst forth in command, and this great fabric is founded and will soon attain its carefully prescribed perfection.

Excuse me for remarking that we mistranslate, irreverently, I think, the Roman saying, *Vox populi vox Dei*. The Romans, like all the heathen ancients, had their *Dii majores* and *Dii minores*, their greater and their lesser gods. They did not know and worship the one true God. They recognized and sacrificed to a host of deities, both male and female, personifying the phenomena and forces of nature, and her productions, and the genius of every human avocation, and art and science. The voice of the people was not to them the voice of God—of *the* Divinity, but that of *a* divinity—majestic, solemn, fearful, full of portent and of power. Its utterances, like the souls of their deities, might be swollen by fury and by malice. Is there in the world's history a recorded cry so fiendish as that one, priest-prompted, of the Jewish populace: *Release to us Barrabas. Crucify him! Crucify him!* What utterance was ever so God-like as the exclamation of our Saviour in his mortal agony: Father, forgive them, for they know not what they do. The motive, the occasion, the soul that finds expression in it, determine the quality of the voice. I am not, I never have been, I believe, a flatterer of the people. Seldom have I recognized the voice of a God in the voice of a people. By our compact, majorities govern, and their behests are entitled to obedience though they fail to command respect. At the dread outset of those times which, more thoroughly than those of the revolutionary war, did try men's souls; when crafty rebellion, fully prepared, broke out into insulting war; when treason threw off all disguise and appeared, like Satan, vast and threatening—then the voice of the true men and women of the North and East and West, unanimous for war in defense of the Union and of liberty, had a tone and compass and majesty, such as the Roman might imagine in the thunder of his fabled Jove. But when that weary, cruel war was over, and the last hope of traitorous ambition was blasted, and the foul rebellion was crushed by our armed heel—when the joy of the crowning triumph was tempered by pity, and, from the very soul of our wounded, exhausted, suffering people, gushed forth the cry for amnesty—was not that magnanimous cry prompted by the spirit of Christ himself? Did not the still small voice within, inform us that the voice of the people was indeed the voice of God?

I cannot say, my friends, that you have done grandly, for you have made no memorable sacrifice to attain this point of honor. Your voice in this was worthy; but I pray that you may speak further and in the same noble strain. Much, very much, remains to be done to secure to Buffalo the good and glory she should aspire to. She looks not like a queen upon the lakes; but she has yet to win the crown. With the most moderate exertion, wealth must flow to her, and she is now very strong, and must grow stronger and stronger. May she never use that strength tyrannously! May she never confound money with wealth, nor rate anything higher than true honor. Her true glory is to be sought in the happiness of her citizens, and that happiness can be assured only by virtue and by knowledge. The dangerous classes must not only be deterred by swift condemnation and inexorable punishment, but must be led from their evil courses by scholarly and priestly hands. How can this rich, proud city deride and condemn the coarse pleasures of the poor, while it does not freely extend to them purer, higher ones. No duty is more exalted, none, in this city, is more urgent, than the extension of pure pleasure and its free diffusion among all classes. It may be mainly sensuous, and it may inform the intellect, but, whatever its character, it tends to regulate the passions and to chasten the heart.

OUR PARK IS A GRAND STEP

in this direction. But this generation, I am free to say, cannot confidently claim that it has done its whole duty while Buffalo remains so undistinguished in science, in learning, in taste. There yet remains to be laid, in order to insure true glory, and, so far as possible, internal order and peace and safety, to our dear city, more corner stones than I can think of; free libraries, and churches, and schools of learning, of art, of the fine arts, of science. The Historical Society should be made assuredly permanent and have a building of its own. The Academy of Fine Arts should have a building of its own, augment its examples of painting and sculpture, secure copies of all the antique statues, and branch forth into schools. The Society of Natural Sciences deserves to be sustained. It can have no assurance of safety for its possessions, no security for its own existence, while it lives at sufferance in the Young Men's Association building. It has been said to me—it is a bitter shame, if true—that the General Hospital languishes for want of an adequate endowment. Speak out my friends, and declare that these weak beginnings of good things shall, for the honor of our city, be saved. And then why has not Buffalo an university? But I am weak and weary with longings for the good of my people and the honor of my city, and I can do nothing. Speak out then, O my people! Be assured that the voice of the people is the voice of God, of our God, only when it is Christian—and is most glorious when it commands works and deeds of charity.

But I will dismiss these vain regrets and idle longings, and rejoice with you, my people, in this auspicious beginning of a long series of popular triumphs. Thank Heaven, we are at least relieved from a most just reproach. When this building is completed, the great county of Erie and our unfinished city will cease to be accused of parsimony and meanness, and want of a proper pride, and of a just sense of the magnitude and worth of their own public and corporate affairs. A noble and commodious edifice will rise here, not by force of a wish, nor in a single night, like Aladdin's palace—but by the persistent toil of swarms of skilled free laborers. Its proportions seem just and beautiful.

IT WILL BE A TRUTHFUL BUILDING.

It will not present to the public eye a splendid front, and hide from it a shabby rear. Standing, as it will, in this ample space, it will show on every side, a truthful face. From turret to foundation stone it will be an honest building. Its construction gives no opening to the plunderer of the public. No slave, no taskmaster, no enforced labor will disgrace this work; no unrewarded sweat will temper its mortar or bedew its ponderous stones. It will bring content and happiness to many willing workmen; it will result in well-won fame to the architect and his assistants; it will impose no unnecessary or unfitting burden upon the tax-paying public; it will confirm and heighten the respect and esteem in which our people hold the Commissioners.

This is not a fit occasion for many words; and if I err in recalling briefly some facts in our history which seem to me fruitful of hope and incentives to humble and energetic action, you must pardon me; and you will please to remember that, in referring more particularly to the city, I bear in mind the fact that the residue of the county has, from the beginning, been so intimately connected with it, that they have acted and re-acted upon each other, and have felt alike and together the changes of the times.

Here was the western end of the long house of the Iroquois. Here the Senecas kept the western door while the Mohawks guarded the eastern. That house remained continuous and unbroken in 1776; and, excepting only the villages of the Senecas, and the patches of land rudely cultivated by the squaws, our country was nearly all dense forest. A few armed explorers had passed through its outer edge, a petty trading post had been planted near it, and few, if any, white intruders had built log huts within our bounds. The country west of us was a wilderness, and our lakes were coasted only by infrequent canoes of the Indians, and by the batteaux of traders; they were, indeed, but desert wastes of water. Councils were usually held in the open air, though their fires, on some occasions, were lighted in a wigwam. The matters of debate were few, and gave but rare occasion for a rude eloquence scarcely worth recording. Romance depicts the red man as noble, and his life as poetical and happy. In truth his life is brutal, and his character far from heroic. I have no tears to shed for him. Unless he becomes civilized, he is not worth preserving, and, in the course of nature, must give way to the wiser, stronger, more energetic white man.

In 1796 there were four houses in Buffalo. In 1801 a small portion of what is now Buffalo was surveyed into village lots, called New Amsterdam, and offered for sale. In 1807 it contained about twelve dwellings. In April, 1813, it was incorporated as the village of Buffalo. Its charter as a city was enacted in 1832. Its population, in 1830, was 8,868; in 1835, 15,561; in 1845, 29,973; and now it exceeds 120,000 largely. In 1822 it was a petty village, and, so far as we can judge, would, at this time, be but little more, had it not been for the

COMPLETION OF THE ERIE CANAL IN 1825.

The growth of half a century has been marvelous; a growth not merely in population, but in everything that adorns and exalts individual life, and gives influence to a municipality. What, if it puts its advantages to use, and exerts its enormous strength judiciously, may we not reasonably hope from the next half century?

But in all this progress, in the very hurry of it, and in the looking forward to more favorable times, nothing creditable was done in the way of providing buildings for municipal purposes. The people were contented with disgraceful make-shifts, probably because they looked upon them as mere temporary expedients, and anticipated the coming of this good time. What a noisy, inconvenient abomination the old Court House is! Time has not made it, cannot make it, venerable. And there is our jail—a thing to be mentioned, but not discussed. And what can be said of the so-called new Court House, except that it is of brick, that it is said to have been constructed with an eye to close economy, and that it gave to the courts and county officers more room, and temporary relief from an almost insufferable pressure. What honorable citizen of Erie County has been able, for many years, to look upon these buildings without blushing?

I do not know where our village fathers held their councils; but very likely they held them, sometimes, in the old school-house, and sometimes in some store or office. In 1836, the city offices and the Council Chamber were upon the Terrace, in the wooden market, which abutted on Main street, and which was, by the judgment of a competent court, abated as a public nuisance. It was a long and indescribably ugly building. The basement was devoted to the sale of vegetables and poultry, the next floor to butchers' stalls, and the attic to our city fathers. This fragment of a mean market was our City Hall, until the corporation acquired full title to this fine square, and adapted the dwelling-houses on the east side to its own proper uses. The square was, in great part, a cemetery, and contained the remains of many well-remembered dead, but of far more of whom no name nor memory survived. All were reverently removed to and interred in other places, and the city took full possession.

In 1848, when our population exceeded 30,000, I, in my impatience, wrote this paragraph: "Our city has no buildings for judicial or civic purposes worthy of its position, or adequate to its wants; but the times seem fully ripe for planning and commencing a City Hall commensurate with the present palmy condition, and worthy of the assured destiny of Buffalo." The times were not ripe for such an enterprise. It was necessary that, from that day to the enactment of the law under which this building was commenced,

WE SHOULD GROAN AND SUFFER AS WE HAVE

under almost intolerable inconvenience and unbounded shame. We counseled and agitated, and devised abortive schemes to secure fit public buildings. But strong men among us were wisely patient. In the fulness of time they appealed to a people who scarcely needed to be persuaded, and the result is the commencement and assured rapid completion of a building worthy of the city and the county.

We must needs die, and are as water spilt on the ground that cannot be gathered up again. Our material works must follow us. They must decay and perish. Flatter not yourselves then that you are building for eternity. You may reasonably doubt whether you are building for a remote posterity. In the early ages of the world men thought to defy time in their works, and to cope with Heaven. Hence the impious attempt at Babel; hence the massive pyramids. Such vain ambition, such foolish hope, no longer stir the souls of men. The great truth is now admitted that time (*edax rerum*) will eventually destroy all our material works, and that he who would build for eternity must build with the spirit. Matter is earthly and evanescent; the spiritual immortal. Prospero spoke truly in saying:

"And like the baseless fabric of this vision,
The cloud-capped towers, the gorgeous palaces,
The solemn temples, the great globe itself,
Yea, all which it inherit, shall dissolve,
And, like this insubstantial pageant faded,
Leave not a rack behind."

True it is that the plan of this great building concurs with its materials to resist decay; that it will combine, in an extraordinary degree, architectural beauty and massive strength. Built, as it will be, of brick, of iron, and of granite, fire cannot consume it, and it would seem that the tooth of time itself can hardly waste or weaken it. But, though the lightning may not rive, nor the earthquake shatter it, and though the tornado fail to dislodge its topmost stone, the ever-wasting hand of time must wear, disfigure and destroy it. The little lichens will eat into the solid rocks, however smooth; mosses will rest upon and draw sapping moisture to it; and wild grasses will find place for their roots in its crevices and crannies. And then, too, no art can stay the invisible forces which war against our works, and, sooner or later, drag them to the ground. Varying moisture and unequal temperature, expanding here and contracting there, the faces and parts of the strongest building, grind, loosen, disintegrate; and it is folly to believe that the wit and strength of man can give birth to an edifice which will effectually resist those powers which are continually degrading the solid hills and casting down the mountains, and which would make the whole earth a plain were they not counteracted by the volcano and the earthquake. But I anticipate the desolation or the abandonment of this great building from no such causes. In fancy I rejoice in the coldness, and perchance the scorn with which a near posterity will regard what we look upon as a wonder—the eagerness with which they will demolish or surrender it to humbler uses. Progress, eternal progress in everything that ennobles and purifies, is the law of every portion of our race where civilization rests upon Christianity. No generation can make assured provision for the needs and tastes of its successors. Were it otherwise there would be stagnation, corruption, moral and intellectual death.

WE SHOULD THANK THE GOOD GOD

for the restless energy, the longing for the further and the higher which He has implanted in our nature. No age ever has been, none ever will be, able to declare to a coming one: "I have attained the highest height, and you can go no higher—repose here and be content."

We are justly proud of our rural population, of their intelligence and virtue, of their liberal thrift, of their ready skill, of the advances in their art and science, by which they make their lands teem with plenty. But their children, and their children's children, to the very end of time, will eschew old ways and old routine, strike out new paths to agricultural success, and open new springs of happiness and wealth. We have great reason to be proud of our young and vigorous city; but the very best of our achievements will pale and fade into forgetfulness in the fresh splendors of our posterity. The passing generation have deserved high commendation, and the coming one—thank Heaven!—cannot. will not prove a sensuous idler; it will far overpass our goal; it will lay deep and strong foundations which we have barely planned; it will be wiser, more virtuous and more liberal than we are, and will shed new lustre on our dear city.

Is Buffalo and Erie county to be content for a century, for half a century, with this noble building as the seat of city and county authority and office? Are they, after their prodigious growth, to suddenly cease growing, and that, too, while the whole country is advancing in prosperity and every city is expanding? What great public building in the United States of America has proved sufficient for the requirements of three successive generations? The City Hall of the city of New York when freshly built, was greeted by its people with rapture as a triumph of architecture, and as sufficient for the city's uses for many ages. What is the judgment of the present generation, and what is the fate of that squat, dingy, worn mass of marble? The Capitol of the nation, once deemed ample and magnificent, has been almost obliterated by addition and superadded richness. Our own State Capitol, fraught with so many great and precious memories, is doomed. One year ago this very day the corner-stone of the new Capitol was laid, and in a few years not one stone of the old Capitol will be left upon another.

Would that the great tower of this new City and County Hall were completed, so that we could rise

TWO HUNDRED FEET ABOVE OUR PRESENT LEVEL

and stand in the observatory, and look around and ponder on the scene. Let us attempt it in imagination! We barely glance at the collossal statues of Justice, Industry, Commerce and Art, for we see the very things themselves in the Heavens above us and in the landscape at our feet. Afar off in the south, blue hills end our extremest view and border the rich expanse of plain, dotted with happy villages and towns which curve eastward and far north. The whole country is alive with labor and with the rush of business and of pleasure. The roads radiating from the city in all directions are thronged with vehicles of every kind. On the west, and apparently so near that we can chuck a biscuit into it, sleeps Lake Erie, the first, if not the fairest of the great chain of mountain lakes—an opening to a navigation of thousands of miles, a ready access to a country almost as broad as Europe and richer far. It is whitened by not unfrequent sails, and above its green waters float the frequent trains of smoking propellers hurrying to and from our harbor. The fair coast of Canada confronts us smilingly. The mighty Niagara like molten silver gleams northward till its own curvings hide it, but the stationary cloud beyond betrays its presence and marks the position of the great Cataract, and proclaims the fact that commerce by water, beyond Buffalo, is barred by nature. On every hand, in every direction upon the land, you see long trains of cars impelled by locomotives toward and from us. You notice, too, that commerce, impatient of the least delay, is bridging, the wide, deep, rushing river. The harbor, once so contracted, is now capacious, and saucy little tugs are pulling leviathans hither and thither with admirable dexterity and ease. And there, too, packed with long lines of freighted boats, towed by slow-paced horses, is the Erie canal, the populator and best friend of the great West—the author, and so far as we know, the sure conservator of the fortunes of Buffalo.

In the city at our feet, here and there, quick puffs of steam, and great steady columns of smoke indicate the positions of our great furnaces and forges, and workshops and factories of innumerous kinds. And then the beauty of the city; but I will not dilate on that. We rest content with stating that the main features of this wondrous picture are the growth of less than fifty years, and that no cause of that growth has ceased to act; that each and every cause of it is now acting, and must act for ages with increasing power. And then we may well remember that the business men and capitalists of Buffalo have enlarged their views. Time was when every one seemed to believe that commerce—meaning thereby the carrying trade—was all in all to Buffalo. Now the great truth that our manufactures are a chief aliment of true commerce is conceded, and they are justly regarded as of cardinal importance to our city. Time was when our citizens seemed to value the Erie Canal rather than the commerce of which it is chief conduit. Now, the beneficence of railroads as instruments of commerce is appreciated, and we seek by them to add to our resources and extend our trade.

I would not undervalue the past, but it seems clear to me that it was not equal to the present power, in energy, in judgment. We have been blessed by Providence. Corn will soon be scattered, and wine and oil be poured upon our selected corner-stone, as emblems of His blessings. Our history seems to show that our material prosperity is largely dependent upon the things themselves. At the outset of her career, corn flowed through Buffalo westward to sustain the crowds of emigrants; but, in a few years, the tide of cereals was reversed, and Buffalo enriched by it. Of late years the wine has become a favorite object of culture and covers our shores and islands; and the wine that gladdens and refreshes the heart of man must find here a central market. We must be content to rely upon the Mediterranean for the oil of the olive; but Buffalo can draw to her that more precious and abundant oil which God stored for us, in the beginning, in the depths of the rocks; and we must not rest until this, too, is achieved.

I fear that I am detaining you too long; but I cannot close without reminding you again that only the spiritual is immortal, and that the house eternal in the heavens is not made with hands, but by the exercise of virtue. This building is now to be consecrated to Justice, and to official fidelity and honor. It will be indirectly devoted to God's worship, a temple for the illustration of these virtues. If they be wanting, His favor will be withdrawn, and the temple will be worse than vacant. May justice never be delayed or bartered here; may honor and honesty and unwearying vigilance guard here our people's rights and interests. The place is holy. My soul is sick with the long delay of punishment, the probable immunity of corrupt judges and plunderers of the public. I pray that the people may watch over these buildings, and if sellers of justice and public cheats should establish here their tables and their trades, who could blame a justly indignant people for scourging them out with knotted chords? May God grant that the corner-stone which will now be proven square, level, and plumb, remain so forever; and that all the work which shall be done in this building may stand at the last day the tests of the unerring square, and level, and plumb.

Then followed the Masonic ceremonies, Grand Master Christopher G. Fox officiating.

INSCRIPTION ON THE PLATE.

The following is the inscription on the plate deposited under the corner-stone:

The Corner-stone of this City and County Hall, erected by the City of Buffalo and County of Erie, was laid in Masonic form by the M. W. Christopher G. Fox, Grand Master of Masons in the State of New York, on the day of the Festival of St. John the Baptist, A. L. 5872, A. D. 1872.

His Excellency, Ulysses S. Grant, President of the United States.
His Excellency, John T. Hoffman, Governor of the State of New York.
His Honor, Alexander Brush, Mayor of the City of Buffalo.
The Commissioners of the Building, James M. Smith, Chairman; Dennis Bowen, Albert P. Laning, Allen Potter, Jasper B. Youngs, James Adams, George S. Wardwell, John Nice and Philip Becker.
Architect—Andrew J. Warner.
Superintendent—Samuel H. Fields.
Clerk—Frederick Masten.

DEPOSITED IN THE BOX.

The following is a list of the articles deposited in the box under the corner-stone.

1. Gold, silver, nickel and copper coins of the United States, of the latest coinage.

2. DAILY NEWSPAPERS.

Buffalo Commercial Advertiser, June 22d.
Evening Courier and Republic, June 22d.
Buffalo Evening Post, June 22d.
Daily Buffalo Demokrat, June 22d.
Daily Buffalo Volksfreund, June 22d.
Buffalo Telegraph (Sunday edition), June 23d.
Buffalo Daily Courier, June 24th.
Buffalo Express, June 24th.

3. BOUND VOLUMES.

The New York Civil List, 1871.
Manual for use of the Legislature of the State of New York, 1872.
Charter and Ordinances of the City of Buffalo (last edition), 1867.
Buffalo City Directory, 1871.
City Comptroller's Report, 1871.

4. PAMPHLETS.

Report of the Superintendent of Education of the City of Buffalo, 1871.
Statistics of the Trade and Commerce of Buffalo, 1871.
Proceedings of the Board of Supervisors of Erie County, 1871.
Revised Charter of the City of Buffalo, 1872.
Third Annual Report of the Buffalo City Water Works, 1871.
Second Inaugural Message of Hon. Alexander Brush, Mayor of Buffalo, 1872.
Annual Report of the Superintendent of the Fire Department, 1871.
Thirty-sixth Annual Report of the Executive Committee of the Young Men's Association, 1872.
Second Annual Report of the Buffalo Park Commissioners, 1872.

5. MANUSCRIPTS.

Sketch of the History of Buffalo, and of the Commission for the erection of the City and County Hall, written in the German language.
Sketch of the History of the City and County Hall, written on parchment, in the English language.
Civil List of the City and County officers for the year 1872, written on parchment.

BY THE MASONS.

6. The Constitution and the General Regulations of the M. W. Grand Lodge of the Most Ancient and Honorable Fraternity of Free and Accepted Masons of the State of New York.

7. A Tableau of the Masonic bodies in the County of Erie, June 24, 1872.

8. A list of the officers of the Grand Lodge for the year 1872.

After the conclusion of the prescribed Masonic rites, came a prayer by the Rev. L. J. Fletcher, an artillery salute, the playing of "America" by the band, and the whole closed with the benediction by the Rev. E. R. Bishop, Rector of St. Luke's church.

THE STATUES.

The four granite statues which adorn the tower were procured at the cost of $22,000, as noted above. The first of these—"Justice"—was raised to its place on the fifth day of July, 1875, and the others within a few days after. The positions occupied by the several figures are as follows:

North-east corner—"Justice."
North-west corner—"Mechanic Arts."
South-east corner—"Agriculture."
South-west corner—"Commerce."

The statues are 16 feet in height, they weigh 14 tons each, and were cut from solid blocks of granite.

HEATING AND VENTILATION.

The heating apparatus, furnished by the Walworth Manufacturing Company, is very complete, and in the arrangement many miles of pipes have been used. The details of the system are quite complicated, and would scarcely be of interest, but a general idea may be gained from the following:

The building is warmed throughout by steam, on the principle of indirect and direct radiation. Indirectly by placing the radiating surface in the basement, and connecting the same with underground plenums, these being supplied with air taken in and forced through by means of two ten-inch fans, operated by the engines, the capacity being sufficient to send through the building 136,000 cubic feet of air per minute. In summer these same fans take in cold air, and force it through the pipes in all parts of the building. This produces a thorough ventilation in all the rooms, which are furnished with registers for taking off the vitiated air into flues which terminate in the attic, from whence it is conducted out through the ventilators on the roof. Registers are also placed in the rooms for the purpose of letting off the air in case it should become overheated. As an auxiliary to this method, direct radiators have been placed under the windows in the different rooms, to be used only in extreme cold weather. The air is taken through cloth screens, so as to eliminate all particles of dirt and dust. The fans can be used so that, if necessary, the air in all parts of the building can be changed once in twenty minutes. The necessary pipes, &c., were put in by Messrs. Hart, Ball & Hart, as agents for the Walworth Company.

THE METHOD OF LIGHTING

includes chandeliers from two lights up to thirty-six, and of a patent designed expressly for this building. There are also a requisite number of desk-lights, side-lights, &c., in the different apartments. The chandeliers are bronzed, with gold and black ornamentation, and when lighted up they certainly look very handsome. These fixtures were furnished by Messrs. Mitchell, Vance & Co., for which firm Messrs. Glenny & Co. are agents. There are two large and graceful standards at each of the entrances, for exterior illumination. These standards are each about sixteen feet in height, and are furnished with five globe lights, each sixteen inches in diameter, the whole finished in silvered bronze.

APPEARANCE OF THE INTERIOR.

The opinion is generally concurred in by those who have visited the building, that it is one which does not "show for what it is worth" on the outside. And now, that it is open to the public, the prevailing sentiment will be that of astonishment both at the magnitude and elegance of the interior. Unquestionably, a much better idea of the extent of the structure can be obtained from the main floor of the first story than from any outside view. The spacious halls, the massive stairways and columns, the marble floors, the finely adorned walls, the handsome black walnut wood-work, must all be seen to be appreciated. One ornamental feature, which may properly be mentioned in this connection, has a peculiarly fine effect. Standing on the main floor and looking up, the spectator will see that the openings under the sky-lights have been filled with beautiful stained glass set in iron frames. This work was done by Messrs. Booth & Reister, of Buffalo.

IN THE FURNITURE

of the different offices, an admirable uniformity is preserved. All the furniture—and the fixtures of every kind—being made according to special plans, this general uniformity is the result. The wood-work, including all the office-desks, chairs, &c., is of black walnut, and what is not walnut—the railings, the finishings of the stairs, &c.—is bronzed. The iron columns throughout are also finished in bronze, and thus all the metal work shows as one quality of metal. In many of the offices are large glass partitions, and the doors are also of glass. It is a gratifying fact that all this fine furniture was made in Buffalo, by Messrs. Weller, Brown & Mesmer, Joseph Churchyard, Clarke, Holland & Co., A. Cutler & Son, and A. Raeker. The carpets upon the floors of the General Term Court room and Mayor's office are of the finest quality of Wilton. In all other rooms, the carpeting is of the kind known as American Brussels, of simple pattern, and the colors harmonizing well with the woodwork.

The name of each office or department is inscribed over its door in large gilt letters, traced on the glass, and each office is numbered. Four large tablets upon the walls near the Franklin street entrance give the "directory" of the offices, also in gilt letters. The corridors are all finished with marble wainscoting, that in the lobby being of the Tennessee and Glens Falls varieties, and inlaid with a border of encaustic tile. The floors in the corridor are marble, and in the first story this extends into the different offices to the line of the counters. The walls in the corridors and offices, and the ceilings are beautifully tinted.

THE COMMON COUNCIL CHAMBER

has been fitted up in the most elegant manner. The central part is exclusively for the members and heads of departments, the seats of the aldermen being arranged in two semi-circles, facing the President's desk, which is raised, and looks considerably like a modern pulpit. In front of this is the City Clerk's desk, and on either side are smaller ones, to be used by newspaper reporters. Back of the President's seat is an entablature, projecting from the wall twelve feet, and forming a lobby for the members' entrance. On either side of the business portion of the Chamber is the space allotted to spectators, provided with comfortable settees, and with sufficient capacity for some six hundred persons. Three tastefully-ornamented committee rooms are located at each end of the Chamber. All the black walnut wood-work is elaborately carved, and ornamented with gold lines. Altogether, the city fathers are to be congratulated upon the elegant and comfortable arrangement of their new apartment.

In the General Term Court room are hung the portraits of about twenty deceased eminent jurists and members of the bar in Buffalo and vicinity. There is also a full-length portrait of the first Mayor of Buffalo, Dr. Ebenezer Johnson, in the Mayor's office.

THE TOWER-CLOCK AND ELECTRIC DIALS.

Among the many features of general interest which the building possesses, not the least is the wonderful system of electric clocks, running in direct connection with the great clock in the tower. There are no less than twenty-eight of these time-pieces, or dials, as they are called, connected with the tower-clock by three electric circuits. By this arrangement absolute uniformity of time is insured throughout the building. This system of electric clocks, is believed to be the largest in the country, and since it has been put in operation, has worked in the most satisfactory manner. The tower clock and electric dials were furnished by Messrs. E. Howard & Co., of Boston, and the work of putting them in was under the supervision of Messrs. Joseph Vreeland and J. Hamblet, employees of the firm. It is claimed by them that the tower-clock is the heaviest and most substantial in the country.

ITS SUPERIORITY TO THE CLOCK

in the New York *Tribune* building consists in the fact that the latter does not strike the hours. The striking apparatus in the City Hall is considered perfect. The hammer weighs one hundred pounds, and the bell—cast by Jones, of Troy—four thousand seven hundred pounds. It is a rather fatiguing experience to climb up the narrow iron winding stairway of the tower to the lofty point where the clock is located, but whoever does so is well repaid, on examining the complicated mechanism. The dials, which look but little larger than the full moon from the streets in the immediate vicinity, are in reality nine feet in diameter. The reflectors by which the light of the gas-jets is concentrated upon the dials, are singularly shaped, with special reference to utilizing all the light. The pendulum is of the kind known as "compensating," and it has a two-second movement. It is hung upon very delicate steel springs, and its movements are made with the utmost precision. Instead of the old "dead-beat" escapement, a far more nicely-adjusted combination is used, being the new gravity-escapement, invented by Mr. Dennison, of London, and introduced in this country by Mr. Howard. The gravity-escapement is connected with the pendulum by simple yet delicate mechanism. By this escapement the motion is communicated to the pendulum. On each side of the pendulum-rod is an iron arm suspended from one end obliquely. As the escapement-wheel turns, small pins on its axes raise the free end of one of these arms by means of levers. As the pendulum reaches the termination of its path, the arm is released, and its weight, pressing against the pendulum, drives it to the other side, where the operation is repeated. The motion is carried to the four dials above by a revolving iron rod. The arrangement for illuminating the dials is very complete, and is regulated by the clock itself. The valve through which the gas reaches the large burners behind each dial is turned by ingenious machinery. A small jet is kept burning all the time, but the amount of gas consumed is very trifling. Screws are so arranged as to turn on the gas at any hour desired. A reverse arrangement automatically turns off the gas at the proper time in the morning.

Since the clock was first set in motion by Mayor Becker, at four o'clock on the afternoon of February 5th, everything has worked satisfactorily. The clock, which has already become the standard of Buffalo time, is warranted not to vary, and a gentleman connected with the firm of Howard & Co. enthusiastically informed the Mayor that it would run with invariable correctness for fifty years, and then an expenditure of fifty dollars would put it in perfect order again.

FURNISHING MATERIAL.

The following is a complete list of the parties furnishing material, &c., for the structure.

The granite for the building, including the statues, was furnished by Mark & St. John, from Clark's Island, Maine.

The brick were furnished by Brush Brothers, of Buffalo.

The sand by Chandler J. Wells, of Buffalo.

The doors and sashes in the whole building were made by Weller, Brown & Mesmer, of Buffalo.

The wainscoting was furnished by Joseph Churchyard, of Buffalo.

The furniture and most of the work in the first story was furnished by Clarke, Holland & Co., of Buffalo. They also furnished the inside shutters.

In the second story by Joseph Churchyard.

In the third story by Weller, Brown & Mesmer.

The marble work has been furnished by John Crawford, of Buffalo.

Mr. Racker, and A. Cutler & Son, of Buffalo, have also furnished a portion of the furniture.

The lead pipe, paint and oil, by the Cornell Lead Company, of Buffalo.

The carpets by Adam, Meldrum & Anderson, L. H. Chester & Co., and Stewart Elder, of Buffalo.

The gas fixtures by Mitchell, Vance & Co., of New York.

The bell by Octavius Jones, of Troy.

The clocks by E. Howard & Co., of New York and Boston.

The plumbing by Irlbacker & Davis, of Buffalo.

The gas-fitting by Hart, Ball & Hart, of Buffalo.

The stone walks by C. H. Rathbun, of Buffalo.

The chairs by Weller, Brown & Mesmer; Schlund & Doll, and Mr. Bensler, of Buffalo.

The iron beams by the Union Iron Company, of Buffalo.

The iron columns by Robert Dunbar, of Buffalo.

The iron stairs, window grates and lamp posts by the Howard Iron Works, of Buffalo.

The safes by Hall's Safe and Lock Company, of Cincinnati.

The plate glass by the Star Glass Company, of New Albany, Ind.

The iron finish to the tower by the Niagara Bridge Works, of Buffalo.

The locks and door hinges by Valentine Brothers, of Buffalo.

The Cement by the Akron Cement Company, of Buffalo.

The conductor pipes by L. P. Beyer & Co., of Buffalo.

The lime by Youngs Brothers, of Buffalo.

The foundation stone by Nicholas Uebelhoer, of Buffalo.

The heating apparatus by the Walworth Manufacturing Company, of Boston.

The slating of the roof by John Galt, of Buffalo.

The slating of the tower by McSheffrey & Maxwell, of Buffalo.

The lettering of the glass over the doors by F. B. Scott, of Buffalo.

The lettering of the tablets in the vestibule by J. C. Rother, of Buffalo.

Jewett & Root, of Buffalo, furnished tin for roof.

W. H. H. Newman, of Buffalo, furnished copper for gutters as valleys.

Hurley & Stygall, of Buffalo, did the copper and tin work of gutter and roof.

Scatcherd & Belton, of Buffalo, furnished the black walnut and Georgia pine lumber.

Laycock Brothers, of Buffalo, furnished the Norway pine roofing timber.

Baker Brothers, of Buffalo, furnished the window weights.

E. Y. Kneeland, of Buffalo, furnished the special stair to the tower.

Mr. James F. Rowley has superintended the painting and finish of the inside work.

The foundation walls and a portion of the first story were laid under the superintendence of Thomas F. Reynolds.

The remaining portion of the walls was laid, and the plastering done under the superintendence of John Druar.

THE TOTAL COST.

The total amount of expenditures for the work up to the first of March, 1876, according to the Secretary's books, was **$1,328,675.78.**

It is believed that the total cost, after removing the old city buildings, improving and beautifying the grounds, and paying all incidental expenses, will be considerably less than the authorized appropriation by the Legislature of **$1,450,000.** This circumstance is so unusual that it deserves special mention, and reflects great credit upon the Building Commissioners.

FROM THE OLD TO THE NEW.

CEREMONIES OBSERVED IN LEAVING THE OLD BUILDINGS AND ENTERING THE NEW HALL.

IN view of the completion of the City and County Hall, the Common Council, at its regular meeting held on the twenty-eighth day of February, 1876, appointed a special committee, consisting of President A. S. Bemis, and Aldermen A. L. Lothridge, Nathan C. Simons, and Elijah Ambrose, and Clerk R. D. Ford, to make suitable arrangements for a formal occupancy of the building.

ACTION OF THE BAR.

Soon after the above mentioned action of the Council, Hon. G. W. Clinton, Chief Judge of the Superior Court, believing that some public demonstration should be made on the part of the legal profession in the matter, prepared and submitted to members of the bar the following paper:

"It is announced that on Monday, the 13th inst., the new City and County Hall will be open for the reception of all our Courts of Record. It seems to us impossible that the gentlemen of our benches and bar can bid farewell to the old Court House without a feeling of regret; and we venture to suggest the propriety of their assembling therein at two o'clock P. M., of Saturday next, for the purpose of a free interchange of memories and social intercourse.

BUFFALO, March 7, 1876.

To this document the names of a majority of the fraternity in Buffalo were soon attached, and a meeting of the bar, to consider the subject, was called, by notice in the daily papers, for Wednesday, the eighth of March, in the Clinton street Court House.

THE FIRST MEETING.

In response to the published call a largely attended meeting of members of the bar of the city and county was held for the purpose of making some arrangements preliminary to a proper observance of the abandonment of the venerable structures in which justice has for so long a series of years been dispensed, and the occupation of the splendid quarters provided for the courts in the new City and County Hall.

The meeting was called to order shortly after four o'clock, and Hon. James M. Humphrey elected chairman. Mr. George Gorham was appointed secretary.

Hon. H. S. Cutting, after the object of the meeting had been briefly explained by the chairman, moved that a committee of five be appointed to prepare a programme of exercises to be observed, and the motion was adopted.

Judge James M. Smith, referring to a paper which had been circulated among the members of the bar, said the explanation was due those who had not signed it, that it was drawn by Judge Clinton, and was intended only for the purpose of ascertaining whether the members were desirous of a public observance of the occasion or not. It simply contemplated that some meeting should be held for that purpose. After being quite generally circulated, the signatures to the paper evidenced that a large number of the lawyers favored the proposed celebration. The paper had thus accomplished its purpose, and on its heels this meeting followed.

Josiah Cook, Esq., was in favor of instructing the committee to have the proceedings wind up with a grand supper, at which the entire bar of Buffalo might unite.

E. Carlton Sprague, Esq., warmly seconded the idea of a banquet. Never had the members of the bar of Buffalo got together in a social way, and he believed it time that a more social feeling, which would be beneficial all around, was inaugurated.

Hon. J. M. Humphrey suggested that the committee of which the appointment had been already ordered would have their hands full, and he advised the appointment of a second committee to ascertain if a supper were advisable, and, if so, to arrange for it. Mr. Cook put this suggestion in the form of a motion, and it was carried. Some discussion was entered into concerning the proposed banquet. The project seemed to receive very general favor, and Monday night was suggested as the proper time for it.

Judge Smith read the paper, drawn by Judge Clinton, above referred to, and asked those present, who had not already signed, to attach their signatures to it if its contents contained nothing objectionable to them. He further stated that it was to be deposited with the Historical Society.

The paper was thereupon signed by those present who had not already done so.

The chair announced as the Committee of Arrangements, Messrs. H. S. Cutting, George Wadsworth, Spencer Clinton, W. C. Bryant and David F. Day; and as the Supper Committee, Messrs. E. C. Sprague, Josiah Cook, Asher P. Nichols, B. H. Williams and Wm. H. Gurney.

The meeting then adjourned to meet on Saturday, the eleventh inst., at 3 o'clock P. M.

THE PROGRAMME.

The Committee of Arrangements appointed on the eighth inst., subsequently published their report of the proposed programme, as follows:

The undersigned committee appointed at a meeting of the bar, held on the eighth instant, have arranged as follows, for taking suitable notice of the occasion of transferring the business of the courts from the old Court House to the new City and County Hall:

The members of the bar of the county are requested to meet at the old Court House, on Washington street, on Saturday next, at 3 o'clock in the afternoon.

Hon. George R. Babcock has consented to preside, and the following named gentlemen have been invited, and have consented to address the meeting: Hon. George R. Babcock, Hon. James Sheldon, Hon. George W. Clinton, Hon. John L. Talcott, and Hon. James M. Smith.

It is recommended that at the close of the proceedings, the meeting be adjourned to Monday morning next, at 10 o'clock, and that the members of the bar then proceed in a body to the new City and County Hall.

BUFFALO, *March* 10, 1876.

HARMON S. CUTTING,
GEORGE WADSWORTH,
SPENCER CLINTON,
DAVID F. DAY,
WILLIAM C. BRYANT,
Committee.

THE SECOND MEETING.

The adjourned meeting of Saturday, March 11th, was largely attended by members of the legal profession, and others interested in the proposed transfer ceremonies. It was called to order by the Hon. H. S. Cutting, who stated its object briefly, and what had been done by the Committee of Arrangements, of which he was chairman. He closed by nominating the Hon. George R. Babcock as chairman, which was carried unanimously. Mr. Babcock then took the chair, and Mr. George Gorham was chosen secretary.

Judge James Sheldon, of the Superior Court, having been requested to prepare some historical statements with reference to the early history of the county and the old Court House, submitted the following paper:

ADDRESS OF HON. JAMES SHELDON.

The old county of Niagara, of which Buffalo was the county seat, was organized by an act of the Legislature, passed March 11, 1808. The present county of Erie was not organized until 1821. By the act of 1808, the erection of a court house and jail in the village of Buffalo, or New Amsterdam, was authorized, provided the Holland Land Company should erect the same within three years and convey the sites to the county. The same act provided that the first Court of Common Pleas and General Sessions for Niagara county should be held at the house of Joseph Landon, in the village of New Amsterdam. In pursuance of the law, the

FIRST COURT HELD IN BUFFALO

was held at Mr. Landon's public house in June, 1808. It was a well known and established tavern-stand, built of wood and situated on inner lot number one on the south side of Crow, now Exchange, street, and a little east of Main street, where the easterly part of the Mansion House now stands, and was destroyed by the British and Indians at the time of the burning of the village in December, 1813. Augustus Porter, of Niagara Falls, was the first judge, and Erastus Granger, of Buffalo, and Zattu Cushing, James Brooks and Martin Prendergast, of Chautauqua, were the *puisne* judges. Asa Ransom was the first sheriff, and Louis Le Couteulx the first clerk of the county. Buffalo, at that time, was a mere hamlet, with but a few hundred inhabitants, and known only as a western frontier settlement. No court had, before that, been held in Western New York, except at Batavia, and the opening of the first term of court at Buffalo was an event of interest and importance.

In Turner's "History of the Holland Purchase," it is stated that "the attorneys of Niagara county, at the time of its organization, were Ebenezer Walden, Jonas Harrison, Truman Smith, John Root, Heman B. Potter, Allen Sharpe, Bates Cook and Philo Andrews. These are all that are recollected as practicing attorneys before the war of 1812." Jonathan E. Chaplin was here in 1812, Albert H. Tracy, James Sheldon and E. S. Stewart came in 1815, and William Hotchkiss, Thomas C. Love, Ebenezer F. Norton and William A. Moseley soon after.

In pursuance of the act of 1808, the Holland Land Company

ERECTED A COURT HOUSE

building and jail in the year 1810. The jail was built of stone, and was situated on inner lots 184 and 185, on the east side of Washington street, between Clinton and Eagle streets, where the Darrow block now stands. The British fired it when the village was taken, but it suffered little damage, and was rebuilt after the war. Our old citizens well remember it, fronting on Washington street, and surrounded on three sides by tall, wooden pickets, sharpened at the top and set firmly in the ground. It was demolished about the year 1834, when Benjamin Rathbun erected the present jail, of which he became, not long after, an occupant as a felon.

The Court House was a wooden structure, standing in front of the present Court House. The deed was executed by Wilhelm Willink and others, who composed the Holland Land Company, and who are therein described as residing in the city of Amsterdam, in the

REPUBLIC OF BATAVIA.

It was dated November 21, 1810, and recorded December 8, 1810, in Liber one of Deeds, at page 62, and conveys to the Supervisors of Niagara County, the property described as follows:

"That certain piece or parcel of land situate, lying and being in the village of New Amsterdam, being one-half of an acre on which the Court House in said village has been erected by the Holland Land Company and accepted by the judges of said county for the Court House of said county, conformably to the fourth enacting clause of an act of the Legislature of the State of New York passed March 11, 1808; the said half an acre of land to be laid out in a circle, the center of the Court House aforesaid to be the center of the circle according to a plan on the margin" of the deed. On reference to the record, the circle is seen, and its center is the center of North Onondaga street, now Washington street, directly in front of the present edifice. This point was the highest elevation of ground in the village of Buffalo, the land descending from it in every direction, and was undoubtedly chosen for a Court House site on account of its conspicuous situation.

JOSEPH ELLICOTT,

the agent of the Holland Land Company, chose to convey the ground in the form of a circle, but no reason has ever been assigned for such a curious proceeding.

The building was built of wood, plain in every respect, but proper for the purposes designed. In addition to its use as a Court House, it was the only place for public assemblages and was generally used for such purposes. The first church of any denomination organized in Buffalo, and which is the one now known as the First Presbyterian Church, was organized in that court-room on the twelfth of February, 1812, by the Rev. Thaddeus Osgood, an itinerant missionary. Judge Townsend, in his description of Buffalo in 1811, mentions "the *old* stone jail on Washington street and an unfinished wooden Court House;" and we find, by reference to the proceedings of the Board of Supervisors of Niagara County, which are on file in the archives of the Historical Society, that on the fifth of October, 1811, only a year after the buildings were accepted by the judges, it was voted that $500 should be raised by tax for the purpose of repairing them, and Nathaniel Sill, Jotham Bemis and Samuel Hill, Jr., were appointed a committee to superintend the work. This Court House continued to be used until its destruction by the British in December, 1813, when the

WHOLE VILLAGE WAS LAID IN ASHES.

In the spring of 1814, the people gradually returned to the village and commenced the work of rebuilding with great ardor. Buffalo was the headquarters of the army, and dwellings, stores and taverns were erected in great haste for the transaction of business and the accommodation of the public. A notice appears in the Buffalo *Gazette* of June 7, 1814, of which this is a copy:

"NIAGARA COUNTY CLERK'S OFFICE, SS:
Notice is hereby given that the Judges of the Court of Common Pleas of said county have appointed the house of John Brunson in the village of Buffalo to be the temporary Court House for said county.
May 23, 1814. ZENAS BARKER, Clerk."

The house referred to was the wood tavern then just erected where the Academy of Music now stands on Main street, and subsequently known as the Farmer's Hotel, kept for many years by Manning Case, who was succeeded by Philip Dorsheimer.

On the seventh of April, 1815, an act was passed by the Legislature authorizing the Judges of the Court of Common Pleas to order and direct the place at which courts should be held until a Court House was erected. In pursuance thereof on the twenty-ninth of April, 1815, the judges "ordered and directed that the courts should be held at the house of Gilman Folsom, at present occupied by Moses Baker & Co. in the village of Buffalo." This house was situate as nearly as can be ascertained, on the east side of Main street, between Mohawk and Genesee streets, and at that place all courts were held until the present edifice

WAS OCCUPIED IN 1817.

On the twenty-fourth of March, 1815, the Legislature authorized the supervisors of Niagara county to raise the sum of four thousand dollars, by taxation, for the purpose of building a Court House, and Samuel Tupper, then first judge, and Joseph Landon and Oziel Smith, were appointed commissioners to contract for and superintend its erection. No action was taken under that law, but another act was passed on the seventeenth of April, 1816, by which the State loaned to the county of Niagara the sum of $5,000, for the purpose of building a Court House, and appointing Joseph Landon, Samuel Tupper and Jonas Williams, Commissioners.

The village authorities had resolved that Washington street should be continued in a direct line through the circle on which Mr. Ellicott had erected the Court House, which left a segment of the circle on each side of the street. By some negotiation the county acquired the title to that part of the block bounded westerly by Washington street, northerly by Batavia street, and southerly by Clinton street, which is now, in part, occupied by this Court House, and the commissioners early in the spring commenced the work of building what was then considered the largest and most beautiful structure in Western New York. The remainder of the block fronting on Ellicott street was subsequently acquired by the county from Sheldon Thompson and others, for the purpose of erecting the present jail.

In the Buffalo *Gazette* of September 24, 1816, the following announcement appeared:

"The walls of the Court House, which was commenced in the early part of the season, are erected; we learn that the carpenter and joiner work of the building are progressing. If the house is finished in the style it has commenced, it will be an ornament to the village; uniting elegance with durability, and will be creditable to the judgment and taste of the commissioners."

Thus was commenced the venerable edifice in which we meet for the last time to-day. It was first occupied early in the year 1817, and the event probably attracted as much attention and elicited as much admiration as the occupation of the new City and County Hall in this centennial year.

THE COURT ROOM

was the same as now, except there was a gallery across the east end of the room for the use of spectators, which was removed in 1826. The stairway led directly up into the room from the hall below, and the jury rooms were finished off in the basement. In 1826, a general improvement of the building was undertaken. The gallery was removed, and the projection at the east end where the stairs now are was built, which added very much to the public convenience. A platform extended the whole length of the front of the building, nearly on a level with the main hall, and the steps were at each end of the platform. The present arrangement for access is comparatively modern. As one entered the main hall, the first door on the right hand opened into the county clerk's office, being the front part of the present sheriff's office. The second door to the right opened into the room occupied as the grand jury room, and by the board of supervisors at its annual meetings. On the left was the sheriff's office, where the district attorney's office now is, and the two small rooms were used for the deliberations of petit juries. On entering the court room, the sheriff's box was located between the doors, and the prisoner's dock was placed immediately adjoining the area reserved for the bar. These were both removed at the time the room was fitted up for the meeting of the old Court for the Correction of Errors about the year 1841, when Lieutenant-Governor Luther Bradish presided. The original bench was not as large as the present one, and was calculated only for three judges, and it is believed that the one now here was built in 1847, to accommodate the General Term of the Supreme Court, then composed of four judges. In other respects, the arrangement of the court room is about the same as originally constructed, excepting that the petit jury box was of enclosed benches, in the same manner as the seats in the rest of the room.

At the time the Court House was erected, it was the finest and most imposing edifice in the village. Situated upon the highest point of land in the corporation limits, it was visible from every direction, and from the cupola or tower, an extensive view was presented of the village and of Lake Erie and the surrounding country. It must be remembered that for many years the adjacent buildings were, with but few exceptions, only two stories in height, so that they offered no obstruction to the view of the splendid scenery which was spread before the observer. Indeed it was the custom of our hospitable people to escort all visitors to the tower, in order to point out for their admiration the

BROAD EXPANSE OF LAKE ERIE,

whitened by the sails of commerce, the beautiful river of Niagara and the shores of Canada where the historic ruins of Fort Erie were already growing gray with the decay of years. The Court House bell, which some of us have heard from infancy, not only rang to indicate the hours for the assembling of courts or religious or other public meetings, but pealed forth many an alarm when conflagrations threatened, and the villagers all hastened, carrying their leathern buckets from their houses, to aid in preventing the destruction of the homes and property of their neighbors.

This room, in which we are now assembled, has been the scene of the deliberations of the people of Buffalo upon unnumbered occasions of public interest. How many meetings have been held here to take measures to counteract the ambitious designs of those who would have made Black Rock the

TERMINUS OF THE ERIE CANAL

and the emporium of the West. Sheldon Smith spoke here very eloquently, on the twenty-sixth day of October, 1825, when Buffalo triumphed, and the Erie canal was opened to the world, and the vast concourse of people who had assembled to witness the departure of the first boats, moved in procession to the Court House to celebrate the grand event. And since that day what anxious deliberations have here taken place with reference to the enlargement of the canal and the various harbor improvements and other matters deemed important to ensure the commercial supremacy of the city.

A record of the political meetings, large, enthusiastic and determined, as if the welfare of the nation and the preservation of the constitution depended upon the fiery eloquence and solemn resolves of the people assembled, would fill a volume. Clintonians and Bucktails, Masons and Anti-Masons, Whigs, Democrats, Loco-Focos, political Anti-slavery and Temperance men, Silver-Grays, Woolly Heads, Republicans, Free Soilers and Hard Shells, have each in turn, resolved and re-resolved, and the Republic yet lives. Here, for more than half a century, were held those annual

COUNTY CONVENTIONS

of the several political parties where the rival claims of patriotic men who were anxious to serve their country in offices of trust or emolument, were determined by the majority vote of the delegates, amid rejoicings and heart-burnings and animosities, the memories of which we all hope have perished.

At the time of its erection and for many years afterwards, there was no other large and commodious room in the village for public exhibitions and entertainments. Here it was that West's world-renowned picture of "Death on the Pale Horse," was shown to the admiring people, and in later days Dunlap's grand historical painting of "The bearing of the Cross and the Calvary," or, as it was commonly called, the "The Crucifixion," attracted the wandering gaze of the untraveled villagers. The "Wandering Piper," celebrated for the harmonies of the strains drawn forth from the Irish and Scotch bag-pipes, as well as for the mystery surrounding his person, paraded in this room in full Highland costume, and entertained the multitudes with his uncouth music and original observations. Concerts of all kinds, instrumental and vocal have here afforded more delicious amusement to the lovers of melody and more gratification to the public, than is now derived from the nocturnes and arias of the modern classical school.

Different religious societies have here been organized, and at an early day, before the construction of any churches, this was the only place in which to assemble for

DIVINE WORSHIP.

Many now living will remember the "meetings" and the Sunday-schools of their youthful days held within these walls, but who shall tell of the good works wrought here, of the sweet influences that have fallen upon the weary and heart-suffering? How many a fevered bosom has here first found consolation and been lifted up by the the strong arms of Hope and Faith to endure with patience the sad realities of life?

The record would not be complete without allusion to those melancholy occasions in all these years, when the members of the bar have been called upon to assemble here and pay their last public tributes of respect to their departed

BROTHERS AND ASSOCIATES.

Some were called when the measures of their years and honors were full; others were taken in the meridian of life and at times of greatest usefulness, and many were cut down in the spring-time of youth, when the beautiful future was just opening before them. We need not recall the names of those who have gone before us and been lamented here in sincere and truthful eulogiums; their memories are present with us this day, as we bid farewell to the scene of their labors. But this we do know, that the recurrence of such events, the saddening influences of the occasions, the contemplation of the near presence of death as it must come to all, were more than sermons to men who understand, and silently acknowledged by them as warnings of the inevitable fate of all humanity.

The history of an edifice of this character might not be complete without allusion to events of historical interest that have transpired within its walls or within the shadow of the lofty columns of the portico. In the year 1823, Ex-President

MILLARD FILLMORE

appeared here before the Court of Common Pleas and was admitted to practice as a member of the bar. Who then anticipated the course of events which culminated in his elevation to the highest position in the gift of his countrymen? In the summer of 1825 at the term of the Supreme Court over which Circuit Judge Reuben H. Walworth, afterward Chancellor of the State, presided, occurred that remarkable trial of the three brothers by the name of Thayer, who were here convicted and sentenced to be hung for the crime of murder. When the affair of the Caroline occurred at Schlosser in December, 1838, the body of Amos Durfee, who was murdered by the British, was brought before the Court House and Henry K. Smith, standing upon the portico, in presence of the excited multitude, delivered that most extraordinary and eloquent funeral oration, which aroused the fury of the populace almost beyond the restraints of authority. These columns witnessed the proceedings of the people when

LAFAYETTE

was received as the nation's guest in the summer of 1825. Before them and in the adjoining park, such Americans as Henry Clay and Daniel Webster, "the old man eloquent," John Quincy Adams,

Silas Wright, Martin Van Buren and Sargent S. Prentiss, and others of great fame, have expounded the political principles of their parties, or acknowledged with eloquent words, the attentions of their admiring fellow-citizens. They stand now, as they stood at that time, when the Free Soil Democrats of the Northern States held that grand and imposing convention which nominated Martin Van Buren for president, in the summer of 1848, and enunciated a platform of principles that led the people to reflect upon the aggressions and barbarisms of slavery, and originated the crusade resulting in the overthrow of that institution.

But time will not allow particular reference to the unnumbered occasions of interest which this venerable edifice has witnessed. One by one they will fade from the memory of living men, and like this forum where our fathers gathered, and where we have now assembled, will be remembered only upon the recorded page of history.

And now, Mr. Chairman and Gentlemen of the Bar, we are soon to bid farewell to this honored edifice, and leave it, a silent witness of the

DAYS THAT ARE NO MORE.

It was erected when this place was but a frontier hamlet of a few hundred inhabitants, and now it stands, in the center of a city of over 150,000 people, and surrounded with all the evidences of wealth and modern civilization. For three score years it served the purposes for which it was intended, but now the exigencies of society demand a change and a new order of things. Like the gray-haired and infirm old man, who once was erect and active in the walks and business of life, but who now totters on the verge of the tomb, it has outlived all usefulness. We do not yield it up without emotion; we cannot sever our particular relations to this place without a thought of the days that are past, but we must say farewell, and to all the clustering memories, *farewell!*

At the conclusion of Judge Sheldon's address, Hon. George R. Babcock, one of the oldest members of the Erie county Bar, read an address, as follows:

A PAPER BY HON. GEORGE R. BABCOCK.

Gentlemen of the Bar: It is eminently fit that the occasion of migrating from an edifice that for a period of nearly sixty years has been the theater of administration of law for an extensive region, should be commemorated by the Bar of Erie county. We go to more elegant and commodious quarters, but memory will linger with the associations of the past which here inhabit. Within these walls have transpired events the most momentous that ever thrilled human bosoms. Questions of life and death; liberty or the felon's cell; honor or shame; competence or penury; bright hope or black despair, have here been debated and settled for all time. Here learning the most profound, research the most laborious, and eloquence the most moving have brought their varied tributes and laid them, a fitting sacrifice, upon the altar of law—that shrine whose worship constitutes the distinction between civilization and barbarism. The proposal to leave the old temple and set up our altar on a new site naturally brings retrospection—solemn if not painful.

You have rendered me an honor to which I am profoundly sensible, in calling me to preside over your proceedings upon this occasion. I assume that I am indebted to this distiction not to my age, but to the fact that

I HOLD THE OLDEST LICENSES

as attorney and solicitor of any member of this Bar who has retained connection with it. Mine are dated in May, 1829. So far as I can learn, there are but four persons living who have, at any period, belonged here, whose date of admission to practice in the Supreme Court is earlier than 1829. One is the Rev. Dr. Lord, of this city, who, after a successful practice of several years, renounced the law for divinity, and is now a resident of this city, honored alike for his talent and devotion to the cause of his Divine Master. Another is Henry C. Van Schaack, now or lately of Onondaga county, who, as early as 1825, was practicing law in our then rural village of Black Rock. He was esteemed a lawyer of fair ability and exemplary character. He did not remain long after the Erie canal was opened to Buffalo. The third is Henry E. Davis, late of the Court of Appeals, and now enjoying a green old age and good practice in the city of New York. He was the attorney of the village and clerk of the Board of Trustees in 1828. Soon he removed to New York, since which time he has occupied several official positions with credit. The remaining survivor is Evert Van Buren, lately, if not now, a resident of Chicago. He was at this Bar a few years, in connection with the late Judge Masten, and achieved a respectable position as a lawyer and advocate.

I have been requested by the committee in charge to give some sketches of the lawyers who practiced here in the early days of this edifice, and of the course of the administration of the law at that time. Had I anticipated the difficulties which I have experienced in the collection of facts in the short time allowed me, I should have at once declined. I rely upon your indulgence for the very imperfect manner in which I shall be able to discharge the duty assigned me. I am compelled to rely largely upon memory and tradition, for the greater portion of the records which ought to be available for the data which I require, are inaccessible, if not lost entirely. I shall be glad to have any errors of fact or opinion corrected by my brethren.

My first acquaintance with the interior of this building was in April, 1825, upon the trial of the three Thayers for the murder of John Love. This trial excited a wider and more intense interest than any ever held here. It has formed an epoch from which many persons, now advanced in years, reckon time and events. The year

1825 had other events of note, such as the execution of the three brothers Thayer, upon one scaffold, erected at the west side of Niagara square; the visit of General Lafayette to Buffalo early in June, and the opening of the Erie canal on the twenty-sixth of October, of that year. Of the actors upon this scene, prior to 1825, I can give little but hearsay. Briefly as to

THE PRESIDING JUDGES.

Before the adoption of the constitution of 1821, Circuit Courts and Courts of Oyer and Terminer were held by judges of the Supreme Court. I remember to have heard that those legal luminaries, Spencer, Van Ness and Platt, had respectively held them here—also Judges Yates and Woodworth, after 1820. William B. Rochester was the first Circuit Judge, under the new constitution, and was succeeded by John Birdsall, in 1826, and the latter by Addison Gardner, in 1829. Judges Rochester and Birdsall were each possessed of fair abilities, and probably had acquirements necessary for a satisfactory discharge of the duties of the office had they been blessed with good health. The business of the Courts in the Eighth District did not proceed to the entire satisfaction of the Bar or suitors under their administration. Judges from other districts came in occasionally and held the courts. The services of Judges Walworth and Betts, who each held terms in 1825, were warmly appreciated by the profession. Judge Gardner held the office nearly ten years, and in the discharge of its duties won fame and the approbation of the profession, as well as that of the public at large. He was, indeed, a model judge at *nisi prius*. Thoroughly versed in the principles of the law, clear in perception, courteous and dignified in manner, he carried on the business of his courts with ease and despatch, while he maintained harmonious relations with opposing counsel, which is often a feat of difficult achievement. Of the first judges of Niagara county, embracing the present county of Erie, Samuel Tupper was appointed, in May, 1812; William Hotchkiss, in November, 1818; Samuel J. Wilkeson, in November, 1820; and continued in Erie county until succeeded by Ebenezer Walden, in February, 1823. Thomas C. Love held the office for less than a year, and was succeeded by Philander Bennett, in 1829, who held the office until 1837. How the duties of the office were discharged by Judges Tupper and Hotchkiss, I have not even a traditionary account.

JUDGE WILKESON

was not a lawyer, but I remember to have heard a competent authority assert that his keen perception and vigorous common sense enabled him, in most cases, to form quite correct opinions of the law from the discussions of counsel and the cases cited. Judges Walden, Love and Bennett were well-trained lawyers, and their decisions usually received the approbation of the profession. They were deficient, according to the present standard, in restraining the personalities of counsel, and in holding them strictly to the discharge of their proper duties in the trial and argument of causes before them. It may be said in their justification that they merely continued, but did not create, this order of things. The Court of Common Pleas, before their day, seems to have been considered a legal arena in which exercises were allowed that were not tolerated at the circuit. If a full history of these gladiatorial contests could be written, it would prove interesting, if not instructive.

The foremost actors, within my recollection, were Root, Sheldon, Love, White, Sherwood, Tillinghast and Barker. They were "cunning of fence," and not to be despised as opponents in any field.

It must attract the attention of any who examines the reports, beginning with the 14th of Johnson and ending with the 13th of Wendell, that comparatively few decisions of the Circuit or Common Pleas of this county were overruled. In part this may be due to the different mode from the present of transacting legal business. There were but four terms of the Supreme Court in each year, and they were held at New York and Albany, until after 1823, when the August term was transferred to Utica. The facilities for travel were decidedly inferior to the present, and our lawyers were usually unwilling to attend General Term when they could, at the best, have but few cases. This involved the expense and inconvenience of employing foreign counsel, and doubtless often led to an acquiescence in decisions with which the parties were not entirely satisfied. Another and perhaps better reason may be assigned. Under the

SYSTEM OF PLEADING AND PRACTICE

then in use, trials were confined to distinct and well-defined issues of fact; consequently, there was no opportunity for such a mass of exceptions to an admission of evidence as characterizes the present system. I forbear to enlarge on this topic lest I incur the opprobrium of many of my younger brothers, now present, for whom I have a sincere liking.

The office of district attorney was filled by John C. Spencer, from February, 1815, to June, 1818; then by Charles G. Olmsted for about six months; then by Heman B. Potter for ten consecutive years. Thomas C. Love filled the place from 1829, to December, 1831, when Henry White succeeded and held the office until his death in August, 1832. George P. Barker was then appointed and held the office until December, 1836. It is enough to say here that the important duties of this office were well discharged by those very competent gentlemen. No county in the State, except New York, had so large a share of criminal business as this—a fact due to its frontier position, rapid growth in population, and the demoralization incident of the war of 1812. The lawyers who were in Buffalo, in 1820, as nearly as I can ascertain, were John Root, Ebenezer Walden, Jonas Harrison, Heman B. Potter, Albert H. Tracy, Thomas C. Love, Ebenezer F. Norton, Joseph W. Moulton,

Jonathan E. Chaplin, James Sheldon, Stephen G. Austin, and William A. Moseley. Harrison went to Louisiana, Moulton to New York, and Chaplin to Northern Ohio, where he became a somewhat distinguished Methodist preacher. In May, 1825, the remaining nine were in Buffalo, and the list was re-enforced by the names of Horatio Shumway, Henry White, Thomas T. Sherwood, Harry Slade, Joseph Clary, Sheldon Smith, Philander Bennett, Roswell Chapin and Major A. Andrews. To these may be added, as belonging to the Bar of the county, Absalom Bull, David Lockwood and Henry C. Van Schaack, of Black Rock, Belden Slosson, of Amherst, Ezra St. John, of Clarence, and Millard Fillmore, of Aurora—the latter belonging to the Common Pleas only. Of these twenty-seven persons, Van Schaack is the only survivor, if, indeed, he does survive. During the next ten years, which is the limit of my retrospect, there were added many names to the list, making the Bar to consist of fifty-three members, excluding those who were admitted to the Common Pleas alone. Of these, twelve survive, viz.: Geo. R. Babcock, Elijah Ford, James McKay, John T. Bush, Seth C. Hawley, L. G. Marvin, John T. Hudson, John L. Talcott, Theodotus Burwell, Orsamus H. Marshall, Evert Van Buren and George W. Johnson. Six of the survivors reside in this city. Surely, the great reaper has gathered a rich harvest.

The practice of riding the circuit, borrowed from England, prevailed in these early days. Eminent lawyers, especially those who had reputation with juries, accompanied the judges from county to county, upon the circuit, to assist on the trial of civil causes and the defense of persons charged with crime. In some cases they were retained beforehand; in others, I think most frequently, they were employed during the sitting of the circuit. They had to rely much upon the preparation which had been made for the trial by the attorney who employed them.

SOME OF THE MOST EMINENT LAWYERS

of the State have tried causes, of greater or less importance, in this room. I may name Elisha Williams, Thomas J. Oakley, John C. Spencer, Dudley Marvin, Vincent Matthews, Ebenezer Griffin, George Hosmer, Joshua A. Spencer, Henry B. Storrs and, I think, Samuel A. Talcott.

The practice, as regards this county, ceased about 1830. If foreign counsel came after that year, it was upon a previous retainer. Our own counselors before 1835, notably Fillmore, Barker, White, Sherwood, Tillinghast and Talcott, attended nearly all the Circuit Courts in the Eighth District. Before 1825, Root, Potter, Love, Tracy, Sheldon, and Sheldon Smith usually attended all the Courts in the adjoining counties of Chautauqua, Genesee and Niagara to try their own causes and such others as might be confided to them. The compensation which able lawers received at this period will seem meager, if not mean, to those who are familiar only with legal charges at the present day. In cases of considerable importance, when the preparation for trial had been made by an attorney, able counsel charged $20 to $25 for the trial, and where several days were employed in the preparation and trial, $50 to $100 was the highest charge for the services, including often a "summing up" more eloquent than Westminster Hall could produce once in five years. When the difference in expense of living is considered the discrepancy lessens. There were comparatively few books to buy; no expensive clerks; no high office rents, and $1 per diem was the highest charge at taverns, as good in all essential particulars as the best at the present day. Although many of them, as at the present time, realize

DANIEL WEBSTER'S DESCRIPTION

of a lawyer's fate, "to work hard, live well and die poor," some of our predecessors failed in each of the particulars, as, doubtless, many of our cotemporaries will persist in doing.

The manners of counsel in trying and arguing causes have changed considerably since my observations began, and, in some respects, improved. The present familiar, colloquial style has succeeded one more formal and stately. Personalities between counsel are less common than they were a generation since. Then it was not uncommon for counsel to keep up a running commentary upon the case or the evidence, during the examination of a witness, and to be in the brisk discharge and receipt of retorts and repartee with his adversary, while the judge was taking down the testimony. Arbitrations were frequent but references rare. Suits in equity were not frequent, and many members of the bar did not take admission to the Court of Chancery at all, or, at least, not until after 1830. There was but little business in the Federal Courts. Such as there was arose chiefly from infractions of the revenue laws. But brief mention of some of the lawyers who played their part on this stage between the years 1825 and 1835. and are now no more, is all that is permitted under the limits which I have imposed upon myself. In respect to many, full biographical sketches exist in the archives of the Historical Society, or otherwise, but for want of time, I have not availed myself of their records. John C. Spencer has often been here. He impressed me as the embodiment of intellectual force; with a knowledge of the law which secured intuition and a logic as inexorable as fate, he went directly at the head of judge and jury, without apparently seeking to excite imagination or awaken sentiment. He was truly a great lawyer. Dudley Marvin came regularly to the Circuit, and was often engaged in civil and criminal cases. He had a grand presence, an imperturable temper, great knowledge of human nature and a commanding eloquence. His ability in examining a witness, especially an unwilling one, was unrivalled, and his arrangement of the evidence in his address to juries masterly. He made little use of authorities either with court or jury, but his skill in transferring such legal weapons from his adversary's arsenal to his own was the subject of mirthful comment in professional circles. Ebenezer Griffin visited us with great regularity and was much employed. He had a majestic appearance, musical voice and pleasing way of presenting himself to courts and juries which, upon occasion, would rise to eloquence. He held high rank as a lawyer and advocate. One of the most exciting trials of this period took place in this room in 1828.

It involved the question of the proper location of Commercial and Water streets, and consequently the title to lands lying between these streets, as now used, and the Little and Big Buffalo creeks. The whole village took an interest in the controversy, and the village election of that year turned wholly upon it. The trustees, represented by Davies, City Attorney, and Henry R. Storrs, were plaintiffs, and Johnson and Wilkeson, represented by Love, Marvin and Spencer, were defendants. A more unpromising subject for the display of eloquence could not well be imagined, and it is difficult to analyze the grounds of the opinion that prevailed within and without the ranks of the profession, that a more brilliant exhibition of classical oratory and logical argument had never been made within these walls than that afforded by

MR. STORR'S ADDRESS TO THE JURY.

I was present, but, really, I was so bewildered that I can tell you nothing about the speech. This, I believe, was the only effort made by Mr. S. at this bar. Some years after I heard him argue a demurrer, with Dudley Marvin on the opposite side, in the Superior Court of New York, and it was a subject of remark that both had more eloquence than knowledge of Chitty's Pleadings. Joshua R. Giddings of Ohio tried a cause here about 1830, growing out of the loss of a cargo of goods by shipwreck near Ashtabula. He then displayed the bold, intrepid and effective oratory which, in after years, upon a wider theater and with larger interests involved, made his name famous. Heman B. Potter, after leaving college, entered the office of Elisha Williams at Hudson, where he was well trained in the principles and practice of the law. He came to Buffalo in October, 1810, and almost simultaneously established a law office, organized a Washington Benevolent Society, a Federal Club, and joined, if he did not organize, a Masonic Lodge. He little thought that the two acts of his earlier life last named would, as they did, form an insuperable bar to political promotion to the end of his days. His appointment as district attorney constituted the only taste of office that he ever enjoyed. He had the kindliest of dispositions, unimpeachable integrity, great industry, united to order and system in all transactions. He soon acquired, what was then considered, a large legal business. He tried and argued his own cases with good success. His addresses to courts and juries were pleasing in manner; his statements of law and fact clear and well arranged, and although he did not often rise to the heights of eloquence, his forensic efforts could not fail to satisfy a moderate ambition. His administration of the office of district attorney, for ten years, was all that could be desired. In one case only had he the assistance of counsel, and that was in the summing up of

THE TRIAL OF THE THREE THAYERS.

The case was one to be made out by circumstantial evidence alone. It was prepared by Mr. Potter, and in after years Chancellor Walworth said that he had never known one so well prepared and tried as this. Thomas C. Love entered into a good business as the partner of Albert H. Tracy. The ill-health of the latter, and his devotion to political life, soon left the law office in Mr. Love's hands. He had great force of character, a strong intellect, courageous temperament, and an industry that shunned no labor. Into whatever he undertook his whole soul was thrown, and, as may well be supposed, he was largely successful. His addresses to courts and juries made up in clearness and earnest force whatever was wanting in taste and elegance. He was regarded as a safe and faithful counselor.

Sheldon Smith had, I think, no marked standing as a lawyer. As an advocate he held high rank. Before a jury he was fluent and graceful—presenting his case with moderation and clearness—in language extremely well chosen and effective. Gibbon was his model for style, and he was a fond reader of the great historian, as much for his ornate rhetoric as for his facts. Smith was better in getting verdicts than in holding them. I remember a case he tried three times, with a verdict in his favor on each trial. I do not know whether his client's adversary was wearied out, or whether so much competent evidence was produced on the third trial that a fourth could not be obtained, but Smith was triumphant.

James Sheldon is probably little known to most of my hearers, and yet he made a prominent figure in this hall for many years. He was the law-partner of Albert H. Tracy, and afterwards of Charles G. Olmsted. Olmsted was here but a short time when he removed to Tennessee. He had the reputation of possessing superior abilities. Sheldon continued his law practice until about 1832. He had a powerful, well-compacted body, an acute intellect, an ardent temper, and an audacity equal to any occasion. He was exceedingly well prepared for his profession, and a thorough-going practitioner. He had a large business in criminal cases and a fair share of civil practice. His speeches to courts and juries were models of conciseness, expressed in terse, forcible words, and in a manner that seemed defiant of contradiction. In the legal frays of justices' courts and the Common Pleas he was foremost—never avoiding an encounter of any description, and seldom coming off without his spurs. He remembered with impartiality his friends and —enemies. Henry White was, in many respects, a remarkable man. He had a subtle and ingenious mind, great industry, and entire devotion to his profession. He read much and thought more of his law books. His entire faculties were devoted to any cause that he undertook, and he was pertinacious to the last degree of any point or proposition that he raised. His temper was perfectly under command, and he always kept it at home if his adversary lost his own. In the begining of a trial he seemed to seek by inuendo, suggestion and comment upon the testimony being taken down, to irritate and perplex opposing counsel, in which he was often successful, and thereafter White remained "cool as a cucumber." If, as sometimes happened, he failed, no one could better assume the *role* of indignation for the wrongs of his client or "tear a passion to tatters" than he. His reputation as a *nisi prius* lawyer had reached a high point and was growing when he was suddenly cut off in August, 1832. Stephen G. Austin had a large share of legal business, and I believe that his learning and ability as a lawyer are not fully appreciated by the present members of the bar. He was well read in his books, and at least down to the time of forming a law connection with Barker, tried and argued his own causes, with a fair measure of success. He was fond of that lost art—special pleading—and delighted to take a case through all its stages, from Narr to Surrebutter before bringing it into this room. Dyre Tillinghast came here in 1826, and at once secured a very respectable standing and business. He was an excellent practitioner, and had great clerical ability. He was a ready, handy man. Whatever he could do at all he could do at once. His first cause here was tried one hot afternoon in August, and he somewhat surprised our lawyers by drawing up a bill of exceptions on the spot and having it settled and signed before the judge took his supper. He was at home in all forums. A justice's court, a board of town officers, an ecclesiastical convocation, a court martial, a trial at the Sessions or Circuit, a case in Chancery or in Admiralty, were equally his delight, and in each he acquitted himself with a fair portion of credit. His reading of law seemed to be without method, although he read much. He had a facility for quoting cases by the book, and sometimes page, that had relation to the subject under discussion, although he did not always hit upon the point or principle decided by them. William A. Moseley was fourteen years at this bar—having entered in 1820, and retired on his election to the Assembly in 1834. He possessed fine ability and acquirements, including a fair knowledge of law and its practice. He tried and argued his own causes, which were most thoroughly prepared, and had good success with them. In the "heavy fights" in the Common Pleas he bore himself well, having the ready wit and biting sarcasm so useful in such encounters. It was thought to be a phenomenon that with such abilities as he possessed he should have been four years in the Senate and four years in Congress without making a speech in either, and four years in the Court for the Correction of Errors without delivering an opinion. It did not arise from inattention to the ordinary duties of the positions, for no one excelled him in punctuality of attendance and knowledge of what transpired in the bodies of which he was a member.

A marked change in the constitution of this bar and in the character of the business began in 1835, and here my way, on this occasion ends. Here began the accession to its numbers whose achievements form

A NEW ERA.

H. K. Smith, Haven, Hall, E. Cook, E. Norton, Stow, Sill, Masten, B. H. Austin, Seymour, Stanley, H. S. Love, Ganson and Verplanck among the dead, and Clinton, Rogers, VanBuren, W. H. Greene, J. M. Smith, Nichols, Putnam, Spaulding and S. C. Hawley among the living, comprise a list whose various talents and acquirements would do honor to any bar in the land. I leave this formidable company of new-comers to other and more competent hands than mine.

To bring this paper at all within reasonable limits, and because other pens have paid them tribute, I omit notices of Root, Tracy, Fillmore, Barker, Sherwood, Shumway and Slade. They are all so well known to the bar, and such justice has been rendered their memories by others, that this cmission will not, I trust, be deemed a defect in this paper. I have discharged the duty imposed upon me as well as the time allowed me, and the data at my command would permit, and I cast myself upon your indulgence in the hope that other hands will supplement my deficiencies, and glean a rich harvest from the unreaped fields that remain.

REMARKS OF JUDGE CLINTON.

When Mr. Babcock had finished his address, he called upon Judge Clinton to make some remarks. As the Judge rose, he was greeted with hearty applause. He spoke extempore, and said: That he very reluctantly declared that he was not going to make a speech upon this occasion, as the previous speakers had stolen all his thunder. They had not only reaped the harvest, but actually gleaned the field. His feelings were of so deep and varied a nature, that he did not know in what order to place them, or how to express himself. He was glad, and yet he was sorry; full of joy, and yet mournful. We stand between tears and merriment. As for this Court-house building, it belongs to the dark ages. It never looked so bare as now, and never was it better graced. It has long been a reproach to the city and county, and its appearance was that of unmitigated ugliness. But when he thought of the memories connected with the old building, his heart was stirred, and he was ready to say, "Burn it to the ground, but don't allow it to be desecrated, and put to common or vulgar uses!"

What contests of wit had enlivened this old building, and where were the men who participated in them? Their sayings, if the speaker should undertake to repeat them, would be as dull and vapid as some things he had seen in magazines, called "Congressional Humor," or something of that sort. The old building had served its day; it was worn out, and effete, and even like the speaker's old hat, which he held in his hand. [Laughter.] And when the time came for him to part with his ancient friend, the old hat, he should do so joyously. Yet the memory of what it was to him would dwell in his heart. So with this building. How many sacred memories were connected with it, which could never be effaced. Here George P. Barker, and the beloved Ganson first felt the grasp of death. Here the speaker's brethren had often assembled to pay feeling tributes to those who had gone before. The memories of those occasions would always be sacred.

In concluding, Judge Clinton said that he believed from his heart of hearts that the Bar of Erie county had never stood higher than now. For the good of the profession, which yielded only in importance to the clerical profession, he would ask, whether it would not be well to draw closer the ties which bound the Bar together socially? He believed it would be well to form an Association of members of the Bar.

Hon. James M. Smith, one of the Judges of the Superior Court, delivered the concluding address of the day, and spoke as follows:

ADDRESS OF JUDGE SMITH.

Mr. President and Gentlemen of the Bar: Your committee has done me the honor to request that I should address you on this interesting occasion, and as I rise to comply with their request, the thronging memories of almost forty years—of all the years of my manhood—crowd my mind with the most varied emotions. As I recall the forms and faces, once so familiar to this place, of the men who elevated the Bar of this city to an equal rank with the ablest of the State, and who here illustrated by their genius, their learning, their eloquence, the highest walks of our profession, and achieved its best rewards, I feel a thrill of pride and pleasure in the recollection of my association with them, that I witnessed their labors and their triumphs, that I rejoiced in the honors which they won, and that I am permitted here to-day to recall their names and to unroll the record which they made. I am indeed sadly reminded that as to almost all of them it must be said the places which have known them know them no more, but their names and memory are cherished by us who survive, and those who succeed us at the Bar and upon the bench, will long remember their achievements and emulate their fame.

> "The dead are like the stars by day,
> Withdrawn from mortal eye;
> But not extinct, they hold their way,
> In glory through the sky."

I first entered these memorable walls early in the winter of 1838. This city had then a population of about seventeen thousand, and, though laboring under the terrible reverses in business which followed the financial crash of 1837, yet its people were full of elastic life and vigorous enterprise; and none more truly so than the members of our profession. The very extensive modifications and changes of the law and its modes of practice which were made by the Revised Statutes, had just become fully understood, adapted to use, and brought into full working order. It may not be without interest to glance at the judicial system of that day, and consider briefly some of its peculiar features, so different from those with which we are familiar now.

THE HIGHEST COURT OF THE STATE

was the Court for the Correction of Errors, composed of the Lieutenant-Governor (or the President of the Senate) who was its presiding judge, the Chancellor, the Justices of the Supreme Court, and the members of the Senate, thirty-two in number. Its jurisdiction was to review the decrees of the Chancellor and the judgments of the Supreme Court. The terms of this court were usually held in the city of New York or Albany, but in the summer of 1846, a session of the court was held in this room, which was specially fitted up for the purpose. Notwithstanding the peculiar character of the court, the large number composing it, and that many of them were not lawyers, its judgments uniformly commanded the respect and confidence of the Bar and the people.

As the Senate always contained some of the most distinguished lawyers of the State, the voice of the professional members of the court had a controlling influence, and there are no more learned, well reasoned and elegantly written opinions upon the pages of our reports than some of those pronounced in that court. Among the most distinguished and most frequently quoted are those written by

THE LATE ALBERT H. TRACY,

when a member of this Bar and a Senator from this district.

The Supreme Court was composed of three justices, held four General Terms each year—two at Albany, one in New York and one in Utica—besides eight Special Terms each year at Albany. Its clerks were four, having their offices respectively at Albany, New York, Utica and Geneva, to one of which all process, pleadings and other papers in that court, requiring to be filed must be sent for that purpose, and where all judgments were docketed, and thus became a lien throughout the State. The State was divided into eight Judicial Districts, with a judge in each to hold Circuit Courts and Courts of Oyer and Terminer. The counties of Erie, Niagara, Orleans, Monroe, Genesee and Chautauqua composed the eighth district, and in each county two Circuit Courts and Courts of Oyer and Terminer were holden each year. Addison Gardiner, who had been Circuit Judge for this district for several years, having resigned in January, 1838, John B. Skinner, an able and accomplished lawyer, a pure-minded and truly good man, whose name should ever be mentioned with reverence and honor, and who was then a citizen of Genesee county, but afterward and for several years a resident and member of the Bar of this city, was appointed to succeed Judge Gardiner. But he declined the appointment by reason of impaired health, and Nathan Dayton was appointed, and honorably discharged the duties of the office until the constitution of 1846 went into operation. The Court of Chancery was composed of Chancellor and Vice-Chancellor for the First Judicial District, and except in that district, each of the Circuit Judges was, *ex-officio*, Vice-Chancellor for his Judicial District.

In each county was a Court of Common Pleas, and a Court of General Sessions of the Peace, consisting of a first judge and four associate judges. It needs but little reflection to perceive how far the State has outgrown such a judicial system, and how wholly inadequate it would be to the exigencies of the present day.

At the time I have referred to, when I became a member of this bar, James Stryker was the first judge of this county, and Frederick P. Stevens, Jonathan Hoyt, Joseph Freeman and Isaac Humphrey were associate judges. Samuel Caldwell was surrogate, Henry W. Rogers, district attorney, Elijah Ford, Horatio Seymour, Jr., Peter M. Vosburgh and Charles H. Bramhall, Masters in Chancery, Dyre Tillinghast, Supreme Court Commissioner. There were then in active practice here, as leading members of the bar, and whose learned and eloquent efforts these venerable walls have so often witnessed, Millard Filmore, Heman B. Potter, Stephen G. Austin, Geo. P. Barker, Henry K. Smith, Nathan K. Hall, Horatio J. Stow, Thos. T. Sherwood, Solomon G. Haven, Benj. H. Austin, Horatio Shumway, Seth E. Sill, Eli Cook, Joseph G. Masten, and Dyre Tillinghast, and in later years as the veterans retired from the field, or yielded to the arch enemy Death, their places were filled by such men as James Mullett, Benjamin F. Greene, Chauncey Tucker, Albert Sawin, James G. Hoyt, Isaac A. Verplanck and John Ganson. I can but recount the names upon this illustrious roll.

I cannot here speak of the individual characteristics of these men or their varied gifts and acquirements, or of the steps by which they took high rank in our profession and in the community of which they were members. These are a part of

THE HISTORY OF THIS BAR

and of this city. They elevated and made more widely and better known the character of both. Many of them were called by their fellow-citizens to fill the places of honor and trust, upon the bench in the halls of legislation, and in various departments of the government. And they carried with them into public life the same marked integrity, energy and industry, as well as the same varied learning, and the same wide range of intellectual gifts which had distinguished them in their professional life. Thus they not only reflected credit upon this bar, and upon the city of their residence, but the fame of some of them has gone forth over all the land, and the nation has risen up to do them honor. But this was the special scene of their professional achievements. They, and their predecessors, the fathers of the bar, of whom honored mention has been made to-day by those who preceded me, have made this building historical, and in spite of its defective architecture and primitive accessories, it has become in our eyes a venerable pile, and this room like holy ground.

I have purposely refrained from the mention of any whose names have not been made sacred by death. I speak not of the living, for I speak to the living. You, Mr. Chairman, and a scanty band of your compeers, alone remain of the eminent men who distinguished this bar when it was first known to me, and who in later days have added luster to its history. Your brethren of to-day, sir, recognize in you

THE LAWYERS OF THE OLD REGIME,

trained in the hardier schools of the past—worthy exemplars of an honored profession. Fortunate as you have been in the associations of the past, and as you are in the rewards of the present, I know that I express the heartfelt wish of your younger brethren, that the years of you who yet survive may be prolonged beyond the common lot, and that as the shadows lengthen with life's declining day, you may repose from care and labor in the consciousness of a well-spent life, and with the blessed assurance that when the night falls, the coming dawn shall break with the splendors of an eternal morn.

At the conclusion of Judge Smith's address, on motion of H. S. Cutting, the meeting adjourned until ten o'clock Monday A. M., the thirteenth inst., for the purpose of taking final leave of the old Court House, and proceeding in a body to the new City and County Hall.

ADIEU TO THE OLD COURT HOUSE.

OPENING OF THE CITY AND COUNTY HALL.

On Monday morning, March 13, 1876, the City and County Hall was thrown open to the public. Most of the officers had taken possession on Saturday previous, and were ready to transact business in their new quarters. There were no formal ceremonies in connection with this branch of the opening of the building.

The Special Term of the Superior Court was opened by Judge G. W. Clinton, and the Civil Trial Term of the same court was held by Judge James Sheldon. The County Court, Judge Albert Haight presiding, also convened. But little business was transacted in either court, and they soon adjourned to participate in the

FURTHER ACTION OF THE BAR.

In accordance with the further plans of the Committee of Arrangements, a very large number of the members of the legal profession assembled at the Old Court House, pursuant to adjournment, at ten o'clock A. M., Monday, March 13, 1876. The meeting was called to order by Hon George R. Babcock, upon whose motion Gen. Gustavus A. Scroggs was chosen Grand Marshal to conduct the fraternity to the City and County Hall. A procession was then formed, headed by Judges Sheldon, Smith and Haight, followed by the members of the Bar admitted previous to the year 1840, and then the balance of the fraternity in order of seniority. In this manner the procession marched to the new City and County Hall, where the Bar were received by Building Commissioners Becker, Wardwell, Laning, Bowen, Hayward, Potter, Youngs and Adams, who escorted them to the Civil Trial Term room of the Superior Court, at the north end of the third floor.

A few minutes after eleven o'clock the meeting was called to order by Hon. Mr. Babcock, who congratulated the members of the Bar that they had come from their old temple of justice to an edifice of which the interior, so far as his observation went, was second to but one in the land; the capitol at Washington was the only building which could compare with it. Mr. Babcock suggested that the proceedings should be opened with an invocation of the Divine blessing, and asked Rev. Dr. Hotchkiss to offer prayer.

Rev. Dr. Hotchkiss offered a prayer appropriate to the occasion.

On motion of Hon. H. S. Cutting, Hon. Sherman S. Rogers was elected Chairman, and Mr. James A. Allen was appointed Secretary.

Upon taking the chair Senator Rogers addressed the meeting, and said:

ADDRESS OF HON. S. S. ROGERS.

Gentlemen of the Bar: It is with but meagre ceremony that the Bench and Bar of Erie county take possession of this goodly temple, and dedicate it to Justice. Here is no imposing pageant; no unwonted display of the glories or the terrors of Authority. No Lord Mayor in gilded coach has lent to our procession the eclat of municipal sanction. The eye searches in vain for the awful shire-reeve, with his bailiffs burly and his tip-staves tall; and where are the judges in their robes of office, and the lawyers in wigs and gowns? And yet the Lord High Chancellor is here, in all but robe and title, and my Lord Chief Justice, too; and perhaps among these ungowned gentlemen are more than one whom future generations may deem not unworthy to be named with the great barristers who have made the history of the English and American bars illustrious. Certainly there are many as truly self-consecrate to the higher duties and obligations of our profession, to truth, to justice, to that loyal recognition of rightful authority which is the

SUPPORT AND SAFE-GUARD OF THE STATE,

as the titled barristers whose escutcheons adorn the walls of the Inns of Court, or any of those untitled, but not less noble worthies, whose unrecorded fame is still the pride of our own bar.

To-day, gentlemen, inaugurates an era in the history, not merely of our fair city, but in some sort also of our own fraternity. I would fain believe that it will also mark the commencement of a higher and worthier professional life.

Not that I expect a material change in our mental or moral characteristics because henceforth we pursue our labors in these elegant and well-appointed rooms instead of the old ones, one of which was always contemptible (I speak, of course, of that in the "New Court-house, so called), while the other had, indeed, become like Judge Clinton's old hat, useful indeed, though never elegant, and tolerable only because for so many years it had been the home of so much good thought.

No; the man is not much changed by the doffing of an old coat or the putting on of a new one; and yet he may be a little more courtly, nay, possibly even more manly in the new than in the old, especially if the coat be supplemented by a good new hat and by nether integuments which are irreproachable both in style and material. Therefore, let us not underrate the probable good effect of these spacious and richly-furnished apartments.

Who shall dare to dull the edge of his pen-knife on these "Centennial chairs," and who among us, with the broad daylight staring at him through these beautiful windows, will not be put a little more upon his good behavior than when he trod the dusty matting and thumped the rickety rail which separated the jury from the bar, under the benign protection of the dear old shabbiness to which we have just said farewell.

But to speak more seriously. Is it too much to expect from the memories of that solemn but delightful meeting which it was our privilege to attend on Saturday last, some enduring and beneficent results? Who among us did not feel his soul kindled and elevated as he listened to the eloquent words of the seniors, as they recited the annals of our local bar? Who was not glad that he, too, was a lawyer? Who of us would not be happy, to think that in some future year, when the Bar of Buffalo shall be gathered on some auspicious occasion, perhaps with a son or grandson to listen, his own name should be found worthy of special mention among the good and great lawyers who have adorned the grand profession of the law in this city of our pride?

The present rarely seems heroic, and Poetry ever turns her beautiful eyes to the past, or, scorning the dull and prosaic present, strains her eager vision towards the future. The dawn and the sunset are her delight. But patience, brethren of the busy, eager, contending, ambitious bar of to-day! We shall all be of the past before long—many of us, indeed, of the forgotten past; but we shall every one contribute something to the character and the reputation of our brotherhood. The mean and ignoble will be more unworthy because of the unworthiness of any of his associates.

THE GOOD AND THE ILLUSTRIOUS

will shine with a purer and brighter glory by the light reflected from the purity of their less successful, though not less worthy brethren.

I congratulate you, gentlemen of the Bar, upon your presence here to-day, and I will not add a word to what I have said to lend a graver tinge to the pleasant and even joyful thoughts which are appropriate to the occasion. Let us enjoy them to the full. Let us with serious but confident anticipation dedicate this noble structure, as we should be dedicate ourselves, to a pure and impartial justice. May all the years of the future witness here the presence of judges, learned, dignified, incorruptible, who fear God alone; of a Bar, able, eloquent, courageous and upright, who shall administer the duties and exercise the privileges of their high vocation as those who know that they stand in the presence of the Judge of all the Earth, of Him by whom princes rule and magistrates execute judgment, and that to Him they must render their final account.

ADDRESS OF HON. A. P. NICHOLS.

Mr. Chairman: This is, surely, an occasion of uncommon interest. That cannot be called common which never, or rarely, happens but once in a lifetime.

The taking down of our altars and household gods in the old temple, and removing and setting them up in the new; this going back for that last, last look, and bidding good-bye to scenes and associations which have grown dearer and dearer, year by year, since the hour we first buckled on spurs for professional conflict, cannot but be full of sadness, even though the star of hope in the future beams ever so brightly upon the transition to our new home. As the soldier looks upon his trusty blade, be it ever so hacked and battered, and, remembering that it never failed him, that its haft never gave way in the supremest crisis; as he looks at his old friend, tried and true—I say, in the presence of a weapon, may be of comelier shape, and glittering in all the glory of strength and undimmed beauty, how his heart instinctively clings to his first love, and if he at last consents to the exchange, it is with a sigh.

"Be it ever so humble, there's no place like home." Ah, those words are but the language of the heart. There is not one among us, Mr. Chairman, I care not how scarred and callous his heart may have become in his long strifes at the Bar, whose pulses do not beat stronger and his breath come quicker as he regretfully bids good-bye to the old camp. There he felt that his foot was on his native heath—how will it be on an untried field? There he felt the first flush of triumph; there he experienced his first defeat; he can never forget them! But here we come, Mr. Chairman, to our new home, to this goodly pile, with its superb architectural effects, its spacious apartments, its complete appointments, rich in all that art and taste and generous expenditure can give, which the generosity of our city and county have furnished, as a temple of Justice, and for the convenience of State, County and Municipal administration. It is, indeed, a noble bounty, worthy of the objects for which it is proposed, worthy of the civilization that prompted it.

I trust that we and all who may be called upon to do honorable service here, in any of the varied departments, may not be unmindful of the scope and meaning of this new phase of life, or of the obligations which grow out of it. You know, Mr. Chairman, that it was said by a Roman poet, in a time that has become immortal, that they who cross the sea change only their external surroundings, not themselves. In coming here, Mr. Chairman, we have changed our forum, but not ourselves. We are no better lawyers, by the simple fact of change; but we may thereby be better, if we prize the opportunity. That depends upon ourselves. We must remember that the Court House is made illustrious by the Bar, not the Bar by the Court House.

As we take possession, then, at this point of a new departure in our professional life, let us, Mr. Chairman, as the noblest recognition of our obligations as a Bar, under which this munificent liberality of our citizens has placed us, and which we so cheerfully acknowledge, as the highest honor we can pay to our noble profession, vow and promise to and with each other that we will not be unmindful of our obligations, for this larger theater and opportunity for usefulness; that, profiting by them, we will strive to be better lawyers and better men; that nothing base or unworthy of the true lawyer shall ever through us wound or sully these noble halls; that, ever striving to mount higher and higher in the walks of our profession, we will insist, day by day, upon a nobler code of ethics and a higher professional tone, and leave this seat of Justice to our successors, honored, not shamed, by our presence. Beneath this dome, what noble ambitions shall have play! How shall the eager aspirants wrestle for the mastery! What momentous issues of life and death, of fame and fortune, shall here be discussed!

And what incitements are here for these efforts! No Bar in the State has surpassed this in the past; shall any surpass it in the future? Think of the line of illustrious names that illuminate it, from its birth to this hour! I will not—I have not the heart—try to enumerate them. We know them, and their names are dear to us all. From its ranks men have been called to spheres of wider influence and usefulness, not only at the Bar and on the Bench, but in civil administration. In the discipline of these Halls, in the high debate and lofty struggles between the Bench and Bar, in our sharp, earnest, but manly, encounters with each other, as in a collision of flint and steel, we shall fit and equip others who may be able, worthily to keep up this line of succession in high places.

In a word, Mr. Chairman, let us but be true to our profession and to ourselves, and we shall not only repay the rich honors and advantages which the public authorities have here confided to our keeping, but have a noble opportunity of showing to our fellow-men how manifold are the benefits which flow to society from a conscientious, learned and upright Bar.

Mr. Henry W. Box moved that Hon. E. Carlton Sprague be chosen to preside at the proposed banquet of the bar of Erie county at the Tifft House to-morrow evening. The resolution having been adopted, Mr. Sprague was called for, and addressed the meeting as follows:

ADDRESS OF E. C. SPRAGUE.

I beg leave to thank the meeting for this expression of its respect. I do so most gratefully, for there are, indeed, few things in this life that I value more than the regard of my professional brethren. And now that I am upon my feet, although I had not expected to say a word upon this occasion, I find it difficult to repress altogether the recollections that are crowding upon my memory, some of which may be interesting, particularly to the students here present. I entered upon the study of the law, in Buffalo, in the summer of 1843, in the office of Fillmore & Haven, then perhaps the leading office in the State, west of Albany. The life of law students then differed in many ways from the same life now. We took turns in the morning sweeping out the office and making the fires. I well remember Mr. Fillmore coming to the office one morning, and finding some dust around the leg of a table unswept (by the negligence of the clerk that morning, who he was I will not say), and exclaiming, that he feared that so negligent a clerk

WOULD NEVER MAKE A LAWYER.

The office hours were from eight A. M. to one P. M., from two to six P. M., and from seven to ten P. M. The pay was nothing the first two years, and two dollars a week the third. Much time was given in those days to chat with country clients and to politics. In the back room was a long high desk upon which the principal newspapers of the State were kept in files, and it was the custom of the press to come to the lawyer's office for counsel and direction as to the political policy to be pursued, and the candidates who should be nominated. And I assure you that our political affairs were not the less purely or ably conducted by reason of the counsel of the profession in those days.

I cannot omit a word in memory of the gentlemen with whom I studied my profession. As a statesman, Mr. Fillmore's name is known as widely as civilization itself; but to the younger men in the profession I wish to bear testimony to his great learning, his profound investigations, his excellent sense, and his unwearied industry as a lawyer. I have not known his superior, upon the whole, as a professional man. I wish also to express my admiration for that strict conscientiousness which I may say that I know governed the most trifling as well as the important actions of his life. Differing from him as I and many of us did in regard to his policy while President of the United States, I have never had the slightest doubt, that he was governed in all that he did by the highest sense of duty, and that he most conscientiously believed that the measures he sustained were calculated to promote the welfare of the country.

I cannot describe to those who did not know him the wonderful tact and humor, the genial conversational power, the unflagging industry, the professional skill, and the peculiar

ELOQUENCE OF SOLOMON G. HAVEN.

He was the prince of jury lawyers, and it is no disparagement to others to say that in my judgment I have never seen his equal in this department of the profession at this or at any other bar. To him, too, more than to any other man, I think, we owe the courtesy and good temper with which the contests in our courts have been conducted by the profession since I have known it. He set a most praiseworthy example in this respect, and it had a marked influence. And in closing let me say that it seems to me that now is a fitting time to congratulate ourselves upon this fact so far as we are deserving of praise, and to resolve that the future shall be an improvement upon the past. As one, I can truly say, after a practice of nearly thirty years in my profession, that I do not carry in my memory a single unkind or uncourteous word expressed to or about me by any member of the profession, during either the trial or the argument of a cause. And I am sure that all will join me in the resolve, that, entering as we are now upon

A NEW CHAPTER OF OUR LIVES

as lawyers, all unkind recollections of the past, if any such there be, shall be cast out from our memories and trodden under foot. As my brother Locke well said the other day, in summing up a cause in which we were the opposing counsel, let us endeavor more and more to bear in mind that success in a law-suit, the reputation of lawyers, the parties to litigation, are of little consequence compared with the maintenance of the laws of the land, and that the highest function of the lawyer is to aid in the pure and intelligent administration of justice.

Hon. A. P. Laning, being loudly called for, said he could only unite his congratulations with those present upon the occupation of their new quarters. How well the Commissioners had fulfilled their obligations he should leave to those present and to a generous public to judge.

Hon. L. L. Lewis was also called upon and responded briefly, reciting some of his experiences in reading law, and in his struggles and difficulties in his early practice. He entered a law-office the same year that Mr. Sprague did, 1843. During his five years of study he received no more no less than one dollar. If law students of to-day think they are inadequately compensated, they may congratulate themselves that they are quite as well paid as he was. He congratulated the Bar, both old and young members, upon the completion of the elegant court rooms in the new Hall, and hoped that their occupancy would inspire the profession to renewed efforts to raise it to a higher plane, both socially and professionally.

Appropriate remarks were also made on behalf of the younger members of the profession by Messrs. C. W. Goodyear and H. R. Squire, after which Mr. George Gorham offered the following resolution:

Resolved, That it is the sense of the Bar of Erie County, that at the sessions of the General Terms of the Supreme and Superior Courts, the Judges should enter in a body; that the Crier of the Court should announce their coming and that the members of the Bar should rise and remain standing until the Judges have taken their seats.

Mr. Gorham supported his resolution with some well-put arguments, citing similar usage in other courts and places to justify the adoption of the proposed practice here. He was followed by Messrs. George Wadsworth, John Norris, General Scroggs, George W. Cothran and M. A. Whitney, in support of the resolution, and by Messrs. L. L. Lewis and J. C. Strong, who thought the matter had better be deferred and referred to the proposed Bar Association, when formed, or to a meeting of the Bar called for the purpose of considering the question.

The resolution was finally adopted by a very decided majority, and the meeting adjourned *sine die.*

THE COMMON COUNCIL.

DEDICATION OF THE NEW CHAMBER.

THE first regular weekly meeting of the Common Council in the magnificent Chamber of the City and County Hall, was held on Monday, March 13, 1876, at 2 o'clock P. M. It was deemed eminently fitting and proper on such an occasion to observe some formalities other than the usual routine of business, which should commemorate an event of no little importance and long to be remembered by the present generation in Buffalo. Accordingly, the programme arranged by the committee was carried out in good order, in the presence of as large a company of ladies and gentlemen as the spacious room would accommodate. Only those to whom tickets had been issued were admitted, as otherwise the crowd who would have sought admission would have been quite too large. Extra seats for the visitors were provided in the lobbies, and also within the railings. The Germania Band, numbering forty pieces and in full uniform, was ranged in front of the platform occupied by the City Clerk and reporters.

Shortly after two o'clock the meeting was called to order by the president, Alderman A. S. Bemis. All the members were present.

His Honor Mayor Becker, the Rev. Drs. J. C. Lord, Wm. Shelton, and A. T. Chester, ex-Mayors Hiram Barton and Chandler J. Wells, and Hon. G. W. Clinton occupied seats upon the dais with the presiding officer.

Dr. Lord opened the special exercises in pronouncing the following prayer:

O, Lord God, our Heavenly Father, we thank Thee that we are permitted to come into this noble edifice and look upon this great work. We thank Thee that in Thy holy and eternal providence Thou hast suffered it thus to be brought to completion; that no fires have devoured it; that no raging whirlwind has torn it apart, and that no trembling of the earth has torn it asunder, and that we have it fully and complete here to-day. We give thanks to God for all His mercies, and implore His divine benediction upon this structure in the years to come, that it may be spared to the city that it may be preserved in Thy providence, that it may remain in future generations as a monument of those of the present age. O, we pray Thee, that the legislators who may assemble in this place from time to time, and year to year, may be guided by Thy good spirit. May they have that spirit of wisdom and understanding which alone can come by Thy divine love. May the counsels of this body be just; may they ever be free from corruption; may they ever seek the good of the great city. O, Lord, we ask Thee to bless them in their incoming and outgoing. Lord, guide and bless and sanctify them. May this fair city grow until no man can count the number of its population ; and may it spread like its sister cities in power and commerce. O, Lord, grant that Thy divine work come, and may the people grow wiser, and may they improve, and may they receive the Gospel of the blessed God, and that this land may be known as a Christian land, and under Christian influence and guided by Christian influence. Now, O, Lord, hear our prayer, as we commend this body to Thee. Be Thou, O, Lord, their guide, their protector and their friend; and do for them bountifully beyond what they are able to ask, or even to think. Amen.

Hon. Philip Becker, Mayor of Buffalo, and one of the Building Commissioners, then spoke as follows:

ADDRESS OF MAYOR BECKER.

Mr. President and Members of the Common Council:

We have assembled here to-day to celebrate the opening of the new City and County Hall, and the duty has devolved upon me as chief executive of the city to welcome you, and through your presiding officer to entrust to your care and custody this beautiful Council Chamber. You have reason to be proud, called as you are by the voice of the people to occupy seats in this room and in this magnificent structure, which is deservedly the pride and ornament of our city.

From a small village, with but few houses, Buffalo has grown to be a beautiful, prosperous and enterprising city, and has attained the name of Queen City of the Lakes, from her position, beauty and importance. The rapid progress, wealth and enterprise of her citizens required, notwithstanding the financial depression of the time, a public building for the accommodation of the different departments of the city government. Immediately upon the appointment of the Board of Commissioners, the matter was promptly taken in hand, and the result of their labors is demonstrated to-day, in the completion of this superb edifice.

Permit me, gentlemen, to say that when you convene in this Chamber, to attend to your official duties, you should lay aside all partisan and personal considerations, and guard the honor and pledge yourselves to be loyal to

THE BEST INTERESTS OF THE CITY.

Responsibilities and duties always important, at times onerous and delicate, rest upon you. Let your actions be animated by a spirit of harmony, and you will not only receive the plaudits, but the gratitude of your constituency. You are the first corporate body to hold its meeting and deliberations in this Chamber, and as it happens to be in the centennial year, an event that will not easily be obliterated from our memory, let all your actions be in conformity with the interests of the taxpayers. You are the

LEGISLATIVE BODY OF THIS CITY.

and to your hands is entrusted the interest of the entire community. Aim toward economy, reduction of taxes and the general improvement and prosperity of the city, and you will have the respect and confidence of every well-minded citizen. I hope and trust that no act or actions of the Common Council will ever disgrace or dishonor this Chamber. It is my most sincere wish that all your proceedings hereafter may be of such a nature as to merit the approval of the executive branch of the municipal government and the citizens at large.

In reply to Mayor Becker, President Bemis said:

ADDRESS OF PRESIDENT BEMIS.

Mr. Mayor: On behalf of the Common Council of the city of Buffalo, and of the people we here represent, I thank you, sir, and the Board of Commissioners, of which you are a member, for the generous and substantial manner in which these spacious accommodations have been provided for this Council, and in accepting the same, I have to ask, that you will please convey to the Board of Commissioners, the unqualified approbation of this body, in all things pertaining to their acts, in regard to the interests of this city in the trust reposed in them.

The Council will undoubtedly take such action in the premises as will give fitting expression to its views upon this subject, to be entered upon the minutes of this Board.

Addressing the Council and those present, President Bemis then spoke as follows:

Gentlemen of the Common Council: This Board assembles to-day, under an agreeable change of circumstances, especially in regard to its place of meeting, and it would seem eminently proper that some fitting recognition of the change that has been wrought should be manifested by this Council, at this, its first meeting here. And as this occasion calls to my mind reminiscences concerning the early history of this Franklin square, which, taken in connection with the history of this building, it may not be deemed inappropriate to relate at this time. I am, therefore, led to ask your indulgence in a few brief remarks applicable to the occasion.

Gentlemen, as I stand here to-day, and view the vast proportions and elegant style of this spacious and commodious Hall that has been provided and set apart for the use of this Council, and contrast the scene of to-day with the sorrowful scenes of long ago that have been witnessed upon the ground whereon this grand structure has been erected, I confess that I feel almost over-awed at the change which the transition from the solemnities of the past to the grandeur of the present has produced.

MEMORY CARRIES ME BACK OVER HALF A CENTURY

to the days of my childhood and early youth, when the land upon which this building now stands, was the common and only burial-place for the dead of the then village of Buffalo, for which purpose it had been dedicated by the Holland Land Company, when laying out the village. My aged mother, who is still living in Buffalo, informs me that her father, Gamaliel St. John and Elias Ransom, organized a "chopping bee," and cleared this ground of its original timber-growth, and laid it out aa s place for the reception of the dead. Mr. St. John had buried his second son here, soon after coming to Buffalo, and he and his eldest son were subsequently buried here in 1813, both having been drowned together in the Niagara river, by the upsetting of the boat in which they and a party of men were crossing from Black Rock to the Canada shore, in the interests of the American army, and in the endeavor to open up and establish communication with a portion of the American forces, then holding possession of Fort Erie and other posts in the vicinity. And here, almost beneath the place where I now stand, the remains of my father reposed for nearly thirty years, having been buried here in 1823. Others of my kindred, also,

SLUMBERED IN THIS SACRED PLAT OF GROUND

for many years; and it is a somewhat singular coincidence, that the kindly acts of my grandfather, St. John, in giving a respectable and sightly appearance to this village burial-ground in its earliest use, became coupled with the fact, that members of his own family were about the first—and the very last that found sepulture in it, his daughter, the wife of the late Judge Samuel Wilkeson, being the last. Judge Wilkeson was the Mayor of this city at the time of his wife's death in 1836, and the Common Council granted him a special permit to bury her here, long after interment in this ground had been prohibited. Many of the early settlers in Buffalo, whose names are now only remembered by a very few of the living of to-day, rested here from their labors, as did also some of their children and their children's children after them. And here also, in this old graveyard, the children of fifty years ago were wont to wander from their sports upon the adjacent green. The village school-house was near by, and this was their favorite place of retreat when let loose from school. Thus, the children of my time became curious lookers-on at many a scene of sorrow and sadness, at times when their sports were interrupted by the lamentations of those bereaved, who brought hither to this once hallowed and holy spot their loved ones to be returned to their parent dust. And such were the scenes here of the long ago, that come up before me to-day in contrast with the present. And what a change! But death, the great harvester of all earthly and human hopes is also a most constant gleaner; and the hand of ambition is seldom if ever stayed, and pays but poor respect at times to the dead or the living.

Buffalo had grown to an incorporated city in 1832, with Ebenezer Johnson for its first Mayor, a portrait of whom has recently been presented by his daughter, Mrs. Dr. Lord, to be hung upon the walls of the Mayor's office in this building.

THE FIRST VISIT OF THE ASIATIC CHOLERA

to the shores of America in 1832, brought a most unwelcome guest to this young and growing city; and the consequences were direful indeed. The capacity of this common burial-place was taxed to its uttermost, and interments in it were therefore soon prohibited. Meanwhile other cemeteries were established, and many of the dead removed thither from this ground, by the voluntary acts of surviving friends; and finally in 1852, the remains of all were removed by order of the Common Council, and at the public expense, to a lot in Forest Lawn, procured for the purpose. The remains of about two thousand bodies were so removed, and with few exceptions were without recognition by surviving friends, and without tombstones or tablets were promiscously interred, where they now sleep unnumbered and unknown, awaiting identification at the final resurrection. The city erected a fitting monument to the memory of a few distinguished officers of the war of 1812, whose remains were among those removed to Forest Lawn, and thus ended the "graveyard scenes" in this time-honored and historic ground. The city having acquired absolute title to this land before the removal of the dead, a new era soon dawned upon the visions of men in regard to its future use. Some agitated the project of a public square or park. The city authorities had also been required by decisions to vacate the Terrace between Main and Pearl streets, then occupied by what was known as the Terrace Market building—the upper story of which was devoted to the use of the Common Council and city offices. Hon. Hiram Barton was then Mayor; and to his foresight and energy, was due the plan of purchasing the Franklin street front of this public ground, and the fitting up of the buildings thereon for city purposes, and with a view also to its ultimate use as a site for a City Hall, when a new one should be required. This project was carried into effect in pursuance of an enabling act of the legislature. The land was purchased and merged with the old burial-ground, and the whole was dedicated as Franklin Square, reserving in the center thereof, a site for a City Hall.

I had the honor of being a member of this body at the time this was done, and voted for the measure; and I have been spared and favored to be here to-day, at the consummation of the plans of nearly a quarter of a century ago, and permitted to take part with you in these ceremonies. The good people of this city, and the county of Erie have most nobly seconded these early efforts that were made. Nay, we might almost say, they have been extravagant and lavish, in these times of financial embarrassment throughout the land, in erecting such a grand and costly structure as this City and County Hall proves to be. But when we consider that the wants and

REQUIREMENTS OF OUR LOCAL GOVERNMENT,

for all time to come, as well as for the present, have formed a chief part of the study of the Commissioners who have been entrusted with the construction of this building, we cannot but say, that their labors have been arduous indeed, and exceedingly well performed; and that the accommodations and conveniences provided for the several branches of the city and county governments, as well as for the judiciary, are all that could be desired, and will prove adequate therefor, while these granite walls shall stand. The various departments of the city government have been transferred to this magnificent edifice; and it remains for the Common Council to inaugurate herein the legislative branch thereof. The session of to-day will, therefore, form a note-worthy event in the history of this city in connection with the dedication of this building in this centennial year; and the record of this day's proceedings will long outlive the members whose names are recorded at this first roll-call of the Common Council in this elegant and spacious Hall.

Gentlemen of the Common Council, we are here assembled, with our fellow-citizens in attendance,

TO SOLEMNLY DEDICATE THIS CHAMBER

to the uses for which it has been set apart; and it were well, indeed, if we, the members of this body, should likewise here dedicate ourselves to the welfare and prosperity of this city, and to its people as well, who have entrusted us with the powers we here possess; vouchsafing to them, if it were possible for us so to do, that the local legislation of this city shall from this day forward, have a new departure, that shall be commendable in their sight, and that shall prove worthy of imitation, by all who shall come after us, to occupy these seats.

At the conclusion of the address of the presiding officer, Hon. George W. Clinton, Chief Judge of the Superior Court, was introduced, and spoke as follows:

ADDRESS OF HON. G. W. CLINTON.

Mr. President and Gentlemen: I feel most deeply the honor you have done me. But I cannot—I know I cannot—adequately express my sense of it, nor my respect for you. Old recollections of the day of little things, when I was Mayor of our then infant city, and of the men, now dead, whose virtues and exertions contributed to confirm its safety and exalt its honor, crowd into my mind and almost overwhelm me. But neither recollections of the past nor exultation in the greatness and goodness of our dear city can make me eloquent. The contrast is too great, the grief too deep. It seems to me, removed as I have been for many years from active public life, that I belong to the puny past rather than to the glorious present. The unwonted magnificence of this noble Council Chamber confounds me, and the solemnity of this audience disturbs me. Were it not for the fact that in you I recognize my own dear friends and neighbors, I might well imagine myself standing in the Roman Senate, this Chamber is so perfect and so grand. Ebenezer Johnson, the first Mayor of Buffalo, went to his reward many weary years ago. But when his son-in-law, the Reverend Dr. Lord, invoked the blessing of Almighty God upon our city and ourselves, the majestic form of that worthy man and faithful citizen rose up before me. My old college friend and room-mate must excuse me. I must say that his presence gives me profound pleasure, and that I, in common, I doubt not, with all who hear me, venerate his well spent life and reciprocate his prayers.

Rightly understood, there is wondrous and solemn truth in the oft-quoted lines:

> "How fares the land, to hastening ills a prey,
> Where wealth accumulates and men decay!
> Princes or lords may flourish or may fade;
> A breath can make them, as a breath has made;
> But a bold peasantry, their country's pride,
> When once destroyed can never be supplied."

Here where the majority forms the government and controls its policy, if the virtues of the masses be sapped, unbounded and irresponsible ruin must be the consequence.

Thank heaven, the people whom we serve are intelligent and uncorrupt. The people of Erie county, and of every part of it, are kind, and liberal, and noble. We office-holders are its servants; and we, in this great City and County Hall, if we are wicked and slothful servants, can never say to it, "Lord, we know thee that thou art an hard man, reaping where thou hast not sown, and gathering where thou hast not strewed." This massive building, famous for all time, with its rich, chaste ornamentation, its admirable appointments for health and comfort, and its perfect adaptations and conveniences for the discharge of all county and city official duties, is, and will remain forever, a witness of the just pride and generous spirit that animates our people, and, we trust, an admonition and incentive to fidelity and honor. Too high praise can hardly be awarded to the Commissioners who have so thoroughly and wisely given effect to the popular will. But to the people of our city and county we and all posterity must attribute the glory of this marvelous achievement.

What, my friends, is the acceptance of office, but a contract? No nobly-minded man seeks any office except for the honor to do some service to the public. He will not take a paid sinecure. He desires, perhaps needs, the emoluments of office, but he feels that his contract binds him to fidelity to the interests and the honor of his master, and is determined to earn them.

THE FAITHFUL OFFICER HAS HIS REWARD

in the respect, perhaps in the affection of the public, and goes down to an honored grave; but the betrayer of a public trust withers under public scorn and private detestation, sinks into a shameful grave, and leaves to his descendants the odious inheritance of his tainted name. Of the infamy that follows the plunderer of the public, we have, alas! a recent example in the late Secretary Belknap. We have another sad example in our city. Better far to die any honest death, though it be to be torn asunder by horses, to be hung, drawn and quartered, to be impaled, than to survive with the unutterable shame that dogs the heels and the intolerable remorse that gnaws, or ought to gnaw, the soul of the perjured thief, of the money entrusted to him by the people.

O, my friends! true and loyal representatives of the generous people that you are—intrusted as you are with the conservation and promotion of their interests, and with the maintenance of the fair fame of our city, you will, we are confident, be always vigilant and faithful, and persistently tenacious of integrity and honor. It is an honor beyond all price to be trusted as you are by the people of Buffalo. This is an epoch in our history—an era worthy of all manner of commemoration. The name of our worthy Mayor ought, with your names, to be engraven, as the first occupants of this Chamber, here on eternal granite, in golden letters; and, somewhere—perhaps in the center of the first floor—a column of granite ought to bear, in detached blocks, the name of any and every officer who now is, or in the far future shall be, basely traitorous to our city.

How strong and beautiful is our great city! How nobly she sits above and looks out upon the lake! How magnanimous she is, and how rich is the reward to those whom she says: "Well done, thou good and faithful servant." May the Almighty inspire me, and you, and all her servants, with a fixed longing for that reward, and give us grace to win it.

CONGRATULATIONS AND THANKS.

When Judge Clinton had concluded his feeling address, Alderman N. C. Simons offered the following resolutions, and moved their adoption:

Resolved, That the congratulations of this Council be and the same are hereby extended to the citizens of the city of Buffalo and of the county of Erie upon the successful completion of this magnificent edifice, in which we to-day meet for the first time, which building is the noblest architectural ornament of our fair city, and may be regarded as the just pride of every citizen of Erie county.

Resolved, That the thanks of this Council be, and the same are hereby tendered, to the Building Commissioners of this City and County Hall, for the commodious and elegant quarters assigned to this body in said building.

Speaking upon the resolutions, Alderman Simons said:

ADDRESS OF ALDERMAN SIMONS.

Mr. President: It is with feelings of the liveliest satisfaction and pride that I rise to speak to the resolutions now pending. The record of this day will long be marked as a red letter page in our history, and in making it a day of jubilee and mutual congratulation, we are but giving expression to the feelings which animate the breasts of all classes of our fellow citizens. It has been well said, Mr. President, that in union there is strength, and the truth of that ancient saying has been strikingly verified in the erection of this magnificent structure, whose towering spire pierces the upper air, a lofty testimony of what such strength may accomplish.

Some years ago it had become manifest that our prosperous and expanding city had outgrown its public buildings, and a bold stand was taken for a City and County Hall which should meet our growing wants, and be an ornament alike to the County of Erie and the Queen City of the Lakes, and instead of dividing the interests of city and county, the wiser plan was adopted, and with the city's co-operation the noble towns comprising the county of Erie came forward with boldness and energy to join in the noble work, the result of which unity we view with just pride in the building in which we this day meet for the first time, and which we to-day dedicate to the use and occupancy of this and coming generations.

The choosing of the site on which to erect the structure became a matter of great moment, and after much thought and investigation, Franklin park was selected, and although to many it is not Zion,

"BEAUTIFUL FOR SITUATION,"

yet I boldly assert that its contiguity to the various railroad depots, from which come vast throngs of people having business with the

County Clerk and Treasurer, the Surrogate and the various Courts, its proximity to the offices of the legal fraternity, and its convenient access to all classes of our citizens, makes the location the most convenient to the greatest number; and when in a few years we shall be able to sweep away the intervening buildings between this and Main street, and when the City and County Hall Park shall bloom in all its loveliness, our chronic croakers will be compelled to admit the wisdom of the choice.

Mr. President, the spot on which we stand is consecrated ground, for the soil beneath our feet was once the resting-place of the remains of many of this county's illustrious dead, but as must always be the case in this live and busy, progressive world, the dead have been crowded out to make room for the living. It is a suggestive fact, the venerable divine who to-day opened with prayer the dedicatory service, officiated at the last rights of him whose mortal remains were last deposited within these grounds. Now they repose beneath the quiet shades of beautiful Forest Lawn, where (almost reverently do I say),. peace be to their ashes, while here upon the soil thus made sacred has risen this massive granite pile, with heavenward pointing spire, to stand as an enduring monument to their energetic work while living, and their resting-place when dead.

Mr. President, we must congratulate ourselves upon the most fortunate selection of the Building Commissioners, for among them were men of large understanding and strict integrity, and thorough business capacity, and under their most careful attention—with closely scrutinized contracts and competitive bids for labor and material—the whole work has been done for the lowest possible pay, and while many who have taken contracts have gone away wounded and limping, but few have gone away with a chuckle that they had taken away many more dollars than they had put down; while all who have had jobs for labor or material have worked chiefly without further profit than that derived from the advertisement of their goods, wares and merchandise, for which this building has afforded a most excellent opportunity.

Among such advertisers may be found representatives not only of our city, but of New York, Boston, New Albany and Hartford, and all have left work here of which they may well be proud.

The materials have been purchased, as far as possible, of our own tradesmen and manufacturers. The various industries of our city and county have been patronized, and the labor in construction has been by our own people; and I here, in the presence of this audience, assert that this City and County Hall

IS THE BEST BUILDING FOR THE MONEY

it cost, that stands on the western continent, for it has been erected without the rings and accompanying stealings that usually prevail in jobs of such magnitude.

Of the Building Commissioners, all of whom have labored so faithfully and well, I am sure the other members will forgive me if I only make mention of one name, and his is inseparably connected with this building, for he has styled it his "baby," and having watched it from its infancy up to full stature, I hope and pray that he will not be led to exclaim, like Simeon of old, "mine eyes have seen thy glory, and now let thy servant depart in peace." It is scarcely necessary to say that the name I allude to is that of Dennis Bowen.

Mr. President, it is altogether probable that some of those who for the first time visit the several apartments exclaim, this is extravagance. This smacks too strong of dollars and cents in many of its details. This chandelier with its colossal proportions, for example, may be thought too large, costly, gorgeous. Yet a glance at the general architectural design of the chamber reveals the fact that it is only in equal and exact proportions. Let it be remembered that this magnificent structure was not built for a day, but for time; and when yonder clock, whose pendulum tells by pairs the fleeting seconds, and whose electric life may be noted by the jumping minutes on twenty-eight dials of which this is one, shall have faithfully marked the cumulative years, and when on the midnight air shall peal forth from that deep-toned bell the second centennial year of America's independence, this granite pile will be found intact from base to dome.

Now, Mr. President and fellow-members of this Common Council, I come to the second resolution, and I may observe that this is where the laugh comes in. The Building Commissioners have bestowed upon us, through our worthy Mayor, this roomy, well-ventilated chamber, having with a lavish hand fitted out and adorned it so magnificently that we find ourselves to-day occupying the most elegant Council Chamber in these United States, and most ungrateful would we be if we did not all most cheerfully and heartily endorse the resolution.

Finally, as we are out of the old house into the new, let us begin our work here with the high resolve so to discharge our duties that when we have been gathered to the land of our fathers, and when the heads of wisdom which now grace and adorn this chamber shall have passed away, and these halls shall echo to the tread of other foot-falls, and when our children shall gather here, it may be said of the Council of the first centennial year of the republic—the first to occupy this chamber—that its record was without spot or stain.

In seconding the motion for the adoption of the resolutions, Ald. A. L. Lothridge said:

REMARKS OF ALDERMAN LOTHRIDGE.

Mr. President and Members of the Council: I heartily second the motion of the alderman of the Ninth. Surrounded by our fellow-citizens, whose faces are an index of the mingled admiration and wonder that possessed them on entering this magnificent building, we can well afford to give toneful expression to their silent congratulations; and we should be derelict in our duties as municipal legislators did we not also convey to those gentlemen, on whom the burden rested, our heartfelt appreciation of the success which has crowned their efforts in presenting at last to the admiration of every beholder one of the noblest temples of justice and law in these United States.

It certainly is a good omen—and one we hope may prove propitious—that this epoch in our municipal history is glorified in the recurrence of the hundredth anniversary of our National Independence. Who will gainsay that to-day's event may not mark the beginning of a renewed life in city government; the ending of strife and party hostility which, unhappily, but too often was manifested in the time-worn structure we have just deserted.

Gentlemen of the Council: Ours the pride denied our predecessors! Ours the glory they fain would covet! In like manner let ours be the task of revivifying the purity of government and integrity of purpose that animated the men who first made the walls of the old Council re-echo with

THE HONEST PLEA OF THE TAXPAYER.

Let us bring into this new temple an ambition to excel only in an unselfish regard of duty and a jealous care for the weal of those who have proclaimed us their representatives. Let the mistakes of the past be buried in the destruction of yonder building, which soon will be among the things of the past.

The time, the scene, the occasion, all these, gentlemen of the Council, I know animate us with a feeling of good-fellowship for one another, and for just and unselfish legislation. If, in the prosecution of our manifold duties, we are actuated by patriotism, and that patriotism is the outgrowth of love of justice, and that justice the parent of honesty, and that honesty the essence of virtue that springs from the fountain of all truth, no man can point at us the finger of derision; no future will blast our reputation! A hundred years hence posterity may not have forgotten the first meeting in this new Hall, and the Council of 1976 may meet and feel as we meet and feel to-day.

The resolutions offered by Ald. Simons were adopted unanimously.

DEDICATION AND DETERMINATION.

Ald. Elijah Ambrose then offered the following resolution:

That in the name of the citizens of Buffalo, whose representatives we are, we dedicate this legislative hall to the exclusive use of the Common Council. As the construction of this splendid edifice marks a new era in the growth and progress of our beautiful city, illustrating a higher order of architectural taste, so may the future action of this Council give evidence of greater devotion to the public interest, of stronger determination to secure a pure and economical municipal government, and more careful and constant endeavor to protect and promote the welfare of our citizens.

In moving the adoption of his resolution, Ald. Ambrose said:

REMARKS OF ALDERMAN AMBROSE.

The resolution just read speaks for itself, and it is a very easy matter for this Council to carry out its instructions. In the first place let each alderman before he enters into this noble building shake the dust from his garments, and at the same time not forget but also shake the politics from his mind, and let no personal favoritism be shown where it is to the injury of others; and this same advice I would also give to the heads of all the departments in our city government, including the judiciary. Let us not strive to gain party advantage over each other, but let us legislate for the greatest good to the greatest number; by so doing we will unite in a common cause, and look to the interest of our taxpayers and to the prosperity of our beautiful city.

Ald. Ferris, in seconding the motion for the adoption of the resolution offered by Ald. Ambrose, addressed the Council and those present as follows:

SPEECH OF ALDERMAN FERRIS.

Mr. President: It is not very often that so distinguished an audience and so well assorted with the fair sex, and those whom we love and honor, listen to the deliberations of the Common Council, and inasmuch as our friend Ambrose proposed to pledge that this Council in the future shall be free, so that when the public shall read in the newspapers the record of its doings that it shall be with satisfaction that every taxpayer shall be satisfied with its proceedings, it seems proper to reply to this resolution. Not in opposition to its sentiment, for I honor the member from the Fifth Ward in his sentiment, but let us pledge before this audience our honest endeavor to do what we believe to be right. I know that at times the taxpayers of the City of Buffalo will have occasion to make complaint. I know that they have had occasion to make complaint at the action of the Common Council in the past. I see before me many men who have occupied the position before me, and I see but few, if any, who have left it with their honor tainted or the maledictions of the public resting upon them. I enter into the sentiments that have been expressed in these resolutions in this Council Chamber with feelings of pride—pride that I have been so long a time a citizen of so proud a city. I can say with a citizen of old,

"I AM A CITIZEN OF NO MEAN CITY,"

but a city of honor, whose name has ever been and ever will be a name of honor among her sister cities.

I am pleased that so large a number of our fellow-citizens have attended with us also at this opening, and I have to thank them, and say we are glad to be recognized by you, and in the future, if you have occasion to find fault with the action of this Council, bear with great consideration with the present, and with the future members of it, for we are of the people. We are not born into any line of nobility by which we acquire any position in this place, but acquire them because of the choice and selection of the people whom we represent, and as we come from them, it seems to me, that when I see the honorable men who sit upon the platform with you, and surround us here, and who so seldom make their appearance at the Council Chamber, unless it is for some personal or private reason—it seems to me that this is an appropriate occasion for every member of the Common Council to make a determination set forth in this resolution, that, so help him God, he will strive to do what is right and honest and just before all men. [Great applause.]

The resolution was then unanimously adopted, and the Council took a recess for mutual congratulations with their constituents present, and to permit a more informal inspection of their spacious Chamber and its rich and beautiful appointments.

RELIGIOUS CEREMONIES.

A MEMORIAL SERMON—AN INTERESTING DISCOURSE BY DR. HEACOCK.

REV. DR. GROSVENOR W. HEACOCK commemorated the event of the completion of the new Hall in the delivery of a historical discourse appropriate to the occasion. The Doctor was born in Buffalo, and, although he is not as old as the venerable Court House, he has, nevertheless, for nearly a third of a century officiated as pastor of the Lafayette Street Presbyterian Church, that has a frontage upon Court House Park in the immediate vicinity of the old and now deserted temple of justice. The Sermon was delivered Sunday evening, March 12, and was especially addressed to the legal profession, a goodly number of whom being present.

The reverend speaker said:

Dear Friends and Brethren: You will excuse my taking notice of an event of so much interest to me, to the county, and to you, as the abandonment of the old Court House, the seat of justice and of judgment among you so many years. You may wonder, indeed, how such an event should find an appropriate place and notice here in a Christian pulpit on the Sabbath day. I hope you may find reason to justify this act before I have done.

IT HAS BEEN OUR NEIGHBOR

for nearly thirty-one years. My recollections of the old and venerable structure, which can be said no longer to grace our streets and park, runs back as far, probably further, than that of most of you. And singular enough, and appropriate to this day and occasion, my first recollections of that old interior are more connected with the gospel than the law. For in the winters of 1831 and 1832, the old Court House was occupied for religious services, and then your speaker—then a lad of eleven years of age—believes that he first began to realize the verities and to feel the power of a religious life. It would be impertinent to dwell at any length upon an experience so personal, but this I may say, that I believe then and there, as far as a boy might realize, I realized the hopes and fears, the anxieties and joys, which attend the beginning of a religious life. The next incident that occurs to my mind, as connected with that old Court House, carries us by a great leap over many years, and was the celebrated

TRIAL OF THE BUFFALO BANK.

George P. Barker, then Attorney-General of the State, and at the height of his fame, was in attendance as prosecutor for the government. The case had awakened a very general and great interest, especially in this community. Hiram Pratt, the president of the bank, was dead. The Court House was crowded to its utmost capacity. I do not remember any of the details of the case. I have heard my genial friend, J. Hyatt Smith, tell of his coming on from Albany to be a witness in the case, in the rude baggage car, where he was compelled to stay to keep guard over a trunk of bank bills he had brought on for testimony in the trial. In the same rude car with him was a plain man, in rough working garb, who had a few express packages with him, which he was personally delivering from station to station. These two took turns with each other, Smith watching his friend's packages when he went out of the car, and the friend his trunk when he wished to go out. They called the man "Fargo," and this was the beginning of that grand enterprize of business energy and skill which has belted the continent with the lines of "Fargo's Express." I have said the bank case had excited a great interest in the community. The intensity of the excitement was too great for Mr. Barker's strength. He was in a community where he had long lived, and it was, I think, his first and last official visit. When he rose to speak at one point of the case, I noticed clearly that he had lost control of his nervous energy—his hand trembled perceptibly as he endeavored to carry a glass of water to his lips, so violently as to make the agitation visible to all. I learned from that simple incident one secret of the true orator's power. There is no doubt that Mr. Barker was an orator, but then, to my mind, he had lost hold for the moment of one of its grandest secrets. He who would control others must be able to control himself. He must not tremble and shrink beneath the cloud, no matter how charged with electricity it may be; he must leap upon the cloud, and turn its thunders upon those whom he would crush or overwhelm. I felt such a pity for him—he could never have aroused within me a nobler sentiment of indignation. An almost perfect contrast to this was another scene I witnessed later in the old court room, and that was the first plea of the late before a jury. Mr. Mullet's fame as a jury lawyer had preceded him here, and many of his friends were gathered to hear his first plea to a Buffalo jury. The venerable ex-President, Mr. Fillmore, so lately deceased among us, was opposing counsel in the trial. I need not allude to the nature of the case. Mr. Fillmore had not risen then to the great distinction he afterwards attained, but was even then a very prominent personage in the political world. He had just returned from Congress where he held the important post of Chairman of the Committee on Ways and Means in the House of Representatives. His plea was marked by that strong sound sense and clear discrimination, which was the characteristic of the man in his profession. When he had closed, Mr. Mullet rose. You could see he was laboring under great excitement, but he, perfectly mastered it—it never for a moment mastered him. Folding his arms across his breast as a measure of self-control, as I thought, he began: "May it please the Court and Gentlemen of the Jury"—and then he went on. I think I could almost give the passage; suffice it to say, that, beginning with a slow and measured movement, the sentence as it went on gathered volume and power—the sighing of the rising tempest, the roll of the approaching thunder was in it—till finally it closed with a burst of indignation and appeal like the crash of thunder over the very heads of the whole audience and jury. There were explanations to be made after that to justify his points, but it seemed to me as if from the close of that first sentence the case was already won.

You may well ask, gentlemen, what have such incidents as these to do with such a time and place as this, and I will tell you. When I think and when you think what

A BRILLIANT ARRAY OF ELOQUENT NAMES,

of matchless arguments and successful pleadings where vice and crime have been overthrown and convicted, and virtue defended and honored; when you think of what a glorious history of all these incidents and names, the memories of that old court room bring back to you, are we not more impressed than ever with the glory, and yet the vanity of men's forensic victories and triumphs. Where are these great names now? Where the memory of their great efforts?

> Like smoke which the tempests in fury have riven,
> Like foam which the waves in their blindness have driven;
> They were, but they are not, their triumphs are o'er,
> And the place that once knew them shall know them no more.

The conscientious pleader in the cause of truth and justice bears with him, indeed, through life, the dear memory, more priceless than jewels, of noble efforts well and worthily made, of noble triumphs well and worthily won. While he who has lent legal skill and study and eloquence to defend the wrong and prevent and defeat justice, memory consumes for him an apple of Sodom, fair to the seeming but ashes and bitterness at the core. This is a lesson for which, God's altars are none too sacred a spot, to learn.

Gentlemen, I was not educated for the profession to which you belong, and it is with the greatest diffidence that I venture to detain you for a single moment longer, to present one single truth which your studies have prepared you more profoundly to realize than even a theologian can.

In turning over the pages of a late autobiography of a distinguished preacher whose ministry was largely effective in your profession, I came across a single statement of one of the topics on which in a course of sermons to lawyers this preacher had addressed them. The topic was this, "That admitting that God was infinitely benevolent, we could not infer from that, on principles of law as administered now in good governments, that sin could be forgiven, but must infer from it on the contrary that incorrigible sinners could not be forgiven." None of the details of the arguments are given—not any of the proofs by which it was made out—yet the statement rested with such power upon my mind, and during this week even my own little legal reading brought up to my mind and memory a course of thought and illustration which seemed to me very conclusive on the point, which I will briefly present to you, only premising if this be the truth that the presumptions under a good and wise human government are

AGAINST PARDON;

they are increased under an infinitely good and wise government, and if the scheme of forgiveness presented in the Bible is not true, we are shut out of all rational hope of any such thing as the forgiveness of real sin or wrong under and against God's government, *i. e.*, if the Bible is not true. Let us look a moment at this case. The civil governments under which we live are and may be regarded as generally benevolent, and yet on what principle are the provisions for pardon based in these governments? Why, manifestly and largely upon the imperfections of human jurisprudence, the native and inevitable imperfections of our procedures for the ascertainment of guilt; that you know is largely and generally the principle. If a man has clearly committed a crime, in a clearly responsible state of mind, has been fairly tried, and his guilt fairly and unmistakably ascertained, why, he goes to his punishment. Suppose you apply to the governor for pardon in such cases. He says to you: Gentlemen, I will hear what you have to say in this case; was this man of sound mind and condition? Did he know clearly what he was doing? Was he fairly tried and fairly condemned? Then how can I interfere? There the case ends—crime and punishment!

The speaker dwelt at some length upon excessive punishment, and argued that it ought to be fairly adjusted to the nature of the crime, and that the pardoning power in a good government is based largely, if not exclusively, upon the apprehended imperfection of human law. He said the hope of pardon for real sin—sin against God's supreme authority clearly and fully recognized it, was a very feeble one without the Bible. And yet, who has not sinned? In conclusion the speaker expressed the sentiment that the gentlemen ought to have no trouble in accepting the grand truth of the Bible—of a great day, of general and final assize and judgment. These things must be in human governments to remove certainly and securely away the evil and dangerous members of society. The public and open administration of justice is needful for its influence on society, the good and the bad. Such a day will come in the history of the universe. It is the judgment of the great day, and man is moving surely and irresistibly toward that day.

THE BANQUET.

A PLEASANT REUNION OF THE ERIE COUNTY BAR.

THE concluding ceremonies in connection with the completion and occupancy of the City and County Hall were observed in a grand banquet or social re-union of the legal profession, at the Tifft House, Messrs. Tuthill Bros., proprietors, on Tuesday evening, March 14, 1876.

The members of the Bar and invited guests, to the number of about one hundred and fifty persons, assembled in the parlors at 8, P. M., and were soon escorted into the banquet hall, where two elegant and bountifully spread tables extended the entire length of the hall, with one at right angles and uniting the tables at the upper end of the room, and forming the head, or post of honor.

The windows and doors were hung and festooned with bunting and the stars and stripes; fresh and fragrant flowers in abundance lent a charm to the interesting scene; and Wahle's Band supplied its choicest music for the occasion.

The company entered the hall under the direction of the Committee of Arrangements, Hon. E. Carlton Sprague, Chairman of the evening, and the Rev. Dr. J. C. Lord in advance, who took their positions at the center of the transverse table at the head of the room. Then came, and were seated upon their right, His Honor Mayor Philip Becker, Hon. G. W. Clinton, Hon. James O. Putnam, Gen. L. W. Thayer, Hon. Geo. R. Babcock, Judge Albert Haight, W. H. Greene, O. H. Marshall, Geo. Wadsworth; and upon their left, Hon. Richard P. Marvin, Judge James M. Smith, Judge James Sheldon, Hon. E. G. Spaulding, Hon. L. L. Lewis, Hon. H. S. Cutting, and Thos. J. Sizer, with other distinguished legal gentlemen, still farther down; while Gen. G. A. Scroggs and Col. J. M. Willett served as Vice-Chairmen at the other ends of the tables. At the right and left extremities of the Chairman's table were stationed District Attorney D. N. Lockwood and City Attorney John B. Greene. When all were in their places, Dr. Lord invoked a blessing upon the occasion.

The company then seated themselves, and gave earnest attention to the bill of fare, which was of the usual "comprehensive" character. Each legal gentleman present proved himself a good judge, so far as this one was concerned, and hence it follows that full and complete justice was done to the substantials and delicacies which it included. At intervals during the hour in which all this was going on, fine music was furnished by the band.

Finally, the bill of fare having been thoroughly "discussed," Chairman Sprague arose and rapped for order, having secured which, he addressed the assembly as follows:

REMARKS OF MR. SPRAGUE.

May it please your Honors, the Judges of the Superior Court, and your Honor, the Judge of the County Court, Brethren of the Bar of Erie county, and Gentlemen: I congratulate you upon the auspicious circumstances which have brought us together this evening. I congratulate our Judges and the elder members of our Bar, upon the possession of constitutions which have enabled them to survive the poisonous atmosphere of the old Court House, and particularly of the dens contained in what has been well called the new Court House, since doubtless it is a perfect novelty in the history of architecture, unprecedented in its ugliness, unparallelled in its inconvenience, and unique in its capacity for the gradual extinction of human life. We can leave them both without regret, for, thank God, our natures are so constituted that we can carry with us all their precious memories while we leave their miseries behind. I congratulate the younger members of our fraternity that the possibility is now afforded them of prolonging their lives through the ordinary term of human existence. I congratulate the Commissioners who have had in their charge the erection of the new City and County Hall, upon its beauty and the convenience of its internal arrangements. Nothing seems to have been left undone by them which could in any way serve the use or comfort of the Bar, and I assure them that their labors in its behalf are fully appreciated and will be always gratefully remembered. Finally, I congratulate all here present upon the fact, that, after more than sixty years of patient waiting, the

BAR OF ERIE COUNTY

has finally succeeded in getting its legs together under the same—I will not say mahogany, for it is our centennial, and I am reminded of the father of our country and cannot tell a lie—but I will say, speaking centennially and patriotically, under the shade of the noble aboriginal, and national tree, the American black walnut.

Why we have waited so long to do so pleasant a thing is one of the topics that I hope to hear discussed this evening. It is not certainly from want of intelligence. The Bar that has produced a President of the United States, a member of its Cabinet, a Lieutenant Governor, cannot admit any intellectual inability either to get up a dinner or get it down. And as to the morality of this Bar, we all know how inadequate the English language is to depict its virtues. But it is a mortifying fact that in the matter of eating and drinking, this Bar as a body, whatever may be said of its individual members, has been sadly degenerate, and that its conduct in this respect calls loudly for reform. This is the more lamentable when we reflect that Bar dinners are one of the time-honored institutions of the profession. Shakespeare tells one of his characters in the "Taming of the Shrew" to do as "adversaries do in law, strive mightily, but eat and drink as friends." Now Shakespeare may not live as long in the memory of mankind as the compiler of "Barbour's Supreme Court Reports," who has lately demonstrated his immortality by the issue of his sixty-sixth volume. But even we lawyers must coincide that Shakespeare was something of an observer, and that when he took pains he handled the English language in a way that will bear comparison with some of the addresses to which the jury of Erie county have been accustomed to listen with such unqualified delight. Now we have his authority for saying that eating and drinking as friends constituted one of the important and well known functions of the legal profession of his time. So all of us who are at all familiar with the biographies of the ancient lawyers and judges of England, of those old leviathans who were accustomed to swim and spout amidst the deepest waters of the common law, will remember how faithful they were to this practice of their tribe. Who does not know that the judges and the Bar of England have always been accustomed to dine together at the assizes; and so in staid New England? My father tells me that when he was a boy he was a page in the courts of New Hampshire, in which Daniel and Ezekiel Webster were wont to strive mightily with Ichabod Bartlett and Jeremiah Mason, but never suffered a term to pass without

BURYING ALL THEIR CONTESTS

and giving to each other the hand of fellowship at the festive board. How it has been generally in New York I do not know; but with a blush I acknowledge the revolting truth that no such flagrant memories make sweet the annals of the Erie County Bar. In view of such a disgraceful record it is not surprising that the moment the message came to our ears, "Awake! Arise! or be forever fallen!" our consciences were stirred to their profoundest depths, that the pangs of remorse became unendurable, and that this festival was inaugurated as a token of our penitence for past unfaithfulness, and our resolution to lead, in this respect, at least, lives more worthy of our vocation and its traditions.

Gentlemen, since I have been a member of the bar, now nearly thirty years, it has been honorably free from petty jealousies and personal hostilities, and its controversies have been conducted with a fair degree of courtesy and mutual respect. But apart from our professional intercourse we have seen little of each other. We do not fully appreciate each other's gifts and virtues. We do not sympathize as we ought with each other's joys and sorrows. We do not aid as we ought those of our brethren who are in trouble, either from unavoidable misfortune, or in consequence of their own weakness or faults. It will be indeed a happy result of our meeting here to-night, if it shall inspire in us a deeper sense of the nearness of our relationship, and of our mutual obligations, and a resolution that in the future our social and other christian duties to each other shall be more faithfully performed. And now, gentlemen, having delivered what I presume will be much the longest and dullest address of the evening, let me say that we will assume that the usual toasts to the

PRESIDENT OF THE UNITED STATES,

the judiciary, the press, and the other dignitaries of the land have been duly offered and drank with all the honors, and in pursuance of the plan of the Committee of Arrangement, let us indulge in personal reminiscences of the history of our Bar, and the other genial table-talk, which shall spring naturally from the occasion, and the enjoyment of which is the principal object of this assemblage.

The chairman then proposed the health of Rev. Dr. Lord, which was drank standing, and with three cheers. As the venerable clergyman rose he was greeted with loud applause.

REMARKS OF DR. LORD.

The reverend and venerable divine commenced by expressing thanks for the kind reception which had been accorded him. His acquaintance with the city was of fifty years' standing, and he had mixed in its affairs, public and private, legal and ministerial. He had ever loved the legal profession, and never had joined with those who had slandered it. Human law was but the offshoot of the divine. The speaker hardly knew where to begin, his recollections were so varied. He might tell stories of John Root by the hour. George P. Barker was a most extraordinary and popular man. The speaker well remembered how affecting it was, at Mr. Barker's funeral services in the North Church, then just erected, to see the poor people, who loved him, crowding into the church to pay their last tribute of respect. The speaker also recollected many things about Thomas T. Sherwood, an irrepressible man, who never stopped talking. Another singular man was Mr. Andrews, the second mayor of the city. On one occasion Mr. Andrews was being cross-examined by Mr. White, and the whole village was aroused on the subject, and the Court House was filled to hear the remarkable duet between the two men.

Mr. George R. Babcock and the speaker began the study of the law at the same time. He afterwards became a partner of Judge Love. The name of Clinton was familiar in Buffalo at that early day, and it was the effort of the people of this village to keep De Witt Clinton in the governor's chair. When Judge Clinton came here, the people received him with great favor. Long may he live to wear the judicial ermine. Dr. Lord then closed by telling some very laughable stories of John Root, and, in taking his leave, said he desired most heartily the welfare of each and all whom he saw before him, and fervently hoped that beyond the storms of this life they would reach that eternal rest which remaineth to the people of God.

The Chairman said:

Gentlemen of the Erie County Bar: There is one man present who, above all others, probably, we desire to hear from on this occasion, and with your permission I will call upon our venerable and distinguished friend, who is justly entitled to be called "The Old Man Eloquent." May his life be kept as fresh and as fragrant as the bright flowers that he loves so well to gather in the spring-time. Gentlemen, I propose the health of Hon. George W. Clinton, and let us all rise.

Judge Clinton responded as follows:

ADDRESS OF JUDGE CLINTON.

Mr. Chairman and Gentlemen of the Bar of Erie County: I cannot, my friends, begin as did my friend Dr. Lord, following the chairman and addressing the judge of this court and of that court, but as to the honor, merit and distinction of the Bar of Erie County—our own Bar—I desire to say that I respect them all; and above all I love the jolly, good-hearted fellows who are gathered around this festive board and are now about to hear the little I have to say. But I confess, gentlemen, that I am a little, a great deal surprised. I have made a false estimate, I fear, of your wisdom and your sense. Why, it seems to me, that you are only distinguished for commercial good sense. Why, we have all read, and we all know, that while speech is silver, silence is golden, and you prefer the silver to the gold; but, gentlemen, paper is said to be better than silver. In our financial statements they tell us that it is no matter at all—that the nation is able to resume specie payment in silver, and that it is not so desirable as paper. Now, I have not got paper —I have nothing but this poor silver. Why, gentlemen, if I could make a speech—but, really, I have talked out all the little talk that I had in me. If I flattered myself that I could on any occasion make a speech, you have taken that wind out of my sails by that meeting of the Bar when they dedicated the City Hall. I, very unfortunately, was prevented from going; and when I came to read the newspapers, I thought that I had sustained a great and almost irreparable loss. I have read those speeches with great interest; they seem to be warm, and come right from the heart. And I was particularly struck with the speech made by

OUR ILLUSTRIOUS SENATOR.

It was a capital speech; it was so fortunate in its allusions. If I had been there I should have been perfectly overwhelmed, and I should have rushed up to him and said, Brother Rogers, I am conquered; Brother Rogers, here, take my hat. [Applause.] Thank Heaven, I have not had time to call on the senator, and as he has gone, too, my good old hat is safe yet. [Applause.]

I cannot tell you, my friends, how happy this makes me. I am thankful to our Committee for a great many things. I am thankful to our host for the bountiful repast which has been spread before us. Everything seems to have been provided, as it ought to have been provided. I am thankful to the Committee of Arrangements for the manner in which they have conducted this banquet. I am duly grateful and sorry that they should have called on me for an address. I am thankful to be permitted to meet them and to meet all those here; it gives me a gratification that I am thankful for. Why, I thought that I should never see such a scene, as I now witness, this side of the grave; to see the Bar of Erie County all together here; men whom I love with all the strong emotions of my heart, and to whom I cannot express the affection with which I hold them.

Now, my friends, I will say that, in respect to this Bar, we are divided into three classes. There are the really old men of the Bar, that are going, and probably their greatest triumphs have been achieved, I will say no more of them; and there are the men of middle age; the men who are in the meridian of their mental vigor, and in their bodily strength also, and who have been winning and who are winning triumphs from day to day, and as to that body of men, I assert it, unblushingly, as

MY STEADFAST AND HONEST OPINION,

that there is no Bar in this State or body of men superior to them, and I doubt if there is anywhere one that is equal to them. And the third class is a class of promise; it is the younger men that are now entering and are about to enter upon the profession, and from the indications which they give here, they are men who have a just appreciation of the obligations of their profession, and will at any rate carry the banner as high as it now stands, and I hope that it may be still higher when their time comes.

Now these classes are all together, for God's sake keep them together, let not this be the last occasion upon which the whole Bar of Erie County shall be brought together, to enjoy themselves at the festive board. This is a Bar to be proud of, but see to it, that its reputation is maintained; form your Bar Association, if you please, or let it go, but do see to the young men, encourage them, that they may maintain the character of the Bar fully up to its present standard. The old Bar is strong, and, as the old men are passing away, see to it that they will have worthy successors.

Now, as to the young men, let me say, there was a man, but I am ashamed to say it, and I believe he was a lawyer too, who said that "A lawyer is one whose trade is to admit nothing, question everything, and talk by the hour." Surely, my young friends, you will follow in the footsteps of those who have preceded you, and you will give the lie to that definition of a lawyer.

Now, gentlemen, I am sensible that I have detained you too long, and I will conclude only by saying this, in regard to the remark made by our reverend friend who has just left us. (Dr. Lord.) He stated of me that I came here in 1836, and was received with warmth by the city of Buffalo. Gentlemen, that is not entirely true; I came here, indeed, that year; I was received by a few, and by a few only. I was unknown; I had done nothing that had made me known; I was known to a very few, and I had to work my way. I have to say this, that although my father's name has been, in some respects, a benefit and an advantage to me, as I have always felt it to be an honor, yet I will say that it has often been to me, in my humble judgment, the greatest impediment that I have had to contend with in my life. Why it should be so I cannot say. I can only say that the bearing of that name, instead of its being a help to the gratification of any ambitious wishes, it has rather been an obstacle, but still I am proud to bear it. And this I will say, and I hold that what sustained me is that from the outset here I met a few friends in the business portion of the community, and a few friends among the Bar of Erie County, and if there has been anything that has kept me on the course of honor, which has kept my heart pure and my affections pure, it has been the

AFFECTION OF MY BROTHER LAWYERS;

and I say to them, God bless them; and I do hope that you will treasure among yourselves a love for every member of the profession. It is the most honorable, except, of course, the clerical profession, and it is in fact the most influential calling in our nation. The lawyers wield more influence than any other body of men in the country.

I say to you frankly, I love this city—I love Buffalo; I shall be proud of it as long as I live. I trust that I shall see you showing a social and friendly spirit towards each other, and moving together in all the interests affecting the honor of our city; moving together as one man for its future glory and advancement.

Mr. Sprague, the Chairman, then said : Gentlemen, we have heard two men that have risen to the summit of their respective professions. We would now like to hear from some of the young men—those who have begun to climb the hill of fame and distinction. I give you, gentlemen, "The rising Bar of Erie County," and I ask my friend, Mr. Philip D. K. Saunders to reply.

MR. SAUNDERS' ADDRESS.

Mr. Chairman, and Gentlemen of the Bar of Erie County: This is indeed a felicitous occasion to the younger members of our profession, and I think it an honor and a privilege to respond to the toast that has just been given by our esteemed brother. We congratulate ourselves that for the first time in the history of the Erie County Bar, the old members of the profession and the young, meet beneath the same roof, and sit around the same festive table, not only for the discussion of the bountiful repast that has been provided here for us, but for a generous interchange of pleasant thought and sentiment. It is but a few years, yet it seems a long while, since the younger members of the profession in this city were gathered beneath the hospitable roof of one who is no longer among us. He has passed from our midst. That noble form of manhood we shall never see again. We shall never again be entertained beneath his hospitable roof. I mention the honored and revered name of the late John Ganson. We were gathered there on the occasion of the admission of one of the members of the Erie County Bar who is now present among us—Mr. Edward R. Bacon. We appreciated the honor that was conferred upon us by the invitation. We were very young then in matters of law, and younger still in the

SUBJECT–MATTER OF DINNER PARTIES.

To be invited to sit at the board of John Ganson was indeed an honor. We had misgivings as to how we should go there, and how we should comport ourselves when there, but we resolved to go, and we went. I well remember the preparations that I made to go to that party. It was the first dinner party that I had ever been invited to attend. I was comparatively without the pale of society, and consequently without a dress coat. And, Mr. Chairman and gentlemen of the Bar, I studied up on the subject of dinner parties for the occasion. I read somewhere that a pair of lavender pants was *the* thing to wear at a dinner party, and I forthwith ordered a pair of lavender pants. I also ascertained that a dress coat was the only thing that could be tolerated in such a mansion as John Ganson's, and therefore a dress coat was ordered. But a vest suitable for such an occasion defied research, and was something that occasioned me more anxiety and trouble than all the rest of my outfit. I finally ordered a very low white vest, and a pair of patent leather shoes, and thus arrayed I went, feeling as Solomon did in all his glory. I was escorted to the dinner by my friend, Mr. Lyman K. Bass. I can well remember the expression of John Ganson's face, and the merry twinkle of his eye, as he took in at a glance my whole make-up. But there was no embarrassment there. We had a noble host, and a most noble hostess. Everyone was made to feel at home, which, let me add, was the very height of entertainment. We had an enjoyable dinner, and we went forth from the mansion of John Ganson with a little old sherry in our heads, peace and good will towards all men in our hearts, and especially toward John Ganson, and thought what a glorious thing it was, after all,

TO BE A LAWYER.

I think that is the only occasion, it is indeed the only occasion that I have been able to find, when any portion of the Bar of Erie County have met together in social intercourse.

Concerning the erection of the new Court House, and leave-taking of the old one, I have few words to say. A great many tears have been shed by the older members of the profession upon leaving the venerable pile of bricks across the way. We have no such tears to shed. We have no endearing recollections of that faded pile of bricks. No thronging memories choke our utterances when we speak of that old Court House, but we do remember that on some occasions we have had our utterances choked inside of those old walls, when we have been endeavoring to convince a court or jury that we were right and everybody else wrong, in the struggle up the rugged hill of our profession. It has been the scene not only of the *struggles*, but the *triumphs* of the older members of the profession, who now are basking in the sunshine of professional eminence earned within its walls. Well may they mourn as they turn away from the venerable structure.

Mr. Chairman, we consider that this new Court House has been given to us by the older members of the profession; it has been built for our occupancy in years to come, when the great gatherer shall have taken to himself a great many of the old members of the profession who are present at this dinner. We appreciate your kindness to us, and the tender solicitude that you exhibit for the wellfare and comfort of the younger members of the profession, but above all other things we congratulate you that you have

STAVED OFF THE DAY OF PAYMENT

for this beautiful and noble structure, until such time in the dim vista of the future, when an increase of clientage and a lucrative practice, will enable us to pay for the same easily and with pleasure.

Mr. Chairman, we appreciate the responsibility that rests upon us. We must maintain the honor, the dignity, and the character of the profession in the future, as it has been sustained in the past. We have received a noble inheritance from the illustrious dead, and we have the living example of the older members of the profession to instruct us in the manner in which we shall practice law in order to merit that respect and confidence of the community which has been so generously bestowed upon them. With these precedents we cannot fail, if we do but follow them.

And now, in conclusion, my friends, the younger members of the profession, pledge that we will maintain the honor and the dignity of the profession of the Erie County Bar.

LETTERS AND TELEGRAMS.

The Chairman announced the receipt of several letters and telegrams of a congratulatory character. The first one presented was from

SENATOR SHERMAN S. ROGERS.

BUFFALO, March 13, 1876.

Gentlemen: It is with very great regret that I am compelled to say that I cannot be present at the Bar banquet to-morrow evening. It will undoubtedly be an occasion of such genuine good feeling, and of such hearty festivity, that it will be remembered many years by the fortunate participants.

I beg to offer the following sentiment and to call on my friend Putnam to respond to it, at the same time desiring that it be distinctly understood that the toast includes none of *us boys*.

Yours respectfully,

SHERMAN S. ROGERS.

The sentiment of Mr. Rogers was—"The Gray-Heads of the Bar," and Mr. James O. Putnam being called upon by the Chairman said:

ADDRESS OF HON. JAMES O. PUTNAM.

I thank you, Mr. Chairman, and the other members of the committee for the grace which has afforded me the pleasure of this hour. I have been so long withdrawn from the active duties of the profession, that your thoughtfulness is doubly kind. You say truly that my early retirement was not a voluntary one, and if I had the strength for its labors, I should regard no future so happy as that which should recall me to its activities.

This is the Centennial year, and I suppose my friend Rogers deemed it necessary to call upon a gentleman of the

REVOLUTIONARY PERIOD

to respond to this gray-haired toast. Well, sir, I realize, as I look around this table of two hundred guests, and recognize not a half-score who were in the profession when I entered it, that I belong to a past generation. Nearly all the men who thirty years ago gave renown to the Buffalo Bar are dead. And what a splendid galaxy of names now come thronging to memory! Tracy, Love, Potter, Fillmore, Hall, Haven, Barker, Sill, Smith, Mullett, Sherwood, Tillinghast, Sawin, Verplanck, Masten, Stow, Austin, Cook, Hoyt, and of a still younger generation, Greene, Norton, Welch. These are but a part of the many names which have made illustrious the Buffalo Bar.

I know it is of the living you expect me to speak, but I am sure you will pardon this brief reference to a past sacred to us all.

As I look around on this assembly my eye rests upon a venerable form full of years and of honor, whose presence among us imparts the highest interest to this occasion.

THE REV. DR. LORD

began his career in Buffalo, as a lawyer, nearly half a century ago But while in the vigor of young manhood, and in the full tide of professional success, he consecrated his splendid genius, his rare talent, his varied learning, indeed all the wealth of his nature, to another profession akin to ours, yet of more exalted dignity. I say akin to ours, for if religion descended from God to men, or if it sprang from that moral consciousness which is a spark struck out of the divinity, is it not true that Law, as good old Hooker declared, "hath its seat in the bosom of God, and its voice is the harmony of the world?" I rejoice in his honored presence among us to-night. It is one of the delightful recollections of my life that it was my pleasure for many years to have intimate relations with him, and that nothing has ever lessened the mutual feeling of kindness which has been, and still is, precious to me.

I see present another representative of the advanced generation, who very appropriately led the commemorative services of the Bar on Saturday. A man who might easily be taken for a Roman Senator in the best days of Rome, when none were for a party, and all were for the State. It was my privilege to be associated with Mr. Babcock when in 1842 I began my professional life in Buffalo.

May the time be a long way in the future before can be fully uttered our appreciation of that constellation of qualities of head and heart which have made the ripe lawyer, the pure and able statesman, the man without guile, and the friend that sticketh closer than a brother.

By my side sits another representative of the earlier time. A man who has added personal renown to ancestral honor—Judge Clinton. He is our universal educator. Not to speak of his eminent professional career, he has taught us the sweet humanities and that unbought grace of life, which are the highest and purest social charm.

NATURE'S OWN CHILD,

he has unfolded to us her mysteries as she has revealed them to him from tree, and shrub and flower, and her myriad schools of life;

for to him Nature unveils her face, and fills his ear with her music, and his soul with her all-pervading beauty. I never think of our venerable friend, and realize the part he is of all we most value among us, that I do not fervently utter the Horatian prayer for Augustus:

> Serus in cœlum redeas, diuque
> Laetus intersis in populo Buffalonis.

Let me ask here if it be not about time that Buffalo remembered her indebtedness to the father of our friend? It was his sagacity and energy that transformed the frontier village into the city which now sits in conscious strength at the feet of these seas. I know Buffalo is De Witt Clinton's monument, but we owe it to ourselves to erect a commemorative work of art to the statesman who saw our possibilities and enabled us to realize them.

I see here my brother Greene who, when I came to Buffalo, had been for two or three years at the Bar. He was my first friend on the most important occasion of my mature life. And when I remember that he was then living in the melancholy condition of a bachelor, and now see around this table his sons who have already won distinction and honor in their father's profession, I realize that my own shadow lengthens and my day declines.

THE HON. E. G. SPAULDING,

who sits at your left, Mr. Chairman, comes under the head of my friend Rogers' toast. He read his profession with my father, and more than forty years ago brought here his learning and his energy to lay the basis and build the superstructure of his distinguished career.

The "gray head" of Mr. T. J. Sizer reveals another of the early men, and recalls our obligation to him for his public and instructive discussion of almost every subject of general local interest.

Near Mr. Sizer I see a "Silver Gray" of the revolutionary epoch; a man without whose life this occasion might never have been. He is the incarnation of that "Aurora" which has so long and so resplendently shone upon our fair city.

After making the fortune of many another man, he has in his last days set out to make the fortune of Buffalo.

Who created our new park? We shake our gory locks at Dennis Bowen, and say, "thou did'st it!" Who urged and supervised the construction of our new City and County Hall which has so opened the flood gates of Buffalo eloquence, and turned the whole city into daily and nightly pilgrimages to this new temple? Who with his own hand let loose from their marble prison those four interesting females who stand perpetual sentinels at the clock tower, henceforth, I suppose, the guardian divinities of the city? If any one man is either to be hung or canonized for all this, Dennis Bowen cannot hope to escape.

Mr. O. H. Marshall, whose useful studies and trusts so constantly associate him with Buffalo institutions, is of the few remaining lawyers of the earlier times.

Judge Smith, whose successful professional career has had its natural and fitting close by his transfer to the Judiciary, and Judge Talcott with the same experience, and Mr. Ford, whom I do not see, and whose ill health I fear has deprived us all of a pleasure, and our brother Stevens who, I presume, is absent rebuking Noah for the introduction of slavery into the United States, almost, if not quite, complete the list.

And here I am sure I may be pardoned a word of reference to one who was long a leader of the Bar, but whom considerations of health have transferred to another State. Henry W. Rogers is still too intimately connected with our institutions of art and charity, and still dwells in too many Buffalo hearts to be regarded as not of us. We rejoice that his closing years are happy, and that he has not forgotten his Buffalo love.

You warned me, Mr. Chairman, off the ground of your decade. I see a goodly number of friends who are rapidly moving

UP TO THE THREE SCORE LINE,

men who are now doing the hard work of the profession and reaping its honors and rewards. And I see around me a little army of young men whose future is all before them, bright to their teeming fancies as a lover's dream.

It would be easy to be sentimental here, but I obey your warning, and close by returning my thanks for the kindness which has permitted me to bid you—"Hail!"

OLD BACHELOR LAWYERS.

In calling upon the next speaker, the Chairman said that the true philosophy of language is to go from the gay to the solemn and severe. We have heard this evening, the good things that have dropped from the lips of the honorable judge, and now I want to call your attention to the doings of our brother Clark. I mean, Delavan F. Clark. He has taken a new departure, although late in life, but still it is better to do a good thing late than not at all. I think brother Clark gave his bachelor brother members a pretty sly slip when he left their ranks and joined ours. I believe that there is but one man left of his class, and he stands now, very much like a hard-hearted oak in the midst of a very large stock of maples. I wish to know from him, from my brother Cutting, what sort of an opinion he has of the practice of the law. And I would like to know something about his affections. It seems to me, if he would explain himself, we might offer him some timely consolation.

SPEECH OF HON. HARMON S. CUTTING.

Mr. Chairman and Gentlemen: Under the most favorable circumstances it would be no easy task to vindicate, before an assemblage like this, the forlorn brotherhood of bachelors. As it is, the wine, for the moment, has vanished from before me; my glass is empty and my throat is as arid as are supposed to be the hearts of the fraternity which I am called on to represent. Doubly difficult, then, is the discharge of the duty which you, Mr. Chairman, have so unfeelingly imposed upon me. In the suddenness of the shock contained in your request, I can make but a lame attempt to defend what is generally regarded as so bad a cause. Indeed, I shall not essay it at all, but will seek to escape from a difficult position by alluding to the deserter whose name you have mentioned, and by calling to your contemplation that still marching procession, marshaled and commanded by this deserter who, up to the very moment of his treason, had seemed to be loyal to our cause. He is gone! He has "squared" his accounts for the loss of a decade, and from the bud of unsophisticated celibacy has suddenly and unexpectedly blossomed into a full-flowered "Benedick."

You, the younger members of the Bar, may read in this startling occurrence such a lesson as the state of your affections shall happen to suggest. As for me, it has added to my importance by bringing me one step nearer to the honors of solitary survivorship; one step nearer to being the officer, standard-bearer and all the rank and file of that great company who, one by one, have disappeared amidst showers of orange flowers and the flutter of white veils. I challenge your congratulations or condolences, whichever you please, for having so stoutly maintained a position that has given me a sort of paramount right to address you on so momentous a topic.

EXAMPLES IN MATRIMONIAL AFFAIRS

are of small consequence. But however you might be affected by such things, I must disclaim all responsibility for any possible effect of my conduct *as a precedent.* Let me explain.

A gentleman not remarkable for his uniform devotion to the principles of Father Mathew, was upbraided by a friend for his folly, and especially for setting so evil an example to the generation which was coming after him. He promptly repelled this imputation of evil and insisted that the value and propriety of his conduct was not understood. Said he: "I seek not to teach by so trite a thing as an example. You must not regard me in that light at all. I am a WARNING! I show what is to be avoided, not what is to be embraced."

Young gentlemen, you see how unnecessary I am, whether for good or ill, as an example, and particularly as an example of what is to be *embraced.* If there is anything in this much maligned bachelorism to be shunned; if half of a pair of scissors is better than a blade however well-tempered; if husbands only are for heaven, then regard me as a warning and not as an example—a warning of what it might be well for you to avoid; a startling image who with figuratively stretched forefinger points away from the solitary paths which he has trodden.

But I give no *cognovit.* I make no confession

TO THE YOUNGER BACHELORS

about me—I mean those not already mortgaged to some fair lady—their condition, I venture to say, is not wholly unbearable; and even when older, it may not be one of unmitigated misery. What my own experience might show, I will not intimate. These wearers of swallow-tail coats and immaculate neck-ties are not those from among whom I shall select my confessor. When I think of this, I can't say that I am particularly proud of being a bachelor. Yet what can one do but make the best of it? In those comfortable old slippers, and with my cigar and book and cheerful fire, it is not so very bad after all. In my solitary apartment, I can pretend to be at home, and keep up the illusion of domesticity by the frequent contemplation of what a *pater familias* I might have been. And as for wooing; why, I can woo the Law. What an opportunity here for the gushing of romantic affection! What ringlets of parchment; what wreaths of red tape; what perfumes of antique mouldiness! But, seriously, though our noble profession may not present the attractions of a bevy of beauty, nor speak in the language of sentiment or song, it is worthy of our most earnest and unremitting devotion; and whether "Benedick" or bachelor, whether blessed or not blessed with a wife or a sweetheart, let us not fail in our affection for our mistress, the Law.

LETTER FROM JUDGE WALLACE.

The Chairman presented the following letter from Hon. Wm. J. Wallace, Judge of the U. S. Court, Northern District, N. Y.:

SYRACUSE, *March* 13, 1876.

Gentlemen: I regret exceedingly that my engagements preclude my acceptance of your kind invitation to be present at the dinner of the Erie County Bar.

I hold it to be one of the paramount duties of every conscientious lawyer to partake of good dinners whenever he can. When dinners are given under the public auspices of the members of the Bar, the lawyer whose seat is vacant should be sent supperless to bed. These occasions, I have observed, are always elevating in their tendencies, and certainly, esthetically considered, improve and educate the taste.

It is a matter for congratulation that these social reunions are becoming more frequent. They cement good-fellowship, soften the asperities of professional intercourse, and promote that *esprit du corps* which is one of the charms and at the same time one of the inspirations of the legal profession.

The pleasure I have derived from my official intercourse with the members of the Bar of Erie County enhances my disappointment at being unable to meet them socially to-morrow evening.

Very truly yours,

WM. J. WALLACE.

Mr. J. D. Husbands, of the Rochester Bar, was requested to speak to the letter of Judge Wallace. He said:

Mr. Chairman and Gentlemen: I came here to the Erie County Bar twenty years ago, sick, as the result of that affliction of the race, chronic rheumatism, but your winters sent me back to my old city—a city that I love on many accounts. I remember your vernal sweetness and your summer pleasures. Buffalo has but two seasons—summer and winter, and to come here is to go where you cannot have four seasons in the year.

I remember, sir, all those old members of the Bar, already referred to. The Buffalo Bar has been extremely fortunate in its

GREAT ANCESTORS.

Let me say to you that you must not rely upon your ancestors, for every young man must rely upon himself. Having practiced for some sixteen or eighteen years in this city, I can say with truth and equal pleasure, that I never saw a Bar that showed a greater measure of talent, or more dignity and respect for human rights, than I have seen here.

Gentlemen, we started sometime ago what we called Bar Parties; we thought them a signal success, and an old friend of mine, a member of the profession, was about to die but he knew it not, he wanted me by his side, and he said to me the last Sunday of his life: I have been thinking a good deal of the want of social life in the profession. We do not visit the families of our brethren of the Bar as we ought to do; he said: As soon as I get well I will go and see the families of the members of the Bar. I wanted to say to you, gentlemen, in the commencement of my remarks to the members of the Bar, I wanted to address you as ladies and gentlemen, because the presence of ladies is really here to-night; you cannot have such a meeting without seeing the influence of wife, of mother, of sister and of sweetheart.

Let this not be the last of your social meetings when you shall get into the new Court House. Go there with a new and nobler purpose, if you can; go there for a nobler future. Do not think that you have nothing to do for the better, but honor the profession that has been honored before you.

I remember that when in Massachusetts, a lawyer put his name in my hat for the purpose of taking it off; there is no such thing in the Buffalo Bar, or in the Erie County Bar, and there is not in the Rochester Bar either. In our city and its surrounding country we sometimes meet with the Buffalo Bar, and we are glad to meet with them, and to see the honest rivalry that exists between the two cities. Let there be no hostility between them. Let there be nothing but generous rivalry of honest hearts, worthily cultivating a purer and a nobler future.

LETTER FROM JUDGE NOAH DAVIS.

The Chairman then announced that he had a letter from Hon. Noah Davis, of the city of New York, formerly a member of this Bar, and who all the older members of the profession and of his age, remember with respect and kindness. Mr. Sprague then read the letter as follows:

New York, *March* 13, 1876.

Hon. E. C. Sprague, Asher P. Nichols and others, Committee:

Gentlemen: I have just received your kind note of invitation to attend a dinner to be given by the Bar of Erie County, at Buffalo, on the 14th instant. I regret that my engagements at the General Term, now sitting, prevent my attendance. Nothing would give me greater pleasure than to be present on that occasion, to meet once more a body of gentlemen with whom I have in the past enjoyed for many years the most friendly professional and official relations. A long separation has in no degree impaired my respect for the Bar of Erie County. I recognize in that Bar many of the ablest and worthiest lawyers of the State.

After a somewhat larger and different experience in professional and judicial life, I recur with greater pleasure than ever to my long service on the bench of the Eighth District, and especially in the courts of Erie county, where the larger share of that service was rendered; and I speak in no disparagement of any other Bar when I say that in ability, courtesy, and in all kindly personal and social relations, I have found no Bar superior to yours.

I should be glad to greet in person every member of it, but as I cannot do that, I beg you will convey to them the feelings of warm regard which I shall never cease to bear. I am, very respectfully,

Noah Davis.

Mr. Sprague said that all wanted to hear one of the oldest members of the profession in response to this letter, and no gentleman is better able to do justice to the occasion than my worthy friend, Hon. R. P. Marvin, of Chautauqua county.

ADDRESS OF JUDGE MARVIN.

Mr. Chairman: Though not a member of the Erie County Bar, I am a member of the profession. I claim to be a brother of the members of the Bar of Erie County; they are my brothers and I claim a recognition from them as they are brothers. I am here upon invitation as your honored guest, and my first acknowledgment should be to the chairman of the committee, and to the members of the Erie County Bar for the compliment and honor bestowed upon me, in inviting me to be here this evening, as a guest. I thought at one time of putting pen to paper and excusing myself. But I said, no, I desire to go and meet the Bar of Erie County personally, and to recognize among them the familiar faces which I have known for so many years.

Brethren, fellow-laborers and soldiers in a good cause, I shall in the few moments allowed me by your Chairman, endeavor to impress upon the younger members of the Bar two or three ideas. If I can daguerreotype them upon your own minds as they have presented themselves to me a thousand times I shall have

ACCOMPLISHED MY PURPOSE.

Gentlemen, mention has been made of the older members of the Bar; I am now among the oldest; I think I rank my friend Babcock, I know I do in age; I think we came into the profession at the same hour, having been admitted in the same class; I say allusion has been made to the past, and sometimes apprehension has been expressed, whether the coming generation and other generations to come, whether they will fulfill their duties as the gentlemen who have gone before have fulfilled theirs; upon that subject I have no desire to speak. I shall dismiss that subject without a single fear. The generation that has gone before us has fulfilled its destiny. They have run their career and performed their duties and offices well. Let me say of them, that their career and their style of doing business was quite different from that which now exists. Well do I remember when I first entered the profession and before that, of listening to the great men, whose names we have heard to-night, and others that I remember, but their style was different from what it is now. I have often been asked the question from the gentlemen of the present day, whether they were equal in talent and equal in ability to those of the past forty or fifty years; and have invariably answered, yes, but the style of doing business has changed, and the men who made great reputations then as advocates would hardly be able to make a living now in this age of lightning and railroads. These men required not an hour only to sum up a case, but it took them a half an hour to pronounce their exordium, and then they went into their narration; then, stating the case briefly, they went into their argument, and then the peroration must be well considered. Not so now. I believe that if some of our ancestors, whose reputations were as wide as the State, were to return to the city of Buffalo, they could not get a living in the profession. It took time for them to get started, and to make a great speech they wanted from three to five hours. You sum up a case in an hour. In that case that was tried out here in Genesee, the Grays, that was in my time, John Griffin, made a speech of five hours on Saturday, and run down within five minutes of Sunday morning, and then the judge stopped him and said: "I regret that this speech is not ended, but this case must go to the jury before Sunday, and I regret that I have

NOT TIME TO CHARGE THE JURY."

And John Griffin got up, and said, "I greatly regret that I have not a couple of hours more in which to finish my speech." Upon this episode the case went to the Court of Appeals.

I have said enough on that subject; I want to say a word in regard to the changes. Has it been better? Has it been a desirable change? I answer, yes, it has been a valuable change. You now come at once to the point that is to be decided by the jury. You come directly to it, and you discuss the evidence and the judge sits and listens, and the lawyers are not allowed to take as wide a range as anywhere between the heavens and the earth. You come at once to the matter in the case. This is an age of business. We have not time to throw away that may be used trying causes. Has the change been beneficial? I say, yes. I have been asked a hundred times in my own courts whether the cases are as well tried now as when the old lawyers used to try them. I say that they are. I will not say why. You will discover the reason why the cases are better tried now than they were then. We come right to the point and the judge comes to the question, and the jury renders a prompt verdict.

Gentlemen, I am nearly through; I want to present another idea: your calling and your profession is the most exalted one that you can have in this land, except perhaps that of the ministry, which teaches us the way of salvation. There is no class of men that are more honorable and honest than the legal profession. You should strive to maintain this reputation, and to exalt yourselves in your high profession to which your duties call you. Among your duties is that of educating the courts. It is that of educating the judges. It is the duty of the Bar to educate the judges. You all know what I mean. It is your duty, you are called upon to address the judge, to inform him, and he in return informs the Bar, and it is in this respect that the reciprocal relations go on. Gentlemen, you are called upon to take an interest in all the affairs of society; everything comes under the observation, to a certain extent, of the legal profession. You are called upon to perform these high duties; you cannot do it with intelligence, without humility. Your profession is one of great labor.

THE LAW IS A SCIENCE;

it must be wooed and won; the law will not come and surrender itself and place itself in the possession of any man unless he wishes it, unless he is to maintain the structure and promises his proper vigils, in order to invite the law, that the law may come and take up its abode with him. You must make it worthy of your ceaseless industry, for unless you do the law will play you some slippery tricks and leave you floundering.

Gentlemen of the Bar of Erie County, I have occupied just double the time that I intended. I thank you for the invitation that has been extended to me and the pleasure which I have enjoyed in meeting you all.

FROM MR. BASS.

The next in order was a telegram from Hon. Lyman K. Bass, Member of Congress from Erie county, which the chairman read as follows:

WASHINGTON, *March* 14.

E. C. SPRAGUE, and others of the Committee:

I send my hearty congratulations to my brethren of the Bar that a new Court House is an accomplished fact, and that the inhalation of the poisoned air of the old ones is of the past. I regret that I cannot be with you this evening.

LYMAN K. BASS.

Mr. Sprague deemed it fitting to call upon District Attorney D. N. Lockwood, Esq., to respond to this message, and Mr. Lockwood did so as follows:

ADDRESS OF D. N. LOCKWOOD, ESQ.

Mr. Chairman and Gentlemen of the Bar of Erie County: I rise with no little embarrassment to respond to the toast proposed by our distinguished chairman. I suppose that I am called upon to reply to the toast of Hon. Lyman K. Bass, mainly for the reason that I hold the office of district attorney, so long and ably filled by him; and, Mr. Chairman, I know that I am but expressing the wish of every gentleman present, when I say, long life and continued prosperity and honor to Mr. Bass.

Mr. Chairman, every subject and thought connected with the change from the old Court House to the new City and County Hall, has already received its full share of praise and eloquence from the honorable gentlemen who have preceded me. It is but little more than ten years since I commenced the study of the law. My experience, if related, would be but the same old story—much work and little pay. I remember how greatly annoyed I used to be by the remark so often made, how much better off the world would be if there were no lawyers, and I have thought to-night how quickly those same persons would change their minds if they could witness this banquet, see all these happy faces, and know, as we know, that a true lawyer ever stands as an impassable barrier between right and wrong, ever the defender and protector of the innocent, and the prosecutor and irreproachable judge of the guilty.

Yes, gentlemen, one of the world's most distinguished historians has written that the reason Rome was great was because her lawgivers were great men, and what more fitting answer, when the people from every quarter of the earth, shall come, as they will in this our Centennial year, to our favored land, and shall ask, as they behold our national greatness and prosperity, what is the cause that has made this young nation so great and powerful, and why does it have so vast an influence among the older nations of the earth

—the answer will be, her lawyers have been and are great men, men who have guarded and defended liberty, and the nation's honor as sacredly as the honor of their own firesides.

And in conclusion, Mr. Chairman and gentlemen, I feel that, as one of the younger members of the Bar of this county, I am warranted in saying for them, that they have pledged themselves anew to maintain the high standing, the honor and dignity, which has ever been maintained by you and your predecessors, and that they will ever maintain and defend the sacred principles of liberty and justice, which have made this nation a land where manhood reigns alone and every citizen is king.

ANOTHER TELEGRAM.

The next message by telegraph was from Hon. Henry W. Rogers, of Ann Arbor, Michigan, formerly of Buffalo, and ran thus:

ANN ARBOR, Mich., *March* 13.

E. C. SPRAGUE:

I regret that I cannot go to the supper, but my heart and thoughts will be there, reverently recalling the memory of the dead who have graced a Bar which for forty years has had few eqnals and no superior in any city of the State. HENRY W. ROGERS.

Hon. Geo. R. Babcock was requested to make response, and, spoke for the older members of the profession, giving many reminiscences, and reciting several anecdotes of the early practice of law in Buffalo.

FROM JUDGE BARKER.

Hon. Geo. Barker, Judge of the Supreme Court, sent this dispatch:

BATAVIA, N. Y., *March* 14.

To E. C. SPRAGUE, Chairman, etc., Tifft House:

Until this moment I intended to be present and participate in the pleasures and festivities that the banquet offers. The train that I was to take is reported late, so I must be content with presenting my respects to the Buffalo Bar, distinguished for its learning, eloquence and integrity.

GEORGE BARKER.

The Chairman said there was a desire to hear from some of the younger members of the profession. He therefore called upon Mr. T. F. Welch, President of the Buffalo Law Society, to respond on behalf of the Association he represented. Mr. Welch did so in a very amusing and felicitous manner as will be seen:

SPEECH OF T. F. WELCH.

Mr. Chairman and Brethren of the Bar: The Buffalo Law Society is so well known to you all, its fame is so wide-spread, that I need take but little time in speaking of it. Organized nine years ago, immediately after the delivery of a law lecture to young men, by His Honor, Judge Clinton, it has continued in vigorous and flourishing life to the present, and though it may not have as great an antiquity as that already historic old hat of the judge's, yet it is now looked upon as, what we would all like that hat and its wearer to be, one of the permanent institutions of our city.

It has well accomplished the object set forth in its constitution, the promotion of mutual acquaintance among its members and their mutual improvement in legal debate and literary discussion, and it has been to younger members of the Bar and law students in many respects, what the proposed Bar Association will be to the profession at large.

The law student, Mr. Chairman, must needs be

FULL OF NOBLE AMBITION,

when, regardless of the many difficulties before him, he places himself among those who are

> "Mastering the codeless science of our law,
> That endless myriad of precedent,
> That wilderness of single instances,
> Through which a few by wit or fortune led,
> May beat a pathway out to wealth and fame."

But every one is confident that he will be among that successful few. Immediately on entering an office, however, he finds difficulty. Expecting to give himself up chiefly to the study of the books, the theory of the law, he is astonished to find that he is required to devote himself mainly to the practice of penmanship, and the manufacture of copies. Thinking he will receive instruction, and have difficulties carefully explained to him, he is simply told to keep his eyes open and he will soon learn. He does soon learn one thing, that he must always know what to do and how to do it, without asking any questions. He learns, too, just how little benefit is derived from making thirteen copies of a complaint, or spending three whole days in copying some long account which is as closely connected with the science of the law as Egyptian hieroglyphics. To such as he the Buffalo Law Society offers great advantages.

In the free intercourse and discussion with his fellow-students which he there obtains, his doubts are removed, his difficulties explained. He gains self-confidence, has an opportunity to use his powers, a chance to expand. Indeed, he sometimes expands so fast that he soon knows more law than old lawyers of long standing at the Bar.

The Buffalo Law Society, Mr. Chairman,

HAS MUCH TO BE PROUD OF

in its history. The old Law Library, where its meetings have been held has often been the scene of impassioned and eloquent debate, of close and powerful argument. Though the words of "learned length and thundering sound" with which its walls have often resounded, may sometimes have been striking only for the length or the sound, yet there have been displayed there by its members such powers of reasoning, such command of logic and analysis, such mastery of wit and humor, as would have reflected honor upon their possessors in any higher field of action. There, too, have been shown, not only such ability, but such constant courtesy and high sense of honor, as to warrant the conclusion that its members will always be honored and respected members of this Bar.

But, Mr. Chairman, the Buffalo Law Society has already produced results which show that it is a power in the land. Not only has it definitely and authoritatively settled many questions of importance in politics and literature, but the decisions of its Moot Court have fixed the law in many points before unsettled, and they have been followed in many cases by the higher courts in this and other States.

"To prove this let facts be submitted to a candid world."

The case of Judd *v.* Seekins, involving an important question in real estate law, tried at the Cattaraugus Circuit, was, pending its appeal, submitted to the

MOOT COURT OF BUFFALO,

and promptly reversed. The General Term soon after acquiesced in this decision.

On the authority of its decision in the great case of Morton *v.* James, the Court of Appeals soon after decided that a complete note altered by filling up blanks left by the maker, was not valid in the hands of a *bona fide* holder.

So the Supreme Court of Massachusetts followed its decision in another case soon after its rendition. As its latest achievement it has recently reversed a decision of the General Term of the Superior Court of Buffalo, and held that sleeping car companies are subject to the liabilities of innkeepers. The decision of the Court of Appeals in the same case, which is soon to be delivered, will follow this, and be but a matter of form. These facts, Mr. Chairman, are full of import.

They as conclusively establish the great authority of the Moot Court of Buffalo, as the strange words "chops and tomato sauce," under the skillful handling of our brother, Sergeant Buzfuz, established the villainy of Mr. Pickwick.

I might show that you, Mr. Chairman, and many of the grayheads here present, are honored honorary members of the Buffalo Law Society, and how most of the younger lawyers of this Bar owe all their success to the training they received in this Society, but I will not trespass further upon your time.

LETTER FROM JUDGE DANIELS.

Hon. Charles Daniels, Judge of the Supreme Court, sent this letter to the Committee:

NEW YORK, *March* 13.

Messrs. E. C. SPRAGUE, JOSIAH COOK, ASHER P. NICHOLS, BENJ. H. WILLIAMS and WM. H. GURNEY:

Gents: I have just received your invitation to the dinner to be given to-morrow evening at the Tifft House by the Bar of Erie County. I can give you no adequate idea of the pleasure it would afford me to be able to comply with this kind invitation. The most agreeable memories I cherish relate to my associations with the members of the Erie County Bar. They are emphatically the associations of a life-time, rendering the place of my home the most hallowed of all localities, and to which I always return, when liberated from the constraints of enforced absence, with the greatest possible pleasure. The Bar of Erie County is second to none other in the State. I do not doubt but the approaching entertainment will prove to be highly agreeable, and pleasantly remembered by those whose good fortune may allow them to participate in it. I am, however, so situated that it will be impossible for me to make one of the number. The business of the court now in session in this city, of which I am a member, excludes me from participation in your festivities. I regret my inability to be present, but can do nothing less than to submit to its necessities. Truly yours,

CHAS. DANIELS.

John Hubbell, Esq., was asked to reply, and did so in a few brief remarks, excusing himself from making a speech, and congratulated himself on his return to the fold of the Buffalo Bar after an absence of years.

LETTER FROM LIEUT.-GOV. DORSHEIMER.

ALBANY, *March* 13, 1876.

Gentlemen: Your invitation to attend the dinner of the Erie County Bar did not reach me until this morning, too late to dispose of my engagements here.

All of us have tender associations with the old Court House, and no one will see it taken away without regret. I never attended a meeting of the Bar except on the occasion of the death of some honored brother. It would give me great pleasure to join in your farewell to the scene of so many struggles, and to listen to the reminiscences, both pleasant and sad, which the occasion will elicit.

I beg you will receive my sincere regrets that I cannot accept your courteous invitation, and believe me

Very truly your servant,

WILLIAM DORSHEIMER.

To E. C. SPRAGUE, Esq., Hon. A. P. NICHOLS, JOSIAH COOK, and others.

The Chairman said that Mr. Dorsheimer had forsaken the law for political honors. He preferred to stick to the practice of the law.

The Chairman thought Mr. L. L. Lewis well qualified to discuss this question, and called upon him to do so.

ADDRESS OF MR. LEWIS.

Mr. Chairman and fellow Lawyers: Our Chairman seems to think my experience in public life and at the Bar entitles me to be heard as to the propriety of forsaking the law for political life. He says he always thought it best to stick to the law. He can't get up any controversy with me on that point. If you have acquired in the practice of the law, even a fair reputation for honesty, and have any desire to maintain it, keep at your profession, and let politics alone, so far as office-holding is concerned. For no matter how honestly you may perform the duties of the office, you will stand nine chances in ten of leaving the office, if it chance to be of a political character, with the reputation of a rogue, and while I think every American citizen ought to take an interest in politics, let some other man hold the office.

But enough on this point. I want to talk about lawyers, and as we grow old we ought to be pardoned for talking about our early experience and observation. I was admitted and came on here in 1848, with an idea of making my home somewhere in the West; but a view up this long lake chilled my ardor, and I stopped here, and went into the office of my brother, Dio Lewis. I did not know anything about law, nor much about anything else, for that matter, but after revolving this subject in my mind, concluded I must have a sign painted, and ordered it. When it was finished I attended to the putting of it up; it read, "*L. L. Lewis, Law Office.*" I took a good look at it after it was hung, and then went into my office, taking an eligible position so that I could see the door, and waited for business, and I don't think it was to exceed one half-hour before the door opened, a young man walked in and inquired if Lawyer Lewis was in. I replied, "That is my name." He was from Canada, and said his father, a resident of this State, had died, leaving some property here, and he wished to know his rights as one of his heirs. I thought it necessary that I should answer at once, if not he might get the impression I was not positive, so I opened my mouth and talked; he listened, or appeared to, for a time, and then looked at me, and asked me, in apparently a confused state of mind, what my charges were.

I PROMPTLY REPLIED, "ONE DOLLAR,"

which he paid. With all the composure I could master, I placed the dollar in my wallet, and, after he retired, I turned my eyes again to the office door, wondering who my next customer might be. I never exactly agreed with my brother, for he insisted that it was precisely six months before another client came in. It was, however, a long time.

The following summer we were visited here with the cholera, and I divided my time between sitting at my office window watching the funeral processions, and in the old Court House, witnessing the struggles of the giants of the Bar. The lawyer whose style and manner of trying causes filled my heart and soul completely full, my beau ideal of a successful jury lawyer, was Solomon G. Haven.

He was unpretending and simple in his manners. In addressing a jury he did not talk over, but between and into their heads; there was an apparent familiarity with the jury, talking to one and then another, till he had convinced them all. His illustrations always came from the farm, the workshop, or their homes, scarcely ever from objects higher than their heads. He convinced the jury that he was in earnest, and believed thoroughly in his client's cause.

He never appeared to make an attempt at oratory, and still he possessed the elements of the true orator, for he swayed and influenced those he addressed, and that, I take it, is the true test of oratory.

There was another man who tried many causes, perhaps more even than Mr. Haven; he was in his demeanor a perfect specimen of a gentleman; he was one of the handsomest men I ever saw, and wonderfully gifted as an orator. I refer to Eli Cook; he was one of the great powers in this county.

There was Henry K. Smith; he did not meet with the success of these other men, and still he was a wonderful man. He was one of those terrible men, who did not stop to convince his hearers. He stormed them;

HE RUSHED LIKE AN AVALANCHE,

and it was hard to withstand his attacks. There was T. T. Sherwood; he was trying a large number of cases; I never could understand him. His manners were strange, just the opposite of Haven and Cook; he seemed to be in a chronic state of madness, in a constant wrangle with the court, and not on good terms with the jury. He would not make one objection, but fifty, and wanted to discuss them one by one, and he acted just as though he believed each objection was fatal to his adversary's case. He was a corpulent gentleman, with a very red face, and, if I may be allowed the expression, he went lummoxing along in the trial of his cases. There were many other men of mark and power practicing here at that time, of whom I cannot detain you to speak. Well, I watched and wondered at the power of these men, and wondered if I could ever attain such a position.

Gentlemen of the Bar, I am glad to be here with you to-night, and hope that this pleasant meeting will prove the beginning of many such gatherings, that we may know each other more intimately in social, friendly intercourse. Our profession is an important and influential one, and it behooves us to hold high its standard of morals and influence.

I have some little acquaintance with the Bar of other cities, and I think I can truthfully say that I know of none so distinguished for friendly and good feeling as ours. Let us all strive to improve this good fellowship and feeling, and may we all live here many years in the practice of our profession.

FROM HON. A. P. LANING.

BUFFALO, *March* 14, 1876.

Gentlemen: I am in receipt of your invitation to attend a meeting of the Bar of Erie County this evening at the Tifft House. Nothing would afford me greater pleasure than to comply with your request and participate with you in the festivities of the occasion, but a pressing prior engagement will prevent my acceptance of your invitation.

Be pleased to present my sincere regrets at my inability to meet my professional brethren. I cordially approve the objects of your meeting, and trust that it may tend to greater fraternal intercourse, and result in the formation of an Association of the Bar of this city, which shall add to its proper influence in the State, and promote the interests of our profession.

Sincerely yours,

A. P. LANING.

E. C. SPRAGUE, Esq., and others of the Committee.

Gen. L. W. Thayer, of Warsaw, Wyoming county, was called upon to speak as hailing from a section of the country near where Mr. Laning came from. The General complied and spoke as follows:

ADDRESS OF GEN. L. W. THAYER.

Mr. Chairman and Gentlemen of the Bar of Erie County: Although highly appreciating your invitation to join you upon this festive occasion, I was at a loss to imagine any cause to which I could attribute it. I had never been a member of your Bar, or held any judicial position that could in any way entitle me to any such distinction. In this dilemma it occurred to me as barely possible that in view of the fact that my name had been mentioned in connection with a judicial position in which you were interested, that with your usual foresight and precaution, you thought prudent at least, in view of my possible appointment, in that way to remind me of your friendship and confidence. If so, I beg to assure you there is not the slightest danger of your being placed in any position where my official action can be of the least importance. Besides I am already under too many obligations to the Bar of Buffalo, which I can never discharge, to require any further manifestations of your friendship and confidence.

I remember, and shall never forget, that nearly twenty years ago when a candidate for a high judicial office, of receiving in this county the enormous majority of six thousand votes over an opponent who afterwards became

ONE OF THE MOST EMINENT JURISTS

in the State. I attributed that gratifying result in no small degree to the influence of the Bar of this city. Four years ago, upon the recommendation of two distinguished members of your Bar (one, alas, now no more) and the eminent jurist alluded to, and wholly unbeknown to me, my name was sent to the Senate, to fill a vacancy in the highest court of the State. But what I chiefly wish to refer to is the active efforts that were made by both the Bar and press of both parties to procure my confirmation, being a Democrat, by a Senate largely Republican. To those efforts on the part of Republican judges and lawyers as well as the Republican press of this city, my worthy friend, Mr. Lewis, then Senator, and to whom I am deeply indebted for his own efforts, can fully testify.

Your friendship and confidence has again and but recently been equally manifested in relation to the judicial vacancy now existing in the district, and with the same disregard of party. Indeed, I am inclined to think that the large support I have received from my Republican friends, not only in this city, but throughout the district, may be one cause of my unpopularity in another quarter, but I assure you that I value it none the less on that account.

Now, Mr. Chairman and gentlemen, I have availed myself of this occasion, and probably the only one I may ever have, to refer to these many evidences I have received of the friendship of your Bar, in order to assure you how fully I appreciate them, and to say from the depths of my heart how sincerely I thank you.

Mr. Chairman: Having lived all my life in an adjoining county I have not been an indifferent observer, either of the rise and eminence of the Bar, or the growth and prosperity of your beautiful city. I have watched the advancement of both nearly half a century with the deepest interest. But I am compelled to admit that there is one event, and but one, in your history that I have never enjoyed. Although

IT OCCURRED OVER FIFTY YEARS AGO,

its history has been told and repeated with short intervals ever since. It has been celebrated in prose and immortalized in poetry. The more I have read, even the poetry, as beautiful as it is, the less I have enjoyed it. And yet I can hardly tell why, unless it be in the name. Whether I was in any way interested in that event, I have never deemed it profitable to inquire. Indeed, in view of that event, I have adopted the advice of the poet Saxe, and have never sought to trace my family line for fear it might

"End in a loop of stronger twine,
To plague some worthy relation."

I have contented myself by denying any relation to any of the name in this county, and consoled myself with the reflection that if three of the same name were hung, that three of the same name came over (as is always the case) in the Mayflower, or some other vessel. I need hardly say I allude to that great and memorable event in your history, the conviction and

EXECUTION OF THE "THREE THAYERS."

Now, I have never wondered that your city should cherish that great event as an epoch in its history. When it occurred you were a mere village without a history, and an event of that importance could not be forgotten. But now as it seems to me, having become a great and prosperous city, with a history made up of events of far more value, and to me at least far more interesting, I should not wonder if you would continue to prosper and advance, even if you should let the "Three Thayers" sleep quietly in their graves for, say, the next half century.

In conclusion, Mr. Chairman and gentlemen, I desire to express my fullest concurrence in the high encomiums that have been pronounced to-night upon those distinguished members of the profession of this county, who have done so much by their learning, integrity, ability and liberality to give to your Bar the high and enviable position it has attained. I knew nearly all of those distinguished gentlemen personally as well as professionally, and testify from my own knowledge of them.

To the younger members of this Bar I wish to say that upon you will soon devolve the honor and responsibility of maintaining that high reputation of your Bar which will be intrusted to your keeping. That you can and will do it, I have seen ample proofs here to-night. You can hardly hope to raise it higher. If you transmit it unimpaired to your successors in the profession, it ought to satisfy your most laudable ambition, and with that result you may well be satisfied.

LAW STUDENTS.

The chairman said he was glad to recognize several law students present, young men that were preparing to enter the profession that had been so highly eulogized this evening. He called upon Mr. James Fraser Gluck, to speak in behalf of the students of the Bar of Buffalo. Mr. Gluck responded and said:

SPEECH OF J. F. GLUCK.

Mr. President and Gentlemen of the Bar of Erie County: In rising I thank you most sincerely for the honor you have conferred, not upon me, but upon the law students of this city by this public recognition of them, on this, the first social gathering of the Bar of Erie County.

The world has indeed moved forward since the time when many of those here present were treated, by those in whose offices they studied, as copying hacks and message boys. It moves further forward to-day when this public recognition is taken of law students in your presence, and the presence of their honors, the judges of this State and county.

But, sir, I hail this, not as an innovation in that most conservative of professions, the law, but rather as a return to its best usages, in its palmiest days, in that nation, distinguished above all others for legal learning and acumen. For, daily, in the streets of Rome, the Imperial City, the great jures-consult might be seen accompanied by their students—by them considered their rarest ornament—engaged in the intervals between cases, in answering their questions and in imparting to them that knowledge of legal principles which books alone could never, can never give.

And, to-night, sir, I forget not the kindnesses which personally it has been my good fortune to experience, when I venture to express the hope that this public recognition is but an earnest of what will in the future be done elsewhere. I would not insult you, sir, nor the learned and dignified assembly here present, by filling up the short time I wish to speak, with glittering generalities or empty platitudes. I have no such desire. I have a purpose in speaking. I have a plea to make, and I stand here to-night and plead, as a student for students, not for better pay, not for more books, not for ampler digests, but for that personal fellowship on the part of members of the Bar, that kindly interest, that willingness to communicate to students that knowledge which reading alone does not afford, which experience alone has given to you all.

No lawyer here present would be willing to admit that he would receive into his office those he deemed unworthy of the profession; knowing them worthy, it is in his power to render them, it is his duty to endeavor to make them ornaments to the profession. It is a mere truism, though seldom fully realized, that the profession is just what its members choose to make it; as they honor the bench, the world will honor it; as they respect themselves, the world will respect them. And the lawyer who honors the bench and respects himself does well; but he, better, who, while carrying with honor the torch of justice, as he runs his own brief race, looks well to it, that he to whom he knows that torch must be handed when he is gone, is not unworthy of that noble task. Surely, if it be man's primal duty to endeavor to leave the world better than he found it, he does much to elevate his profession, and through it, the world, who, by generous sympathy, does all he can to stimulate and encourage those who will one day constitute that profession.

But the first advance should come from the superior. There is thereby no loss of dignity. He indeed honors himself more than him whom he serves, who descends from his own clear and sunny perceptions of the law to the student, lost in the fog-land of text-books and the confusion worse confounded of our early law.

But enough of this. Let me speak on a more pleasant theme. Let me assure you, sir, that this kindness in inviting us and according us recognition to-night as students will not be without its effect upon us. To-night we have had recalled to our minds by the venerable men who have spoken, those who are our ancestors—the great and good men of the past; our ancestors, I say, for there is a lineage of mind that is truer than that of blood; we have listened to the record of their noble deeds, we are roused to emulate the glory of their characters; and we dedicate here to-night, our energy, our enthusiasm, our loftiest ambition to the upbuilding of a noble profession, a purer and grander republic.

The ancient Lombard kings, as they placed upon their heads the iron crown of their kingdom, were wont to say, "God has given it me; let him beware who would take it from me." And so each of us to-night, resisting the insane thirst for wealth, and the insidious whisperings of a corrupt and time-serving ambition, place upon our heads the ideal crown of a pure professional life; and exclaim like the kings of old, "God has given it me; not all the world shall take it from me!"

In response to repeated calls, Mr. Geo. Wadsworth said:

ADDRESS OF GEO. WADSWORTH, ESQ.

Mr. Chairman and Brethren: I think that the orange has been squeezed, and the juice and pulp distributed, and that calling me up, at two o'clock in the morning for a speech, is like asking me to make some delectable beverage from the rejected and despised rind of the fruit.

The praises of our new Court House have been sung here this evening, but little or nothing has been said about the old one; this is natural, the dead are soon forgotten, we smooth down their resting places, and go our way, and they soon pass from our memories, and so it seems as if

OUR VENERABLE OLD COURT HOUSE

were forgotten already; we have been to its funeral; allow me to say a few words about it.

When I came to Buffalo, in 1852, the old Court House was standing in almost precisely the same condition it is now, the so-called new Court House, on the corner of Clinton and Ellicott streets was nearly new in fact, as well as in name.

Small, narrow, contracted and insufficient for the business of to-day as the old Court House is, and especially as it seems to us when contrasted with the superb Hall, into which we have removed, yet when erected, it was more than sufficient for its designed purposes.

I am told by James D. Sheppard, Esq., the pioneer in the profession and business of music here, that in the year 1827, he could not find a suitable place in the village of Buffalo in which to open his music store, and that John G. Camp, then sheriff of Erie county, leased to him the north-east corner room on the ground floor of the old Court House for that purpose, and that he carried on his business of a music dealer there for some time; whether his music had charms to soothe the savage breasts of the counsel and litigants who thronged the other rooms of the old building we are not told, but it may have had its share in bringing about that amelioration of the manners of the Bar, which has been spoken of.

You will remember that the chairman of our meeting on Saturday mentioned many of the lawyers who flourished here in the infancy of Buffalo; among them he named Hon. Henry E. Davies, late Judge of the Court of Appeals, who was City Attorney and clerk at the time of the great controversy concerning the location of Commercial and Water streets, which Mr. Babcock also mentioned; that controversy left a long legacy of litigation to the city; even so late as the year 1860 or 1861, when I was City Attorney, I argued in the Court of Appeals, a case which was originally brought in the year 1844 by the city against Jonathan Sidway, and which grew out of the Commercial and Water street matter, and when the facts were stated at the opening of the argument,

JUDGE DAVIES AROSE AND LEFT THE BENCH,

saying that he could not sit in the case, as he had been attorney for the city in those matters.

I have thought that a brief mention of the changes which have taken place in the Bar might interest you. The list of attorneys in Buffalo in 1856, comprises one hundred and seventy names; of these fifty-one are dead, thirty-four have removed to other localities, three remain with us, but are not in practice, and of ten others I have no knowledge, leaving but seventy-two who are still connected with the profession, either on the bench or at the Bar. Our present roll of attorneys includes over two hundred names. Thus it appears that nearly two-thirds of the lawyers of this city have commenced their professional lives within the last twenty years, and that, while our city has doubled in wealth and population, the number of members of our profession has not increased in anything like the same proportion.

And now that "Ichabod" is written upon the portals of the old Court House, now that its glory has departed, and we bid farewell to it, and to all the memories and associations which cluster so thickly around it, let it be our aim to maintain and if possible elevate still higher the honorable position which the Bar of Erie County has always sustained, and see to it that the dignity and honor of our profession suffer no detriment at our hands, in the elegant surroundings of our new Temple of Justice, to which we go with mingled feelings of sorrow for the past and gladness and hope for the present and the future.

Mr. Box was called for, and spoke as follows:

SPEECH OF H. W. BOX, ESQ.

Mr. Chairman and Brethren of the Bar: At a banquet where so much has been appropriately and eloquently said, I confess I am embarrassed in attempting to add a single word.

I am profoundly grateful to the movers of this re-union of the Bar of Erie County.

We have been made to feel to-night that ours is a glorious profession, and to rank well with its best members is no ordinary privilege. Surely, a little self-glorification on such an occasion as this is pardonable; besides, self-praise has one great element of advantage over all other kinds of praise, it is always convenient; and if we do not take it in sufficient doses, the fault is our own.

I am sorry the world has not always held so high an estimate of our profession as we place upon it ourselves to-night.

CROMWELL'S BAREBONES PARLIAMENT

cherished no such exalted notions concerning our profession, and regarded the whole fraternity with suspicion.

But, gentlemen, whatever may have been the prejudices against lawyers in the early days of our civilization, it is certain none exist to-day. No pursuit in life appears more captivating to the aspirant for fame than the profession of the law as it is followed and rewarded in our American courts.

It is the great avenue to political preferment and reputation; its honors are among the most splendid which can be attained in a free country, and its emoluments and privileges are prizes to be contested for by all its members. The rolls of our own County Bar celebrate many individuals who have risen from the humblest ranks by patient labor to wealth and station.

If the younger members of this Bar imagine they perceive in the elevation of these men much due to fortuitous circumstances, they are sadly deceived. These men are the architects of their own respective fortunes. Let us submit ourselves to the same tests, the same unremitting toil; if we do not attain their greatness, we can acquire distinction. The dream of indolence must be dissipated; we must awaken to the truth that there is no excellence without great labor.

The young men here to-night will soon be called to take the places of the sages of the Bench and Bar whose splendid achievements they now daily witness with admiration and surprise. In remembrance of the past, who would dare venture a prediction as to who present will occupy the future places of honor, trust and emolument! The genius at the college, think you? The young gentleman who answered every question asked by the examining committee for admission? The young man of high family position?

The child of wealthy parents? The history of the past furnishes no affirmative answer.

We have seen the genius sink and perish in poverty, obscurity and wretchedness, while on the other hand we have observed the *mediocre* plodding his slow but sure way up the hill of life, gaining steadfast footing every step, and mounting, at length, to eminence and distinction, an ornament to his family, a blessing to his country.

SIR JOSHUA REYNOLDS SAID:

"If a man has great talents industry will improve them; if he has but moderate abilities industry will supply their deficiency." The Spartan youth who complained to his mother that his sword was too short, was told to add a step to it; and so must our scant capacity be increased by diligence, and a more earnest determination. If it be not literally true that "nothing is denied to well directed labor," it is certain that "nothing is to be obtained without it."

To those of my young professional brethren who have just entered upon the practice of the law, and who scarcely know where the next installment for board is to be obtained, take courage from the success of your seniors who have triumphed over similar obstacles and reached the highest positions in our profession. They appreciate your embarrassments and annoyances, they sympathize with you, and in their heart of hearts bid you God's speed.

Learn to labor and to wait, and you shall verify the truth in your own lives of the declaration of the great dramatist:

> "Sweet are the uses of adversity,
> Which like the toad, ugly and venomous,
> Wears yet a precious jewel in its head."

Mr. E. C. Pattison was called upon, and his address was as follows:

ADDRESS OF E. C. PATTISON, ESQ.

Mr. Chairman and Gentlemen: As we have left the old Court House, and, professionally speaking, left it forever, it seems to me that the occasion requires and is entitled to a poet; and, although I've not been published as one whom the Muse has looked upon with favor, still I cannot let the opportunity pass without contributing my verse. But I trust, gentlemen, you will not lay aside your Shakespeare, Milton, Byron and Burns, to welcome

A POET FROM THE BUFFALO BAR.

I say the occasion demands a song, celebrating it, as we do around this festive board, and those venerable old buildings should by right be embalmed in verse, for, be it known, they must be embalmed in something to keep them together, although I fear my verse won't preserve those old benches and bars from the decay that will visit them from henceforth.

We've had many a happy time there, sometimes feeling keenly sensitive of our defects, at other times reveling in our triumphs. Justice has been meted out there, I hope, at all times with an even hand, and, as occasion required, it has been tempered with mercy, by those who have graced our Bench, as shining lights in the legal firmament, but who have now gone down the tide of returnless years; others have filled their places, and our Bench is now the pride and glory of the Bar, and one which we may justly feel proud of. But, sir, on this joyous occasion, celebrating our possession of the new City and County Hall, we can look back at the old Court House and say:

Farewell to the rooms, where Justice held sway,
Farewell to walls, that begin to decay,
Farewell to its Bench, farewell to its Bar,
Welcome, thrice welcome, our new "Temple Bar."

We've left the old Court House, entered the new,
And look back over mem'ries bright as the dew,
To where battles hard have been fought and won,
And others been lost, to all and each one.

There scenes were acted we ne'er can forget,
And hopes were blasted, bright suns were set;
There young legal lights have made their first plea,
Proud of their triumphs, as gems from the sea.

There the Judge, Lawyer, Sheriff and Clerk,
Met to solve problems that puzzled old Quirk;
Old Gammon and Snap have taken a hand
In troubles of those who belong to our band.

The Fillmores and Havens, Gansons and Halls,
Have wrestled for justice within those walls;
Verplanck and Masten, Mullett and Grover,
Have graced the old Bench, now left forever.

We left the old Court House, left it in pairs,
And thought of the fun we've often had there;
Ah! what's that glistens? a tear in the eye—
Farewell, old homestead! we bid you good-bye.

Another call was made for the younger members of the Bar, and Mr. H. B. Greene answered for them, and made one of the best speeches of the evening. It was original, thoughtful, and instructive. His address was sufficiently interlarded with anecdote to make it amusing and relishable, and it was listened to with the deepest interest.

Mr. Greene was followed by Mr. J. G. Milburn, another young, promising and rising member of the profession, who acquitted himself nobly in a manly and thoughtful address, that evinced extensive reading, and a well-stored mind.

Mr. Perry G. Parker was loudly called for, and gave the following address:

ADDRESS OF P. G. PARKER, ESQ.

Mr. Chairman and Brother Lawyers: I have never delivered a Fourth of July oration in my life; never have read an essay or an address before an agricultural society, although the son of a farmer and brought up at farmers' work.

This is my native county, and this city has been my home during all my legal labors, and will be until those labors are ended. In September, 1841, I entered the office of Fillmore and Haven as a student-at-law, and remained there until I was admitted to practice in November, 1844, at the October term of that year held at Rochester, N. Y. Lucien Hawley, Isaiah T. Williams, James M. Haven and E. Carlton Sprague were associate clerks and students in the same office. Of Mr. Sprague I need not speak; he has done that for himself. Mr. Haven, a younger brother of S. G. Haven, died in April, 1844; he did not live long enough to be admitted to practice in his chosen profession. He was talented, kind-hearted, and amiable as a young woman. Hawley and Williams, were admitted to the Bar at the same time I was, in 1844. Of Hawley, let me say he is a good lawyer, the incorruptible government official, an honest man—a valued friend. Williams was bound to succeed, and he has accomplished success,

STANDING IN THE FRONT RANK

of the profession in the city of New York, and has few superiors as an advocate. The friendships formed in our student life have existed ever since. The life of the student then was not what it is now. It was very rare that the student was allowed, like my brother Lewis to pettifog before he was admitted.

The lawyer has a profession which is second to none other; and in its ranks are to be found the ablest and the best in every community of this enlightened country.

In 1842, Reuben Hyde Walworth, was Chancellor of the State; Samuel Nelson, was Chief Justice of the Supreme Court; Nathan Dayton, Circuit Judge; Nathan K. Hall, First Judge of Erie County; Horatio J. Stow, Recorder of the City of Buffalo; Henry W. Rogers, District Attorney of Erie County. Among the old law firms of Buffalo I remember at that time, were Fillmore, Hall & Haven; Barker, Hawley & Sill; Potter, Babcock & Spaulding; Austin, Love & Vedder. This union of strength was desirable because it permitted a division of labor, as every variety of business was done in each law office,—civil and criminal in law, equity and admiralty, through all the different stages of litigation.

I tried my first case in a Court of Record in December, 1845, before H. K. Smith, Recorder and a jury. Judge Daniels was my opponent. I was in excellent health and perfectly sober, and yet I remember that it was with great difficulty that I could stand upon my feet when addressing the court or jury; there was a weakness in my knees, and a general feeling of feebleness. I was defeated by a decision of the court upon a question of law; but on appeal to the Supreme Court I reversed the Recorder and succeeded in the case.

ALL MY ASSOCIATIONS

with the Bar of Erie County have been pleasing and enjoyable. I have received the greatest kindness from Bench and Bar. In many a warm contest honorable blows have been taken and given; and self-respect and friendship maintained. I think this Bar is noted for its liberal practice; and I commend this to its younger members as more profitable and agreeable in the long run than technical or sharp practice.

The code and rules furnish a general guide in the practice; but there are constantly springing up matters for which there is no written rule and you must rely upon the word of promise of your adversary; see to it that your promise be kept. In all things involving the merits of your case, consult your client's interest; in matters of practice consult your own convenience and pleasure.

Before me, on my right, is a small band of my brothers, with gray hairs. I am hastening on and will soon join them. I see the crowd coming up the hill on the other side; I say to you, welcome; but hasten slowly; do not turn us away. Be kind to us; we would linger yet awhile about the scenes with which we have been so long familiar. This social gathering marks an era in the Bar of Erie County. The movement to form a Bar Association meets with my hearty approval. Let it embrace all; and its object be to elevate and improve us all, not to push down any. From the social feeling which begins here to-night the best of results will flow, if properly cultivated. Therefore, cherish this and organize. I thank you for the attention you have given me, and bid you all good-night.

Mr. Gurney, being called upon, said:

ADDRESS OF W. H. GURNEY, ESQ.

Mr. President and Gentlemen of the Erie County Bar: I did not expect to be called upon to speak to you to-night, indeed, in all this talk about the "old members" and the "young members" of the Bar, I hardly know where I belong. Until the last few days I supposed I ranked with the young members—among the boys—but when we took leave of the old Court House, and were formed by Gen. Scroggs in Military order, or in Masonic order, the boys in front and the old men in the rear, I was, to my surprise, nearer the rear than the front; there were more boys in front of me than old men behind me.

Mr. Chairman, I was admitted in the class of 1860, a class entitled to some recognition at your hands, and I believe, sir, I am the only representative of that distinguished class present this evening, and I propose to say something in its defense. We have heard to-night of those admitted prior to 1850, and of the young members —but of the class of '60, we have, until now, heard nothing.

For the last four days we have been constantly reminded of the old members—of how those old men practiced law. Why, Mr. President, those old fellows undoubtedly, did nobly in their day and generation—we do nobly in ours. When they point us to their eloquent Barker, we can show them a dozen eloquent Barkers. When they point to their Dudley Marvins, we can point to a score of Marvins. When they point to lawyers who won verdicts from juries by the mere force of their eloquence, we can show a dozen who do that every day. When they show you a lawyer who could get verdicts and could not keep them, we can show his counterpart to-day. When they point with pride to the honest and able judges, with an equal degree of pride we can direct attention to our accomplished, honest and able judges.

Practicing law in those days and to-day is a different matter; as an illustration, in those days when they desired to follow their causes to the Court of Last Resort—then the Court for the Correction of Errors—it took them a week, by the then most expeditious mode of traveling, the stage-coach or the packet-boat, to reach Albany. Now we go to bed in Buffalo in the evening, and are in Albany the next morning, ready to argue our causes. There has been a change in mode and manner of practicing law. Those old men so noble and efficient in their age and day of the world, would be as much out of place in this, as would the stage-coach and packet-boat as a mode for speedy travel.

It seems proper for the class of '60 occupying the prominent middle position that they do, to say this. We can say, to the old men of our day that we do not think you have passed the days of your usefulness, but that your opinions are not as vigorous as they were formerly. We can say to the boys—but in view of the able speeches we have had from them to-night, it would be a bold man that would say anything to them, except to congratulate them—to the student we say, it is to the class of '60 that they must look for the redress of those unpleasant things which surround the life of the student; the members of that class have not forgotten the days when they were students. Many of the obstacles that the class of '60 encountered exist no more—the life of a student now, is comparatively pleasant, when contrasted with the time when the class of '60 were students. But evils still exist, and it shall be the special mission of the class of '60 to see them removed.

Mr. Josiah Cook, after being excused two or three times, finally yielded to the call for a speech, and spoke thus:

ADDRESS OF JOSIAH COOK, ESQ.

Mr. Chairman and Brethren of the Bar: I thank you for the compliment you have been pleased to pay me in calling upon me to address you. I do, indeed, appreciate the compliment, when I look about me and see the vast number of learned gentlemen I am addressing.

Brethren, I have met the members of the Erie County Bar on more than twenty different occasions, called together to exchange condolences upon the death of some brother, and to walk in procession to the depositing of the remains of those deceased brethren in their last resting-place. I remember the last meeting for that purpose was to pay the last tribute of respect to that bright spirit, the lamented Folsom.

And when we gathered at the "Old Court House" for the purpose of marching from there to the new Temple of Justice, was there one in that vast assemblage who did not heave the sigh of bereavement as they took the last look at the old structure? Not one. And it occurred to me that, as every occasion upon which the Erie County Bar had met in a body, had been one of sorrow, it was about time that we met for the purpose of having a social time. It was these reflections which prompted me to offer the resolution that we meet at this banquet table. We are here, and I have been pleased by the general good-feeling which has prevailed, and again to see the large attendance here to-night. This is a meeting of the Erie County Bar, which will not soon be forgotten; it is the first of the kind, and, I hope, not the last. I am pleased at the very large attendance here, of what may be termed, the young members of the Bar, and, while listening to the speeches of several of them here this evening, it occurred to me that Erie county might well be proud of the young men who are coming up to associate with and take the places of the older members, when they should be called to their fathers. In conclusion, allow me to suggest to the younger members who have been talking much about Roman law and lawyers, that they had better give their attention to Buffalo law and lawyers, for, after they have practiced at the Buffalo Bar for twenty years, as I have, they will find that the Buffalo lawyers will keep them so busy, that they will have little time to devote to Justinian *et al.*

Gentlemen, I bid you good-night.

The chairman referred to the law firm of Fillmore, Hall & Haven and to Thomas J. Sizer as having been a student with them and having for a time the charge of their law business, and asked to hear something from him. Mr. Sizer in response said:

ADDRESS OF T. J. SIZER.

The chairman's allusion to my former connection with the distinguished law firm requires me to say something. I had not thought but that many others present, as Mr. Sprague, Mr. Parker, and others, were students with that firm, but, thinking of it, there is only Dennis Bowen present whom I remember as a student with me.

Mr. Fillmore was one of the best of lawyers. It seemed so to me then; and I know it better as I have had better opportunities for observation and comparison. It has, by many, been supposed that he was chiefly a statesman. I think him more pre-eminent as a lawyer—one of the best, if not the best, whom I have ever personally known. His method was admirable. He seemed rather slow and cautious, but in reality progressed through his examination of a case with dispatch, and came to his conclusion with remarkable certainty and confidence, because his system was so good and thorough. He noted, but laid aside, each irrelevant question, and, following the principle of the case, knew, with confidence, the true conclusion when it was reached. I know this from my own good opportunities for observing. He was always a student, always a learner, always acquiring.

Judge Hall had remarkable qualities. His instinctive knowledge of law was wonderful; and his off-hand opinion on any point almost invariably accurate. He wrote a beautiful hand, and more rapidly than any one I ever knew, and could transact business with wonderful dispatch and correctness. If cornered, or pressed for time, he could do more in an hour, and do it well, than many a one could do in a whole day.

In my opinion, as a judge, he erred in elaborating his decisions, and in the conscientiousness with which he investigated authorities. I think he would have been entirely safe in relying more on the excellence of his own intuitive perceptions and knowledge, and that his great abilities would have been better appreciated, and his health preserved.

Mr. Haven was perhaps more known as a lawyer than either of his partners by those here present, and he has already been well and truly described. His pleasant manner in all his professional work most agreeably impressed everybody, and undoubtedly had a most excellent effect on this Bar. But Mr. Haven was a remarkable worker. He seemed to love work for its own sake; and I think he erred in making it too constant and continuous. He would to the very last, spend long evenings in his office in the work of copying papers.

I have felt very much interested here to-night in the appeals of the students and younger members of the Bar for sympathy and encouragement. It is not always easy to find satisfactory methods by which to express these. The young must not suppose that they alone are subject to embarrassment, and that they alone experience these wants.

Since the Banquet, the chairman has received a letter from Hon. Henry E. Davies, formerly a Buffalonian, but now of New York. The older residents of Buffalo will remember Mr. Davies as a promising young lawyer, who began his professional career a half a century ago, and who held the office of clerk and attorney of the village corporation of Buffalo in 1826, or fifty years ago. Judge Davies has since then become eminent as a lawyer and jurist, and has been a member of the Court of Appeals. It is to Judge Davies that Mr. Geo. Wadsworth referred in his address at the Banquet, as having left his seat on the Bench, when a Buffalo case was called, in which he had been counsel many years before. Judge Davies is now full of years and is crowned with well-earned laurels, won in the profession, and on the Bench. His letter to Mr. Sprague here follows:

LETTER OF HON. HENRY E. DAVIES.

New York, *March* 27, 1876.

Hon. E. C. Sprague, Buffalo, N. Y.:

My Dear Sir: On the afternoon of the fourteenth of March, instant, I had the honor to receive from the committee of the Bar of Erie County an invitation to a dinner, to be given that evening at the Tifft House. For this remembrance of the Bar of Erie County, permit me to express my grateful acknowledgments, and the regret I have deeply felt that it was not in my power to be present on this interesting occasion.

I have read with great interest the proceedings of the meeting of the Bar of Erie County, held at the old Court House, in Buffalo, on Saturday the eleventh day of March, inst. It would have been peculiarly gratifying to my feelings to have been present on that occasion. The scene calls back to my memory the fact, that fifty years since I made my first professional speech in that room, before the Court of Common Pleas of Erie County, and the subsequent events of my professional life have never effaced the interest of that, to me, memorable occasion.

You will permit me to express to the Bar of Erie County, through you, and to the chairman of the meeting referred to, my grateful acknowledgments for the notice taken of my connection with the Bar of your county. I shall hope, at no distant day, personally to interchange congratulations with you upon your removal from the old to the new Court House, where I hope you will all achieve great professional honors and be rewarded with the approving voice of a grateful and faithfully served community. I have the honor to be, with great respect,

Very truly yours,

Henry E. Davies.

ANOTHER BANQUET.

THE ATTACHES OF THE COUNTY CLERK'S OFFICE CELEBRATE THEIR REMOVAL.

THE gentlemen connected with the County Clerk's office celebrated the transition from the old to the new, in a somewhat select and private social reunion. The affair was confined to the clerk, his deputies and employees, the ex-county clerks, and former attaches of the office, with a few invited guests, and came off Thursday evening, March 16.

The party assembled in the old clerk's office at half-past seven o'clock and organized, by the appointment of George L. Remington, Esq., the County Clerk, as chairman. On taking the chair, Mr. Remington said that in leaving the old quarters he had no regrets to offer. There was nothing about it to claim endearment except the recollections and associations formed there. In leaving this old building for the more noble structure, he said: Let us determine to so shape our lives that in the end we go to buildings more spacious, to palaces more grand and which shall remain eternal.

Mr. Noah P. Sprague was appointed vice-president and made brief remarks. In connection with the old building he had recollections both pleasant and sad. He came to Buffalo in 1824. In 1831 he became County Clerk, which office he held for three years, and, beginning with 1840, he held it for a second term. The first clerk of the county was Louis Le Couteulx, a polished gentleman of the old school, one of the French nobility, courteous and dignified, a very genial, excellent old man. When Mr. Sprague came to Buffalo it was a village of about two thousand inhabitants. He remembered talking with Gen. Joseph Clary, Mr. Barker, and David Burt, regretting the shabby appearance of the square in front of the Court House. Mr. Barker, then County Clerk, proposed that they should get some trees to plant there; the next day they went out to the chestnut ridge and procured some trees which they planted in the square, some ten or twelve of which the speaker could recognize to-day. He thought it due to the Clerks of Erie county to say that they had been a line of honorable men, and he hoped that in the future the same integrity and capacity might be shown.

Mr. S. Cary Adams was chosen secretary, and in assuming the duties of the station, he said:

ADDRESS OF MR. ADAMS.

Mr. Chairman and Gentlemen: I thank you for the honor of this appointment. For months I have been anxiously waiting and hoping to see the change take place, from the old to the new, as to all departments of public business, but as to none of them, with as much eagerness, as I have with respect to this office. As an outsider during several years, I have witnessed the crowded condition of affairs within these walls, and have felt that the records and files were being ruined for the want of proper accommodation. I remember well but a few years ago when the commissioners turned this then new building over to its uses as a Court House and Clerk's office. I felt then, as now, that it was a monstrosity, and wholly unfitted as a place in which to store public records.

My connection with this office began in January, 1859, and ended January, 1865. It was with me, as it is, and has been with all who are, and have been connected with it,

A TIME OF STEADY HARD WORK.

I found as you who are connected with it now find, that it is not a matter of pastime, but "that eternal vigilance is the price of safety," that the public interests require constant, continuous watchfulness so that no mistakes shall be allowed to creep into the records; that nothing shall be lost, and that all, so far as possible, may be kept as good as new.

It was my experience during my entire continuance in this office to find a public, willing to give all due credit for all honest endeavors to fairly discharge the duties of the position. Particularly was this the case with the gentlemen of the legal profession with whom I was brought in daily contact. These are the bright points in my memory connected with this building to which we are now about to bid farewell. These are the redeeming features connected with it. Robbed of these its memory would be hateful. As with myself, so no doubt it is with the rest of you.

But these memories, these recollections we shall take with us, and always cherish them. And as the new rooms to which we go are the more bright and the more beautiful, so also shall be these memories and these recollections.

Mr. Marcus Bartlett, the affable and obliging deputy clerk, was called upon to address the meeting in behalf of the employees of the office, and said:

ADDRESS OF MR. BARTLETT.

Mr. President and Gentlemen: I thank you for your courtesy in calling on me to make a few remarks on this occasion, and as I have not much to say I hope not to tire your patience. It may perhaps be thought by some that we are rather late in formally leaving our old place of business and taking possession of the new. But did they know the amount of labor that was necessary to be performed to remove the things that belong to this office to their new position, did they know that the County Clerk's office was kept open for business and transacted all that came promptly up to five o'clock Saturday evening, its usual hour of closing, and that it was open at the new building and everything in place and ready for business at the usual opening hour nine o'clock on Monday morning, they would know that work had to be done, and when informed that there were eighty-three wagon loads of records and documents, they will discover just cause for this delay, and acknowledge that the work was performed quickly and quietly without even delaying any act of official business for a moment. And for this, great praise is due not only to the officials and employees, but to many of our outside friends whose business had made them familiar with the office, and who, taking an interest in its affairs, promptly tendered assistance and rendered efficient aid. And now we are ready to unite with our friends in taking a formal leave of our old quarters, and a formal possession of the new.

And here I beg leave to read a few lines of verse that I have hastily jotted down for the occasion:

Years ago I am told when our city was new,
When our county was young and its records were few,
Good men of the age, quite discerning and wise,
In the light of the past saw the future arise.

With a keen sense of need and an honest good will,
And perhaps of those times with an architect's skill,
They planned and erected, by diligent work,
This building, for Court House and office of Clerk.

'Twas a safe, noble structure, no doubt for its time;
No doubt its projectors e'en thought it sublime,
As a place for the records of mortgage and deed,
The Clerk's office sure must be all they would need.

But Time, the great teacher that many despise,
Gives knowledge and wisdom ofttimes to the wise,
And happy the man, and the people, indeed,
When truth comes so plain that though running they read.

This awkard, contracted, unhealthy, dark place,
To both county and city became a disgrace,
When those who kept pace with the marches of time,
Planned and reared its successor, a model sublime.

And therefore we leave this old castle alone,
With a joy in our hearts we are willing to own;
Though memory whispers of many things here,
Which time and our friendships have made doubly dear.

But ere we depart let us briefly review
Those deeds of the past, we here learned to do,
And see if perchance while the watchman has slept,
Naught bad was engrossed where the records are kept.

Through dockets of judgments and libers of deeds,
Through mortgage foreclosures and intricate leads,
We have searched for the titles of houses and lands,
To help those in trouble and strengthen their hands.

Faithful scribes we have been, at least tried to be,
And to leave the best page where others could see,
On the books of this office we oft would compete,
But that does not prove all our records complete.

For the unwritten page to our minds may reveal
Certain deeds which displayed less of wisdom than zeal.
And the thought of them often our feelings have stirred,
But we never were human unless we had erred.

If we often did wrong, we as oft would deplore,
And like other transgressors the same things do o'er.
So with good and with bad we have jostled along,
Ever striving for right but at times doing wrong.

May our good deeds stand forth in the strength of their might,
And our bad ones be buried in Oblivion's night;
And as we go forth from these walls with a sigh,
Drop a tear of regret with our parting good-bye.

Messrs. Thomas B. Wright and Amos B. Tanner were then appointed marshals, and the employees and their guests, having been formed in procession, marched to the office in the new building, where the meeting was re-organized, and the exercises opened with prayer invoked by Rev. James Remington, of Lancaster, father of the County Clerk.

Hon. Albert Haight, County Judge, then made some pleasant remarks, in the course of which he spoke of the City and County Hall as surpassing any other building in the country constructed for similar purposes. Heretofore the people of Buffalo had referred to the public buildings with mortification, but now they were possessed of a structure of which they might well be proud. He congratulated the County Clerk and his employees upon the beautiful office to which they had been removed.

Alonzo Tanner, Esq., considered the new City and County Hall an honor to the citizens of Erie county and of Buffalo. There was no building that he knew of, unless it might be the Capitol at Washington, that could compare with its magnificence. Mr. Tanner spoke of his familiarity with the County Clerk's Office, and of the great increase of the business of the county since 1850. He agreed with what had been said, that there should not be a great amount of murmuring upon leaving the old quarters.

Mr. Bartlett, the deputy clerk, was again called upon and spoke as follows:

Mr. President and Gentlemen: Again I thank you for this mark of favor, and again, as I said before, I will endeavor to be brief, but it is well for me and perhaps better for you who are here assembled, that I am not a man of words; that I am not an orator. For were I thus gifted I should endeavor at this time, in this place and on this occasion, surrounded as we are by all this grandeur and magnificence, to attempt in words to do justice to this building, its equipments, its architects, its projectors, its builders, and to all to whom we are indebted for its usefulness and beauty. But words as well as ideas fail me. We have here a safe receptacle for the most important documents of all the people of our county, the titles to their very homes; and I am proud to live in a county where its leading men conceived and carried out so successfully such a worthy and laudable undertaking. I am proud to be a tax-payer in Erie county in this one hundreth anniversary of our nation's independence that I may assist in the erection of so noble a structure.

I will again conclude what I have to say in verse:

We have passed from the old, we have entered the new,
And behold what a change, what a sight meets the view!
And the truth stands before us in splendor sublime
That mind has kept pace with the marches of time.

A temple where wisdom should sit on the throne,
A temple where fraud should be always unknown!
A temple where justice should never be dumb;
And a place for our records for long years to come.

Words fail on my tongue half its beauties to tell,
Of its firm granite walls from the basement to bell,
Of its spacious apartments where neatness appears,
Of its glittering columns and grand chandeliers.

From the tip of the turret to foundation stone
Each part in itself is a model alone ;
All forming combined (and which none should destroy)
A grand thing of beauty, forever a joy.

These things in our hearts should awaken anew
A faith in our kind, a resolve to be true.
We are men with a title to honor and fame,
Let our life records prove we are worthy the name.

What is wealth without wisdom and that from above?
What is man without honor and life without love?
For the joy of well doing will never depart
From the thankful in spirit, the grateful in heart.

We will thank all the builders that none feel aggrieved,
From the hand that performed to the head that conceived;
Especially those through whose wisdom and will
We are blest with this model of architect skill.

How they guarded the funds as they reared the strong wall,
Is an honor to them and a blessing to all.
And they each should be proud every fact to reveal
In these days of lax morals when honest (?) men steal.

But of earthly rewards nothing richer is gained
Than to know that their fingers have never been stained;
Then like just men and true we'll resolve here to-night—
God giving us strength—we will always do right.

If we seek for the favors of bounteous Heaven,
Our bad deeds repented will all be forgiven ;
Then like mortgages paid or outlawed judgment rolls,
We shall feel they're no longer a lien on our souls.

And the good, when the bad to oblivion have passed,
Will all be recorded for ever to last,
In letters of gold in those Libers of love,
Kept only by Angels in mansions above.

When the last page is reached and the last line is laid,
The world will be blest by the records we've made.
And with naught to upbraid, and no sorrow to feel,
We will pass from this earth to the land of the leal.

At the conclusion of Mr. Bartlett's address, a procession was again formed, and leaving the stately building the company pursued their way to

THE OCEAN HOUSE,

where the scene was exchanged for a banquet room in which a most inviting table was spread. The bill of fare was excellent, and the guests were in good condition for doing justice to it. After appetites were satisfied, a "feast of reason" was declared in order, and regular toasts were proposed and responded to, as follows:

"The County of Erie," responded to by Judge Albert Haight.

"The Building Commissioners," George S. Wardwell, Esq.

"The Old Settlers of Erie County," Rev. James Remington.

"The Superior Court," John C. Graves, Esq.

"The District Attorney's Office," District Attorney D. N. Lockwood.

"The Sheriff's Department," Under Sheriff E. R. Chase.

"The Surrogate's Office," C. W. Goodyear, Esq.

"The County Treasurer's Department," R. C. Titus, Esq.

"The Board of Supervisors," A. B. Tanner, Esq.

Impromptu toasts and a general interchange of sentiment were then in order, and the late hours of the evening were passed in the most pleasant manner.

APPENDIX.

CIVIL LIST OF THE VILLAGE AND CITY OF BUFFALO

FOR SIXTY YEARS.

THE following is a list of the names of persons who have filled the principal offices under the charters of the village and city of Buffalo, for a period of sixty years, or from 1816 to 1876, inclusive :

1816.

Clerk—Jonathan E. Chaplin.
Treasurer—Josiah Trowbridge.
Collector—Moses Baker.
Trustees—Oliver Forward, Charles Townsend, Heman B. Potter, Ebenezer Walden, Jonas Harrison, Samuel Wilkeson.

1817.

Clerk—Jonathan E. Chaplin.
Treasurer—Josiah Trowbridge.
Collector—Moses Baker.
Trustees—Ebenezer Walden, Jonas Harrison, John G. Camp, Samuel Wilkeson, Elias Ransom.

1818.

Clerk—Stephen K. Grosvenor.
Treasurer—Elijah D. Efner.
Collector—Moses Baker.
Trustees—Joseph Stocking, Charles Townsend, Heman B. Potter, Oliver Forward, Abraham Larzelere.

1819.

Clerk—Stephen K. Grosvenor.
Treasurer—Elijah D. Efner.
Collector—Leonard P. Crary.
Trustees—Charles Townsend, Samuel Wilkeson, Joseph Stocking, Heman B. Potter, Joseph Landon.

1820.

Clerk—Stephen K. Grosvenor.
Treasurer—Elijah D. Efner.
Collector—Moses Baker.
Trustees—Charles Townsend, Cyrenius Chapin, Samuel Wilkeson, Joseph Stocking, Wm. T. Miller.

1821.

Clerk—S. K. Grosvenor.
Treasurer—E. D. Efner.
Collector—E. F. Gilbert.
Trustees—Charles Townsend, Samuel Wilkeson, Joseph Stocking, Cyrenius Chapin, Heman B. Potter.

1822.

Clerk—Gorham Chapin.
Treasurer—Henry R. Seymour.
Collector—Moses Baker.
Trustees—Ebenezer Johnson, Oliver Forward, John B. Hicks, John Scott, Henry M. Campbell.

1823.

Clerk—Joseph Clary.
Treasurer—Henry R. Seymour.
Collector—James Higgins.
Trustees—Oliver Forward, Chas. Townsend, David Burt, Abner Bryant, Benjamin Caryl.

1824.

Clerk—Joseph Clary.
Treasurer—Henry R. Seymour.
Collector—Lorin Pierce.
Trustees—Heman B. Potter, David Burt, Joseph Stocking, Nathaniel Vosburgh, Oliver Forward.

1825.

Clerk—Joseph Clary.
Treasurer—Henry R. Seymour.
Collector—James Higgins.
Trustees—Oliver Forward, David Burt, Heman B. Potter, Ebenezer Johnson, Nathaniel Vosburgh.

1826.

Clerk—Henry E. Davies.
Treasurer—Henry R. Seymour.
Collector—James Higgins.
Trustees—Oliver Forward, Benjamin Rathbun, William Hollister, Joseph D. Hoyt, Major A. Andrews.

1827.

Clerk—Henry E. Davies.
Treasurer—Henry R. Seymour.
Collector—Leonard P. Crary.
Trustees—Benjamin Rathbun, Joseph D. Hoyt, William Hollister, Oliver Forward, Major A. Andrews.

1828.

Clerk—George P. Barker.
Treasurer—Henry R. Seymour.
Collector—James Higgins.
Trustees—Bela D. Coe, Anthony Beers, Jos. Clary, Hiram Pratt, Moses Baker.

1829.

Clerk—George P. Barker.
Treasurer—Henry R. Seymour.
Collector—David E. Merrill.
Trustees—Joseph Clary, Hiram Pratt, Bela D. Coe, Moses Baker, Anthony Beers.

1830.

Clerk—George P. Barker.
Treasurer—Henry R. Seymour.
Collector—David E Merrill.
Trustees—Moses Baker, Theodore Coburn, John W. Clark, Jos. Clary, William Ketchum.

1831.

Clerk—Elijah Ford.
Treasurer—Henry R. Seymour.
Collector—David E. Merrill.
Trustees—Bela D. Coe, Moses Baker, John W. Clark, James Sheldon, Theodore Coburn.

1832.

Clerk—Elijah Ford.
Treasurer—Henry R. Seymour.
Collector—Gilman Smith.
Trustees—John W. Clark, Wm. S. Waters, Cyrus Athearn, John D. Harty, Jos. Sheldon.

NOTE.—The village of Buffalo was incorporated as a city by an Act of the Legislature of 1832, which divided the city into five wards, and authorized the election of two Aldermen in each ward, who, with the Mayor as the presiding officer, constituted the Common Council. The Council elected the Mayor, Clerk, Treasurer, Attorney, Street Commissioner, Surveyor, and other corporation officers. The first election under the charter was held on the twenty-sixth of May, 1832, when the following board of officers was elected and superseded the village officers, above named, for the remainder of the year.

1832.

Mayor—Ebenezer Johnson.
Clerk—Dyre Tillinghast.
Treasurer—Henry R. Seymour.
Attorney—George P. Barker.
Surveyor—J. J. Baldwin.
Street Commissioner—Edward Baldwin.

WARDS. ALDERMEN.

First—Isaac S. Smith, Joseph W. Brown.
Second—John G. Camp, Henry Root.
Third—David M. Day, Ira A. Blossom.
Fourth—Henry White, Major A. Andrews.
Fifth—Ebenezer Walden, Thomas C. Love.

1833.

Mayor—Major A. Andrews.
Clerk—Elijah J. Roberts.
Treasurer—Henry R. Seymour.
Attorney—William A. Mosely.
Surveyor—James J. Baldwin.
Street Commissioner—Edward Baldwin.

WARDS. ALDERMEN.

First—Stephen Clark, Jos. W. Brown.
Second—John G. Camp, James Durick.
Third—Geo. B. Webster, Darius Burton.
Fourth—Philander Bennett, Moses Baker.
Fifth—Sheldon Smith, Sylvester Matthews.

1834.

Mayor—Ebenezer Johnson.
Clerk—Elijah J. Roberts.
Treasurer—Orlando Allen.
Attorney—Wm. A. Mosely.
Surveyor—James J. Baldwin.
Street Commissioner—Edward Baldwin.

WARDS. ALDERMEN.

First—Isaac S. Smith, Stephen Clark.
Second—Squier S. Case, Henry Root.
Third—Birdsey Wilcox, John T. Hudson.
Fourth—Moses Baker, Elijah Ford.
Fifth—Sylvester Matthews, James Miller.

1835.

Mayor—Hiram Pratt.
Clerk—Theodotus Burwell.
Treasurer—Henry Root.
Attorney—Nathaniel K. Hall.
Surveyor—Wm. B. Gilbert.
Street Commissioner—Sylvester Matthews.

WARDS. ALDERMEN.

First—Jno. W. Clark, Jno. Prince.
Second—Squire S. Case, Orlando Allen.
Third—Ira A. Blossom, Wm. F. P. Taylor.
Fourth—Elijah Ford, Noyes Darrow.
Fifth—Manly Colton, Nathaniel Vosburgh.

1836.

Mayor—Samuel Wilkeson.
Clerk—Elbridge G. Spaulding.
Treasurer—A. J. Douglas.
Attorney—John L. Talcott.
Surveyor—William B. Gilbert.
Street Commissioner—Alanson Webster.

WARDS. ALDERMEN.

First—John Prince, Aaron Goodrich.
Second—James Durick, M. L. Faulkner.
Third—S. K. Grosvenor, Silas Sawin.
Fourth—Nathaniel Wilgus, Harlow French.
Fifth—D. F. Kimball, Jeremiah Staats.

1837.

Mayor—Josiah Trowbridge.
Clerk—Theo. C. Peters.
Treasurer—Hamlet D. Scranton.
Attorney—Theodore C. Peters.
Surveyor—William B. Gilbert.
Street Commissioner—Wm. K. Scott.

WARDS. ALDERMEN.

First—Wm. Valleau, Wm. J. Mack.
Second—Jacob A. Barker, Geo. E. Hayes.
Third—Walter Joy, Edward L. Stevenson.
Fourth—Nathaniel Wilgus, Moses Baker.
Fifth—Pierre A. Barker, Nathaniel K. Hall.

1838.

Mayor—Ebenezer Walden.
Clerk—T. C. Peters.
Treasurer—Hamlet D. Scranton.
Attorney—Theodotus Burwell.
Surveyor—W. K. Scott.
Street Commissioner—W. K. Scott.
* *Superintendent of Schools*—O. G. Steele.
Police Justice—James L. Barton.

WARDS. ALDERMEN.

First—D. F. Kimball, C. S. Pierce.
Second—S. S. Case, Lucius Storrs.
Third—Wm. F. P. Taylor, James McKay.
Fourth—Nathaniel Wilgus, Moses Baker.
Fifth—Charles Winne, Alonzo Raynor.

1839.

Mayor—Hiram Pratt.
Clerk—T. C. Peters.
Treasurer—Wm. Moore.
Attorney—Harlow S. Love.
Surveyor—W. K. Scott.
Street Commissioner—Wm. K. Scott.
Superintendent of Schools—O. G. Steele.
Police Justice—James L. Barton.

WARDS. ALDERMEN.

First—F. W. Atkins, Henry Lamb.
Second—Lucius Storrs, Thos R. Stocking.
Third—W. Hollister, Jr., Ed. L. Stevenson.
Fourth—M. L. Faulkner, F. Dellenbaugh.
Fifth—Peter Curtiss, Augustine Kimball.

1840.

†*Mayor*—Sheldon Thompson.
Clerk—Squier S. Case.
Treasurer—John R. Lee.
Attorney—Harlow S. Love.
Surveyor—W. K Scott.
Street Commissioner—Wm. K. Scott.
Superintendent of Schools—Daniel Bowen.
Police Justice—Horace Clark.

WARDS. ALDERMEN.

First—Henry Lamb, C. A. Comstock.
Second—N. H. Gardner, Wm. Evans.
Third—Wm. Williams. Horatio Shumway.
Fourth—Philander Bennett, F. Dellenbaugh.
Fifth—Peter Curtiss, I. R. Harrington.

1841.

Mayor—Isaac R. Harrington.
Clerk—John T. Lacy.
Treasurer—William Williams.
Attorney—George W. Houghton.
Street Commissioner—Henry Lovejoy.
Superintendent of Schools—Silas Kingsley.
Police Justice—Horace Clark.

WARDS. ALDERMEN.

First—Henry Lamb, E. S. Havens.
Second—Edward Root, N. H. Gardner.
Third—Richard Sears, E. G. Spaulding.
Fourth—Philander Bennett, O. G. Steele.
Fifth—John R. Lee, Henry Roop.

* By Act of Legislature in 1837, the offices of Superintendent of Schools and Police Justice were created, and the Council authorized to fill the same.

† By an amendment of the charter the Mayor was elected by the people, and Mr. Thompson was the first Mayor so chosen.

1842.

Mayor—George W. Clinton.
Clerk—John T. Lacy.
Treasurer—John R. Lee.
Attorney—Samuel Wilkeson, Jr.
Surveyor—Henry Lovejoy.
Street Commissioner—Abram Hempstreet.
Superintendent of Schools—Samuel Caldwell.
Police Justice—Horace Clark.

WARDS. ALDERMEN.

First—E. S. Havens, E. D. Robinson.
Second—N. H. Gardner, L. H. Pratt.
Third—John Wilkeson, O. H Marshall.
Fourth—O. G. Steele, Nelson Randall.
Fifth—H. W. Pierce, Asahel Camp.

1843.

Mayor—Joseph G. Masten.
Clerk—John T. Lacy.
Treasurer—George C. White.
Attorney—A. P. Nichols
Surveyor—Henry Lovejoy.
Street Commissioner—Charles S. Pierce.
Superintendent of Schools—Samuel Caldwell.
Police Justice—Horace Clark.

WARDS. ALDERMEN.

First—John Cummings, Patrick Smith.
Second—F. S. Ellas, Alex. McCulloch, Jr.
Third—A. M. Grosvenor, Manuel Taff.
Fourth—W. R. Andrews, Thompson Hersee.
Fifth—H. W. Pierce, Elbridge Farwell.

1844.

Mayor—William Ketchum.
Clerk—John T Lacy.
Treasurer—Robert Pomeroy.
Attorney—Seth E Sill.
Surveyor—Henry Lovejoy.
Street Commissioner—Isaac T. Hathaway.
Superintendent of Schools—Elias S. Hawley.
Police Justice—E. A. Maynard.

WARDS. ALDERMEN.

First—John Cummings, Patrick Smith.
Second—Samuel F. Pratt, F. S. Ellas.
Third—Daniel Bowen, Hiram Barton.
Fourth—James DeLong, Thompson Hersee.
Fifth—L. L. Hodges, S. G. Walker.

1845.

Mayor—Joseph G. Masten.
Clerk—John Stringham.
Treasurer—William Lovering.
Attorney—Eli Cook.
Surveyor—Henry Lovejoy.
Street Commissioner—Abram Hempstreet.
Superintendent of Schools—O. G. Steele.
Police Justice—E. A. Maynard.

WARDS. ALDERMEN.

First—W. W. Stanard, Patrick Smith.
Second—Orlando Allen, S. S Jewett.
Third—Daniel Bowen, Chas. A. Van Slyke.
Fourth—Thompson Hersee. Chas. Esslinger.
Fifth—William Williams, Robert Russell.

1846.

Mayor—Solomon G. Haven.
Clerk—M. Cadwallader.
Treasurer—James Crocker.
Attorney—James Mullett.
Surveyor—Henry Lovejoy.
Street Commissioner—Samuel G. Walker.
Superintendent of Schools—Daniel Bowen.
Police Justice—P. A. Child.

WARDS. ALDERMEN.

First—Patrick Smith, J. W. Banta.
Second—S. S. Jewett, S. T. Atwater.
Third—George R. Babcock, Lester Brace.
Fourth—Nelson Randall, Harlow French.
Fifth—B. Thompson, Samuel Haines.

1847.

Mayor—Elbridge G. Spaulding.
Clerk—M. Cadwallader.
Treasurer—John R. Lee.
Attorney—James Sheldon, Jr.
Surveyor—Henry Lovejoy.
Street Commissioner—Samuel G. Walker.
Superintendent of Schools—E. S. Hawley.
Police Justice—P. A. Child.

WARDS. ALDERMEN.

First—J. W. Banta, Patrick Smith.
Second—Orlando Allen, L. A. Burrows.
Third—Calvin Bishop, Hiram Barton.
Fourth—A. S. Merrill, O. G. Steele.
Fifth—L. K. Plimpton, Watkins Williams.

1848.

Mayor—Orlando Allen.
Clerk—Jesse Walker.
* *Comptroller*—M. Cadwallader.
Treasurer—J. R. Lee.
Attorney—J. F. Brown.
Surveyor—Henry Lovejoy.
Street Commissioner—Samuel G. Walker.
Superintendent of Schools—E. S. Hawley.
Police Justice—P. A. Child.

WARDS. ALDERMEN.

First—W. W. Stanard, J. M. Smith.
Second—Daniel Bowen, D. M. Vanderpoel.
Third—Levi Allen, Paul Roberts.
Fourth—A. S. Merrill, H. H. Matteson.
Fifth—L. K. Plimpton, Watkins Williams.

1849.

Mayor—Hiram Barton.
Clerk—Jesse Walker.
Comptroller—M. Cadwallader.
Treasurer—John R. Lee.
Attorney—Charles D. Norton.
Surveyor—Henry Lovejoy.
Street Commissioner—Samuel G. Walker.
Superintendent of Schools—Daniel Bowen.
Police Justice—P. A. Child.

WARDS. ALDERMEN.

First—W. Lampman, H. Thomas.
Second—S. S. Jewett, M. P. Bush.
Third—S. A. Bigelow, C. F. Miller.
Fourth—A. S. Merrill, Harrison Park.
Fifth—W. K. Scott, L. F. Tiffany.

1850.

Mayor—Henry K. Smith.
Clerk—Horatio Seymour.
Comptroller—M. Cadwallader.
Treasurer—Daniel T. Marcy.
Attorney—James Wadsworth.
Surveyor—Henry Lovejoy.
Street Commissioner—Albert S. Merrill.
Superintendent of Schools—Henry K. Viele.
Police Justice—P. A. Child.

*Council was authorized in 1843 to appoint Comptroller, but none was chosen until 1848.

WARDS. ALDERMEN.

First—J. W. Banta, John Walsh.
Second—M. P. Bush, M. W. Hill.
Third—Paul Roberts, Miles Perry.
Fourth—Harrison Park, A. S. Swartz.
Fifth—L. F. Tiffany, G. L. Hubbard.

1851.

Mayor—James Wadsworth,
Clerk—W. G. L. Smith,
Comptroller—M. Cadwallader.
Treasurer—Cyrenius C. Bristol.
Attorney—Eli Cook.
Surveyor—Henry Lovejoy.
Street Commissioner—Abram Hempstreet.
Superintendent of Schools—O. G. Steele.
Police Justice—P. A. Child.

WARDS. ALDERMEN.

First—C. S. Pierce, John Walsh.
Second—M. W. Hill, M. P. Bush.
Third—Alexander McKay, Paul Roberts.
Fourth—A. S. Swartz, Harrison Parks.
Fifth—L. F. Tiffany, G. L. Hubbard.

1852.

Mayor—Hiram Barton.
Clerk—R. L. Burrows.
Comptroller—M. Cadwallader.
Treasurer—George R. Kibbe.
Attorney—Cyrus O. Poole.
Surveyor—Henry Lovejoy.
Street Commissioner—James Howell.
Superintendent of Schools—Victor M. Rice.
Police Justice—Charles R. Gold.

WARDS. ALDERMEN.

First—John Walsh, C. S. Pierce.
Second—J. R Evans, M. W. Hill.
Third—A. S. Bemis, Alexander McKay.
Fourth—J. C. Harrison, A. S. Swartz.
Fifth—A. L. Baker, L. F. Tiffany.

1853.

Mayor—Eli Cook.
Clerk—R. L. Burrows.
Comptroller—M. Cadwallader.
Treasurer—George R. Kibbe.
Attorney—Cyrus O. Poole.
Surveyor—Henry Lovejoy.
Street Commissioner—James Howell.
Superintendent of Schools—Victor M. Rice.
Police Justice—Charles R. Gold.

WARDS. ALDERMEN.

First—C. S. Pierce, John Walsh.
Second—C. J. Wells, J. R. Evans.
Third—Alexander McKay, A. S. Bemis.
Fourth—Dan. Devening, Jr., J. C. Harrison.
Fifth—H. S. Chamberlain, A. L. Baker.

1854.

**Mayor*—Eli Cook.
Comptroller—William Chard.
Treasurer—John R. Evans.
Attorney—John Hubbell.
Surveyor—George Cole.
Street Commissioner—Jacob L. Barnes.
Superintendent of Schools—Ephraim F. Cook.
Police Justice—George Drullard.

* By an amendment of the charter in 1853, the city limits were extended so as to include the town of Black Rock, and the territory as enlarged was divided into thirteen wards. The term of city offices was made two years, and elective by the people

WARDS. ALDERMEN.

First—J. H. Bidwell, C. S. Pierce.
Second—D. D. Bidwell, C. J. Wells.
Third—George W. Barker, Samuel Slade,
Fourth—Hiram Chambers, J. J. Weber.
Fifth—Edward Bennett, Henry Lamb.
Sixth—Harry Miller, Solomon Scheu.
Seventh—A. S. Plumley, Edwin Thayer.
Eighth—Z. Bonney, B. Logan.
Ninth—A. S. Bemis, C. F. Miller.
Tenth—Michael Clor, Watkins Williams.
Eleventh—F. A. Alberger. James Haggart.
Twelfth—S. W. Howell, Fayette Rumsey.
Thirteenth—J. A. Bridge, Sam. Twitchell, Junior.
**President*—Stephen W. Howell.
Clerk—R. L. Burrows.

† 1855.

WARDS. ALDERMEN.

First—J. H. Bidwell, C. S. Pierce.
Second—L. J. Waters, C. J. Wells.
Third—Samuel Slade, Geo. W. Barker.
Fourth—Hiram Chambers, J. J. Weber.
Fifth—F. Dellenbaugh, Edward Bennett.
Sixth—Solomon Scheu, Harry Miller.
Seventh—A. J. McNett, A. S. Plumley.
Eighth—Geo. J. Rehm, Z. Bonney.
Ninth—J. F. Lockwood, C. F. Miller.
Tenth—Dennis Bowen, Watkins Williams.
Eleventh—F. P. Stevens, James Haggart.
Twelfth—L. P. Dayton, Fayette Rumsey.
Thirteenth—W. C. Prescott, J. A. Bridge.
President—Charles S. Pierce.
Clerk—R. L. Burrows.

1856.

Mayor—Frederick P. Stevens.
Comptroller—Charles S. Pierce.
Treasurer—Wm. L. G. Smith.
Attorney—A. J. McNett.
Surveyor—George Cole.
Street Commissioner—Patrick Smith.
Superintendent of Schools—E. F. Cook.
Police Justice—George Drullard.

WARDS. ALDERMEN.

First—J. H. Bidwell, Jarvis Davis.
Second—L. J. Waters, C. J. Wells.
Third—N. Hagerman, James O'Brian.
Fourth—H. Chambers, H. P. Thayer.
Fifth—F. Dellenbaugh, Edward Bennett.
Sixth—Lorenzo Gillig, P. Rechtenwalt.
Seventh—A. S. Plumley. Wm. Hellriegel.
Eighth—G. J. Rehm, Thomas Merrigan.
Ninth—J. F. Lockwood, H. T. Chamberlain.
Tenth—Dennis Bowen, Miles Jones.
Eleventh—E. S. Dann, H. P. Clinton.
Twelfth—L. P. Dayton, John Ambrose.
Thirteenth—W. C. Prescott, J. A. Bridge.
President—Lewis P. Dayton.
Clerk—W. H. Albro.

1857.

WARDS. ALDERMEN.

First—Michael Hagan, J. H. Bidwell.
Second—C. J. Wells. James B. Dubois.
Third—James O'Brian, Joshua Barnes.
Fourth—H. P. Thayer, Stephen Bettinger.
Fifth—Edward Bennett, Edwin Thayer.
Sixth—P. Rechtenwalt, C. Rodenbach.
Seventh—Wm. Hellriegel, H. A. Goodrich
Eighth—Thos. Merrigan, Thos. O'Grady.
Ninth—H. S. Chamberlain, S. W. Carpenter.
Tenth—Miles Jones, Henry Martin.
Eleventh—H. P. Clinton, E. S. Dann.
Twelfth—John Ambrose, L. P. Dayton.
Thirteenth—J. A. Bridge, Benj. Dole.
President—L. P. Dayton.
Clerk—W. H. Albro.

1858.

Mayor—Timothy T. Lockwood.
Comptroller—Charles S. Pierce.
Treasurer—C. A. W. Sherman.
Attorney—Edwin Thayer.
Surveyor—Gustavus G. Berger.
Street Commissioner—Levi J. Waters.
Superintendent of Schools—Joseph Warren.
Police Justice—Geo. Drullard.

WARDS. ALDERMEN.

First—J. H. Bidwell, Michael Hagan.
Second—Jas. B. Dubois, C. J. Wells.
Third—Joshua Barnes, Jas. O'Brian.
Fourth—S. Bettinger, Harry Hersee.
Fifth—B. H. Colegrove, D. Devening, Jr.
Sixth—C. Rodenbach, Harry Miller.
Seventh—A. S. Plumley, Geo. F. Pfeifer.
Eighth—Thos. O'Grady, Thos. Truman.
Ninth—S. W. Carpenter, H. S. Chamberlain.
Tenth—Henry Martin, Alonzo Tanner.
Eleventh—E. S. Dann, H. P. Clinton.
Twelfth—L. P. Dayton, John Ambrose.
Thirteenth—Benj. Dole, Geo. Moore.
President—Daniel Devening, Jr.
Clerk—W. H. Albro.

1859.

WARDS. ALDERMEN.

First—Michael Hagan, Patrick Walsh.
Second—C. J Wells, J. B. Dubois.
Third—Jas. O'Brian, J. G. Turner.
Fourth—Harry Hersee, Jacob Beyer.
Fifth—D. Devening, Jr., J. A. M. Meyer.
Sixth—Harry Miller, William Messing.
Seventh—Geo. P. Pfeifer, F. M Pratt.
Eighth—Thos. Truman, P. F. Barton.
Ninth—H. S. Chamberlain, F. A. Alberger.
Tenth—Alonzo Tanner, A. S. Bemis.
Eleventh—H. P. Clinton, A. A. Howard.
Twelfth—John Ambrose, S. H. Howell.
Thirteenth—Geo. Moore, Lewis L. Wilgus.
President—Alonzo Tanner.
Clerk—Charles S. Macomber.

1860.

Mayor—Franklin A. Alberger.
Comptroller—Alonzo Tanner.
Treasurer—John S. Trowbridge.
Attorney—Geo. Wadsworth.
Surveyor—Peter Emslie.
Street Commissioner—Levi J. Waters.
Superintendent of Schools—Sanford B. Hunt.
Police Justice—D. D. Bidwell.

WARDS. ALDERMEN.

First—John Hanavan, Patrick Walsh.
Second—Nathaniel Jones, J. B. Dubois.
Third—Z. G. Allen, J. G. Turner.
Fourth—Everard Palmer, Jacob Beyer.
Fifth—Chas. Beckwith, J. A. M. Meyer.
Sixth—Paul Goembel, Wm. Messing.
Seventh—J. F. Swartz, F. M. Pratt.
Eighth—Rob. Mills, P. F. Barton.
Ninth—Jas. Adams, J. L. Barnes.
Tenth—Geo. R. Yaw, A. S. Bemis.
Eleventh—Jacob Crowder. A. A. Howard.
Twelfth—Wash. Russell, S. W. Howell.
Thirteenth—Thos. Savage, L. L. Wilgus.
President—Asaph S. Bemis.
Clerk—Chas. S. Macomber.

---

*By a charter amendment the Council was authorized to elect a presiding officer from their own number.

† City officers same as 1854.

1861.

WARDS. ALDERMEN.

First—John Hanavan, Patrick Walsh.
Second—Nath. Jones, Joel Wheeler.
Third—Z. G. Allen, Nathaniel Brush.
Fourth—Everard Palmer, Edward Storck.
Fifth—Charles Beckwith, Andrew Grass.
Sixth—Paul Goembel, Jacob Scheu.
Seventh—J. F. Schwartz, F. M. Pratt.
Eighth—Robert Mills, C. E. Felton.
Ninth—James Adams, E. P. Dorr.
Tenth—G. R. Yaw, A. S. Bemis.
Eleventh—J. Crowder. A. A. Howard.
Twelfth—W. Russell, S. W. Howell.
Thirteenth— Thos. Savage, Thos. Rutter,
President—Asaph S. Bemis.
Clerk—Otis F. Presbrey.

1862.

Mayor—William G. Fargo.
Comptroller—Peter M. Vosburgh.
Treasurer—Joseph K. Tyler.
Attorney—Harmon S. Cutting.
Surveyor—Francis F. Curry.
Street Commissioner—James O'Brian.
Superintendent of Schools—John B. Sackett.
Police Justice—Alonzo Tanner.

WARDS. ALDERMEN.

First—P. Walsh, J. Hanavan.
Second—J. B. Dubois, Joel Wheeler.
Third—J D. Colie. Alex. Brush.
Fourth—O. C. Hoyt, Edward Storck.
Fifth—C. Beckwith, Andrew Grass.
Sixth—Paul Goembel, Jacob Scheu.
Seventh—F. Bangasser, W. A. Sutton.
Eighth—C. E. Felton, Robert Mills.
Ninth—E. S. Warren, E. P. Dorr.
Tenth—Geo. R. Yaw. A. S. Bemis.
Eleventh—J. Crowder, N. K. Hopkins.
Twelfth—L. P. Dayton, Peter Burgard.
Thirteenth—R. M. Taylor, Thos. Rutter.
President—Charles Beckwith.
Clerk—Charles S. Macomber.

1863.

Police Justice—W. H. Albro.

WARDS. ALDERMEN.

First—P. Walsh, J. Hanavan.
Second—G. B. Gates, J. B. Dubois.
Third—W. P. Moores, S. D. Colie.
Fourth Richard Flach, O. C. Hoyt.
Fifth—Elijah Ambrose, C. Beckwith.
Sixth—J. Scheu, Paul Goembel.
Seventh—Wm. A. Sutton, F. Bangasser.
Eighth—H. C. Persch, Robert Mills.
Ninth—W. J. Mills, E. S. Warren.
Tenth—Seth Clark, Geo. R. Yaw.
Eleventh—N. K. Hopkins, J. Crowder.
Twelfth—L. P. Dayton, Peter Burgard.
Thirteenth—Christian Klink, R. M. Taylor.
President—Charles Beckwith.
Clerk—Charles S. Macomber.

1864.

Mayor—Wm. G. Fargo.
Comptroller—Ralph Courter.
Treasurer—John Hanavan.
Attorney—Chas. Beckwith.
Surveyor—F. F. Curry.
Street Commissioner—James O'Brian.
Superintendent of Schools—H. D. Garvin.
Police Justice—W. H. Albro.

WARDS. ALDERMEN.

First—D. Fitzgerald, P. Walsh.
Second—P. S. Marsh, G. B. Gates.
Third—Alex. Brush, Wm. P. Moores.
Fourth—Geo. Fisher, Richard Flach.
Fifth—Henry Nauert, E. Ambrose.
Sixth—P. Goembel. J. Scheu.
Seventh—J. L. Haberstro, Thos. Clark,
Eighth—Geo. Bamler, H. C. Persch.
Ninth—J. D. Sawyer, W. I. Mills.
Tenth—Geo. R. Yaw, Seth Clark.
Eleventh—Jno. Auchinvole, N. K. Hopkins.
Twelfth—Peter Burgard, L. P. Dayton.
Thirteenth—Angus McPherson, C. Klink.
President—Lewis P. Dayton,
Clerk—Chas. S. Macomber.

1865.

WARDS. ALDERMEN.

First—D. Fitzgerald, James Ryan.
Second—P. S. Marsh, Jonathan S. Buell.
Third—Alex. Brush, Wm. P. Moores.
Fourth—Geo. Fisher, Richard Flach.
Fifth—Henry Nauert, E. Ambrose.*
Sixth—Paul Goembel, J. H. Pfohl.
Seventh—J. L. Haberstro, Thomas Clark.†
Eighth—Geo. J. Bamler, Jno. P O'Brian.
Ninth—J. D. Sawyer, W. I. Mills. ‡
Tenth—G. R. Yaw, W. C. Bryant.
Eleventh—John Auchinvole, N. K. Hopkins.
Twelfth—P. Burgard, H. A. Schwartz.
Thirteenth—A. McPherson, John Kelly.
President—Nelson K. Hopkins.
Clerk—Charles S. Macomber.

1866.

Mayor—Chandler J. Wells.
Comptroller—Wm. F. Rogers.
Treasurer—Joseph Churchyard.
Attorney—Geo. S. Wardwell.
Surveyor—John A. Ditto.
Street Commissioner—Jeremiah Mahony.
Superintendent of Schools—John S. Fosdick.
Police Justice—W. H. Albro.

WARDS. ALDERMEN.

First—James Ryan, Thomas Whalen.
Second—J. S. Buell.§ P. S. Marsh.‖
Third—Wm. P. Moores, Alex. Brush.
Fourth—R. Flach, Jacob Beyer.
Fifth—J. H. Shepard. August Hagar.
Sixth—J. H. Phohl. Solomon Scheu.
Seventh—Geo. J. Buchheit, J. L. Haberstro.
Eighth—J. P. O'Brian, G. J. Bamler.
Ninth—S. S. Guthrie, Henry Morse.
Tenth—W. C. Bryant. Geo. R. Yaw.¶
Eleventh—N. K. Hopkins,** J. Auchinvole.
Twelfth—H. A. Schwartz. John Glassar.
Thirteenth—John Kelly, Jr., A. McPherson.
President—Joseph L. Haberstro.
Clerk—Charles S Macomber.

---

* Resigned, Oct. 23d.
† Resigned, Oct. 23d, and Geo. J. Buchheit elected to fill the vacancy.
‡ Resigned Oct. 16th, and S. S. Guthrie elected to fill the vacancy.
§ Resigned, April 23d. to assume the duties of Police Commissioner.
‖ Resigned, Oct. 1st, and Joel Wheeler elected to the vacancy.
¶ Resigned, Sept. 24th, and John Walls elected to the vacancy.
** Resigned, Oct. 16.

These are the first vacancies that were ever caused in the council.

1867.

Police Justice—Isaac Vanderpoel.

WARDS. ALDERMEN.

First—Thomas Whalen, James Ryan.*
Second—Joel Wheeler, John Pierce.
Third—Alex. Brush, J. A. B. Campbell.
Fourth—Jacob Beyer, A. Stettenbenz.
Fifth—August Hagar, J H. Shepard.
Sixth—Solomon Scheu, Felix Bieger.
Seventh—J. L. Haberstro, G. J. Buchheit.
Eighth—G. J. Bamler, Edward Madden.
Ninth—Henry Morse, S. S. Guthrie.
Tenth—John Walls, W. C. Bryant.
Eleventh—Jno. Auchinvole, N. B. Hoyt.
Twelfth—Jno. Glassar, J. W. Parsons.
Thirteenth—A. McPherson, J. Kelly, Jr.
President—William C. Bryant.
Clerk—J. D. H. Chamberlain.

1868.

Mayor—William F. Rogers.
Comptroller—R. D. Ford.
Treasurer—Joseph L. Haberstro.
Attorney—David F. Day.
Surveyor—George Vom Berge.
Street Commissioner—Alexander Brush.
Superintendent of Schools—Samuel Slade.
Police Justice—Isaac Vanderpoel.

WARDS. ALDERMEN.

First—Edward Byrnes, George Chambers.
Second—W. B. Smith, John Pierce.
Third—Z. G. Allen, J. A. B. Campbell.
Fourth—Frank Colligon, A. Stettenbenz.
Fifth—P. Rechtenwalt,† J. H. Shepard.
Sixth—Paul Goembel, Felix Bieger.
Seventh—John Gisel, G. J. Buchheit.
Eighth—John Sheehan, Edward Madden.
Ninth—Henry Morse, S. S. Guthrie.
Tenth—D. C. Beard, W. C. Bryant.
Eleventh—John Auchinvole, N. B. Hoyt.
Twelfth—John Ambrose, J. W. Parsons.
Thirteenth—A. McPherson, J. Kelly, Jr.
President—Paul Goembel.
Clerk—Charles S. Macomber.

1869.

WARDS. ALDERMEN.

First—Edwd. Byrnes, George Chambers.
Second—W. B. Smith, John Pierce.
Third—Z. G. Allen, G. G. Newman.
Fourth—F. Colligon, P. P. Miller.
Fifth—Charles Sauer, John Dietzer.
Sixth—P. Goembel, Henry Dilcher.
Seventh—John Gisel, Donald Bain.
Eighth—John Sheehan, Michael Keenan.
Ninth—Henry Morse, James Van Buren.
Tenth—D. C. Beard, Robert Carmichael.
Eleventh—John Auchinvole, E. S. Hawley.
Twelfth—John Ambrose, Elisha Safford.
Thirteenth—A. McPherson, George Orr.
President—John Auchinvole.
Clerk—George S. Wardwell.

1870.

Mayor—Alexander Brush.
Comptroller—R. D. Ford.
Treasurer—J. L. Haberstro.
Attorney—Benjamin H. Williams.
Surveyor—John A. Ditto.
Street Commissioner—George W. Gillespie.
Superintendent of Schools—Thos. Lothrop.
Police Justice—Isaac Vanderpoel.

WARDS. ALDERMEN.

First—George Chambers, Wm. B. Smith.
Second—John Pierce, John Booth.
Third—George G. Newman, S. G. Peters.
Fourth—P. P. Miller, Edward Storck.
Fifth—John Dietzer, Charles Groben.
Sixth—Henry Dilcher, Michael Lang.
Seventh—Donald Bain, John Werrick.
Eighth—John Sheehan, M. Keenan.
Ninth—Henry Morse, Frank A. Sears.
Tenth—D. C. Beard, Lewis M. Evans.
Eleventh—John Auchinvole, Jacob Scheu.
Twelfth—John Ambrose, I. I. Van Allen.
Thirteenth—A. McPherson, A. T. Patchin.
President—John Pierce.
Clerk—George S. Wardwell.

1871.

Police Justice—Oliver J. Eggert.

WARDS. ALDERMEN.

First—W. B. Smith, Patrick Walsh.
Second—John Booth, John Pierce.
Third—S. G. Peters, John Kelly, Jr.
Fourth—E. Storck, W. S. Ovens.
Fifth—Charles Groben, Joseph Bork.
Sixth—M. Lang, J. H. Fischer.
Seventh—John Werrick, George Rochevot.
Eighth—John Sheehan, Daniel Cruice.
Ninth—Frank A. Sears, James Van Buren.
Tenth—L. M. Evans, R. Carmichael.
Eleventh—J. Scheu, George W. Zink.
Twelfth—I. I. Van Allen, C. L. Dayton.
Thirteenth—A. T. Patchin, William Dawes.
President—John Sheehan.
Clerk—Thomas R. Clinton.

1872.

Mayor—Alexander Brush.
Comptroller—Lewis M. Evans.
Treasurer—Joseph Bork.
Attorney—Frank R. Perkins.
Surveyor—John A. Ditto.
Street Commissioner—James Franklin.
Superintendent of Schools—Josephus N. Larned.
Police Justice—D. D. Nash.

WARDS. ALDERMEN.

First—John Doyle, Patrick Walsh.
Second—Benj. Dickey, John Pierce.
Third—J. A. Seymour, John Kelly, Jr.
Fourth—E. Storck, L. P. Reichert.
Fifth—Frank Sipp, Joseph Bork.
Sixth—Jacob Bott, J. H. Fischer.
Seventh—J. P. Einsfeld, George Rochevot.
Eighth—M. Keenan, Daniel Cruice.
Ninth—F. A. Sears, James Van Buren.
Tenth—Joseph Churchyard, R. Carmichael.
Eleventh—Wm. Baynes, George W. Zink.
Twelfth—John Frank, C. L. Dayton.
Thirteenth—A. B. Angus, A. Prenatt.
President—Edward Storck.
Clerk—Walter C. Winship.

1873.

WARDS. ALDERMEN.

First—John Doyle, Timothy Cotter.
Second—Benj. Dickey, Ellis Webster.
Third—J. A. Seymour, J. W. Dennis.
Fourth—Louis Herman, L. P. Reichert.
Fifth—Frank Sipp, William Henrich.
Sixth—Jacob Bott, J. H. Fischer.
Seventh—J. P. Einsfeld, Geo. Reinheimer.
Eighth—M. Keenan, Charles Jessamin.
Ninth—F. A. Sears, James Van Buren.
Tenth—J. Churchyard, R. Carmichael.

* Resigned, Oct. 21, and George Chambers elected to the vacancy.

† Died September 22, and this was the first vacancy in the Council by death.

11

Eleventh—Wm. Baynes, Archibald McLeish.
Twelfth—John Frank, Christopher Laible.
Thirteenth—J. J. Weber, A. Prenatt.
President—Frank A. Sears.
Clerk—Walter C. Winship.

1874.

Mayor—Lewis P. Dayton.
Comptroller—Thomas R. Clinton.
Treasurer—Joseph Bork.
Attorney—Frank R. Perkins.
Surveyor—George E. Mann.
Street Commissioner—A. Stettenbenz.
Superintendent of Schools—William S. Rice.
Police Justice—D. D. Nash.

WARDS. ALDERMEN.

First—Timothy Cotter, John Doyle.
Second—Ellis Webster, Benjamin Dickey.
Third—J. W. Dennis, J. N. Mileham.
Fourth—L. P. Reichert, G. F. Zeller.
Fifth—William Henrich, C. P. Drescher.
Sixth—J. H. Fischer, Joseph Jerge.
Seventh—Geo. Reinheimer, J. P. Einsfeld.
Eighth—Charles Jessamin, Joseph Galley.
Ninth—James Van Buren, N. C. Simons.
Tenth—R. Carmichael, P. J. Ferris.
Eleventh—A. McLeish, George W. Zink.
Twelfth—Christian Laible, I. I. Van Allen.
Thirteenth—A. Prenatt. N. H. Lee.
President—Benjamin Dickey.
Clerk—Walter C. Winship.

1875.

Police Justice—Thomas S. King.

WARDS. ALDERMEN.

First—John Doyle, John Hanavan.
Second—Benjamin Dickey, Wm. V. Woods.
Third—J. N. Mileham, Michael Danahy.
Fourth—G. F. Zeller, Charles Persons.
Fifth—C. P. Drescher, E. Ambrose.
Sixth—Joseph Jerge, Jacob Heimenz.
Seventh—J. P. Einsfeld, J. C. Weber.
Eighth—Joseph Galley, Michael Keenan.
Ninth—N. C. Simons, C. D. Simpson.
Tenth—P. J. Ferris, M. Nichols.
Eleventh—Geo. W. Zink, John Auchinvole.
Twelfth—I. I. Van Allen, William Farmer.
Thirteenth—N. H. Lee, Charles Dickman.
President—Elijah Ambrose.
Clerk—R. D. Ford.

1876.

Mayor—Philip Becker.
Comptroller—Lewis M. Evans.
Treasurer—Henry D. Keller.
Attorney—John B. Greene.
Engineer—George E. Mann.
Street Commissioner—Charles Jessemin.
Assessors—Oliver G. Steele, Jr., John Zoll, John C. Sheehan.
Superintendent of Education—Wm. S. Rice.
Overseer of the Poor—John C. Level.
Police Justice—Thomas S. King.
Justices of the Peace—Geo. G. Newman, W. H. Albro, Frederick Rickert, John O'Brian.

WARDS. ALDERMEN.

First—John Hanavan, John White.
Second—Wm. V. Woods, A. L. Lothridge.
Third—Michael Danahy, Alfred H. Neal.
Fourth—Charles Person, Asaph S. Bemis.
Fifth—Elijah Ambrose, Jacob Benzinger.
Sixth—Jacob Hiemenz, Henry J. Baker.
Seventh—John C. Weber, Donald Bain.
Eighth—Michael Keenan, John Pfeil.
Ninth—Clarence D. Simpson, N. C. Simons.
Tenth—Merritt Nichols. Peter J. Ferris.
Eleventh—John Auchinvole, Chris. Smith.
Twelfth—Wm. Farmer, Isaac I. Van Allen.
Thirteenth—Chas. Dickman, M. Shannon.

President—Asaph S. Bemis.

Clerk—Rensselaer D. Ford.

Deputy Clerk—Timothy W. Crowley.

Messenger—George Frederick Bender.

Sergeant-at-Arms—John Long.

Commissioner of Public Buildings—Wm. Henrich.

Auditor—Robert Hollister.

Superintendent of Fire—Thomas B. French. Louis Hermann, 1st Assistant; George W. Hibsch, 2d Assistant.

Clerk of the Markets—John Mahony.

Sealers of Weights and Measures—George N. Brown, William Ferris, Peter Funk.

Harbor Masters—Samuel Eldridge, Hawley Klein, John Connell.

Pound Keeper—Anthony Canfield; Henry P. Gale, Assistant.

Park Keepers—Philip J. Murphy, Court House Park; Andrew Mahony, Johnson Park; Jacob Fisher, Heacock Park; John Batch, B. G., North Street.

Porters of Markets—Edward Toumey, Elk Street; John Gibson, Assistant. Henry Stewart, Washington Street; John Wander, Assistant. Anthony Brosso, Clinton Street.

Inspector of Oils—John Codling.

Inspector of Dredges—Wm. T. McCormick.

Bridge Tenders—Michigan Street—William Ring, Martin Bahen, Patrick Doyle, Dennis O'Brian. Ohio Street—Patrick Mahony, Patrick Kennedy.

Jubilee Water Commissioners—Philip Fredenburg, P. J. Meyer, Matthias Soomers.

Sexton—Francis J. Kraft.

Scavenger—John Peters.

Board of Health—Asaph S. Bemis, President Common Council; Lewis M. Evans, Comptroller; George E. Mann, Engineer.

Health Physician—E. C. W. O'Brien, M. D.

DIST. DISTRICT HEALTH PHYSICIANS.

First—Stephen S. Green, M. D.
Second—Edward N. Brush, M. D.
Third—Bernard Bartow, M. D.
Fourth—S. G. Dorr, M. D.
Fifth—Francis A. Burghart, M. D.
Sixth—J. C. Elliott, M. D.
Seventh—W. C. Earl, M. D.
Eighth—William H. Slacer, M. D.

Street and Health Inspectors—Michael Shinzius, 1st Ward, Badge No. 1; William Taggert, 2d Ward, Badge No. 2; Hugh Mooney, 3d and 13th Wards, Badge No. 3; Carl Hornung, 4th Ward, Badge No. 4; John Quattlander, 5th Ward, Badge No. 5; Philip D. Baetz, 6th Ward, Badge No. 6; Jacob Croesmen, 7th and 12th Wards, Badge No. 7; John O'Connell, 8th Ward, Badge No. 8; Job King, 9th and 10th Wards, Badge No. 9; Henry Lickert, 11th and 12th Wards, Badge No. 10.

Board of Water Commissioners—George B. Gates, George Truscott, Edwin Hurlbert.

Board of Police Commissioners — Philip Becker, Mayor, ex officio; John Pierce, Jacob Beyer.

Superintendent—John Byrne.

Surgeon—Byron H. Daggett, M. D.

City and County Hall Commissioners—Geo. S. Wardwell, Chairman; James Adams, Dennis Bowen, Philip Becker, Albert P. Laning, John Nice, Allen Potter, George W. Hayward, Jasper B. Youngs. Clerk, A. P. Mason.

Commissioners for Care of City and County Hall—His Honor the Mayor, the Comptroller, the Chairman of Board of Supervisors.

Park Commissioners—His Honor the Mayor, Pascal P. Pratt, Edward Bennett, Britton Holmes, Cooley S. Chapin, Edwin T. Evans. Patrick Smith, Joseph L. Fairchild, Dennis Bowen, Joseph Bork, Sherman S. Jewett, Michael Mesmer, DeWitt C. Weed, Joseph Warren, Daniel D. Harnett, Augustus Fuchs.

President—Pascal P. Pratt.

Secretary and Treasurer—Wm. F. Rogers.

Consulting Landscape Architect—Frederic Law Olmsted.

General Superintendent—William McMillan.

SUPERIOR COURT.

By an Act of the Legislature passed in 1839 a Recorder's Court was created for the city of Buffalo, and the appointment of the Recorder was vested in the Governor. The term of office was four years, and it was held by Horatio J. Stow from 1840 to 1844; Henry K. Smith from 1844 to 1848.

By the Constitution adopted in 1846, the office was made elective by the people, under which it was held by Joseph G. Masten from 1848 to 1852; George W. Houghton from 1852 to 1854.

An act was passed in 1854 by which the Court was reorganized and merged into the present Superior Court with three judges, whose term of office was fixed at six years. Provision was also made that the incumbent of the office of Recorder at the time of the reorganization, should serve as one of the Judges of the Superior Court for the remaining portion of the term for which he had been elected. Recorder Houghton was therefore under this arrangement entitled to serve two years as judge of the new court.

At the first election under the new law George W. Clinton and Isaac A. Verplanck were chosen as the other judges, and upon casting lots for the long and short terms, Judge Clinton secured the full term of six years, and Judge Verplanck that of four years. The judges of the reorganized court have been:

George W. Houghton	1854 to 1856
I. A. Verplanck	1854 " 1858
George W. Clinton	1854 " 1860
Joseph G. Masten	1856 " 1862
I. A. Verplanck	1858 " 1864
George W. Clinton	1860 " 1866
Joseph G. Masten	1862 " 1868
I. A. Verplanck	1864 " 1870
George W. Clinton	1866 to 1872
Joseph G. Masten	1868 " 1871
James M. Humphrey	1871 " 1872
James Sheldon	1872
I. A. Verplanck	1870 " 1873
James M. Smith	1873 " 1874
James M. Smith	1874
George W. Clinton	1872

Judge Masten died in the spring of 1871, after serving two terms and a half, or fifteen years, and James M. Humphrey was appointed by Gov. Hoffman to fill the vacancy. At the succeeding election in November, 1871, James Sheldon was elected as the successor of Mr. Humphrey.

Judge Verplanck died in the spring of 1873, after serving two full terms and two fractional terms, or a little more than eighteen years, and James M. Smith was appointed to the vacancy by Gov. Dix. At the succeeding election in November, 1873, Judge Smith was chosen his own successor.

By the constitutional amendments of 1870 the term of office was extended to fourteen years, and it is also provided that the judges shall be elected for the full term of fourteen years, whether chosen to fill a vacancy or otherwise. Instead, therefore, of Judges Sheldon and Smith being now serving out the unexpired terms of Judges Masten and Verplanck, they will hold for the full term of fourteen years from the date of their election. The present terms of Judges Clinton and Sheldon will expire December 31, 1886, and that of Judge Smith December 31, 1888.

The clerks of the Court have been:

M. Cadwallader..................1839 to 1844
Nelson Ford......................1844 " 1846
C. M. Cooper......................1846 " 1848
William Davis.......................1848 " 1851
Jared S. Torrance..................1851 " 1856
Dyre Tillinghast.................1856 to 1862
Thomas M. Foote................1862 " 1863
Amos A. Blanchard..............1863 " 1875
John C. Graves...................1875

CIVIL LIST OF ERIE COUNTY.

Buffalo was the county seat of Niagara county from its organization in 1808 to 1821, when Erie county was created from portions of the former county. Below will be found a list of the names of persons who have held the principal offices in the original county of Niagara and the county of Erie, since its organization:

1808.

Judge—Augustus Porter.
Sheriff—Asa Ransom.
Clerk—Louis Le Couteulx.
Attorney—Wm. Stuart.
Surrogate—Archibald S. Clarke.

1809.

Judge—Augustus Porter.
Sheriff—Asa Ransom.
Clerk—Louis Le Couteulx.
Attorney—Wm. Stuart.
Surrogate—A. S. Clarke.

1810.

Judge—Augustus Porter.
Sheriff—Samuel Pratt, Jr.
Clerk—Juba Storrs.
Attorney—Daniel W. Lewis.
Surrogate—A. S. Clarke.

1811.

Judge—Augustus Porter.
Sheriff—Asa Ransom.
Clerk—Louis Le Couteulx.
Attorney—Wm. Stuart.
Surrogate—A. S. Clarke.

1812.

Judge—Samuel Tupper.
Sheriff—Asa Ransom.
Clerk—Louis Le Couteulx.
Attorney—Wm. Stuart.
Surrogate—Otis R. Hopkins.

1813.

Judge—Samuel Tupper.
Sheriffs—Nathaniel Sill, Cyrenius Chapin.
Clerk—Zenas Barker.
Attorney—Vincent Matthews.
Surrogate—Amos Callender.

1814.

Judge—Samuel Tupper.
Sheriff—Asa Ransom.
Clerk—Zenas Barker.
Attorney—Vincent Matthews.
Surrogate—Amos Callender.

1815.

Judge—Samuel Tupper.
Sheriff—Asa Ransom.
Clerk—A. J. Clarke.
Attorney—Daniel Cruger.
Surrogate—Ebenezer Johnson.

1816.

Judge—Samuel Tupper.
Sheriff—Asa Ransom.
Clerk—Fred. E. Merrill.
Attorney—J. C. Spencer.
Surrogate—Ebenezer Johnson.

1817.

Judge—Samuel Tupper.
Sheriff—Asa Ransom.
Clerk—F. E. Merrill.
Attorney—J. C. Spencer.
Surrogate—E. Johnson.

1818.

Judge—William Hotchkiss.
Sheriff—James Cronk.
Clerk—F. E. Merrill.
Attorney—Chas. G. Olmstead.
Surrogate—E. Johnson.

1819.

Judge—Wm. Hotchkiss.
Sheriff—James Cronk.
Clerk—John E. Marshall.
Attorney—Heman B. Potter.
Surrogate—E. Johnson.

1820.

Judge—Samuel Wilkeson.
Sheriff—James Cronk.
Clerk—J. E. Marshall.
Attorney—Heman B. Potter.
Surrogate—E. Johnson.

1821.

Judge—Samuel Wilkeson.
Sheriff—Almond H. Millard.
Clerks—Jas. L. Barton, Oliver Grace.
Attorney—Heman B. Potter.
Surrogates—Roswell Chapin and Rufus Spaulding.

The foregoing were officers of Niagara county before its division and the formation of Erie.

1822.

Judge—Samuel Wilkeson.
Sheriff—John G. Camp.
Clerk—James L. Barton.
Attorney—H. B. Potter.
Surrogate—Roswell Chapin.

1823.

Judge—Ebenezer Walden.
Sheriff—Wray S. Littlefield.
Clerk—Jacob A. Barker.
Attorney—H. B. Potter.
Surrogate—Roswell Chapin.

1824.

Judge—Ebenezer Walden.
Sheriff—Wray S. Littlefield.
Clerk—Jacob A. Barker.
Attorney—H. B. Potter.
Surrogate—Roswell Chapin.

1825.

Judge—E. Walden.
Sheriff—Wray S. Littlefield.
Clerk—Jacob A. Barker.
Attorney—H. B. Potter.
Surrogate—Roswell Chapin.

1826.

Judge—E. Walden.
Sheriff—John G. Camp.
Clerk—Jacob A. Barker.
Attorney—H. B. Potter.
Surrogate—Roswell Chapin.

1827.

Judge—E. Walden.
Sheriff—John G. Camp.
Clerk—Jacob A. Barker.
Attorney—H. B. Potter.
Surrogate—Roswell Chapin.

1828.

Judge—Thomas C. Love.
Sheriff—John G. Camp.
Clerk—J. A. Barker.
Attorney—Heman B. Potter.
Surrogate—Ebenezer Johnson.

1829.

Judge—Philander Bennett.
Sheriff—L. Wasson.
Clerk—Elijah Leech.
Attorney—Thos. C. Love.
Surrogate—Ebenezer Johnson.

1830.

Judge—Philander Bennett.
Sheriff—L. Wasson.
Clerk—E. Leech.
Attorney—T. C. Love.
Surrogate—E. Johnson.

1831.

Judge—Philander Bennett.
Sheriff—L. Wasson.
Clerk—E. Leech.
Attorney—T. C. Love.
Surrogate—E. Johnson.

1832.

Judge—Philander Bennett.
Sheriff—Stephen Osborne.
Clerk—N. P. Sprague.
Attorney—Henry White.
Surrogate—Martin Chittenden.

1833.

Judge—Philander Bennett.
Sheriff—Stephen Osborne.
Clerk—N. P. Sprague.
Attorney—Geo. P. Barker.
Surrogate—Israel T. Hatch.

1834.

Judge—Philander Bennett.
Sheriff—Stephen Osborne.
Clerk—N. P. Sprague.
Attorney—Geo. P. Barker.
Surrogate—I. T. Hatch.

1835.

Judge—Philander Bennett
Sheriff—Lester Brace.
Clerk—Horace Clark.
Attorney—Geo. P. Barker.
Surrogate—I. T. Hatch.

1836.

Judge—Philander Bennett.
Sheriff—Lester Brace.
Clerk—Horace Clark.
Attorney—Geo. P. Barker.
Surrogate—Samuel Caldwell.

1837.

Judge—James Stryker.
Sheriff—Lester Brace.
Clerk—Horace Clark.
Attorney—H. K. Smith.
Surrogate—Samuel Caldwell.

1838.

Judge—James Stryker.
Sheriff—Chas. P. Persons.
Clerk—Cyrus K. Anderson.
Attorney—H. K. Smith.
Surrogate—Samuel Caldwell.

1839.

Judge—James Stryker.
Sheriff—C. P. Persons.
Clerk—C. K. Anderson.
Attorney—H. K. Smith.
Surrogate—Samuel Caldwell.

1840.

Judge—James Stryker.
Sheriff—Chas. P. Persons.
Clerk—C. K. Anderson.
Attorney—H. K. Smith.
Surrogate—Samuel Caldwell.

1841.

Judge—N. K. Hall.
Sheriff—Lorenzo Brown.
Clerk—N. P. Sprague.
Attorney—H. W. Rogers.
Surrogate—Thos. C. Love.

1842.

Judge—N. K. Hall.
Sheriff—L. Brown.
Clerk—N. P. Sprague.
Attorney—H. W. Rogers.
Surrogate—Thomas C. Love.

1843.

Judge—N. K. Hall.
Sheriff—L. Brown.
Clerk—N. P. Sprague.
Attorney—H. W. Rogers.
Surrogate—Thos. C. Love.

1844.

Judge—N. K. Hall.
Sheriff—Ralph Plumb.
Clerk—Manly Colton.
Attorney—S. G. Haven.
Surrogate—Thomas C. Love.

1845.

Judge—Fred. P. Stevens.
Sheriff—Ralph Plumb.
Clerk—Manly Colton.
Attorney—S. G. Haven.
Surrogate—Peter M. Vosburgh.

1846.

Judge—Fred. P. Stevens.
Sheriff—Ralph Plumb.
Clerk—Manly Colton.
Attorney—G. P. Barker.
Surrogate—Peter M. Vosburgh.

1847.

Judge—F. P. Stevens.
Sheriff—T. A. Hopkins.
Clerk—Moses Bristol.
Attorney—Geo. P. Barker.
Surrogate—Peter M. Vosburgh.

1848.

Judge—F. P. Stevens.
Sheriff—T. A. Hopkins.
Clerk—Moses Bristol.
Attorney—B. H. Austin.
* *Treasurer*—Christian Metz.
Surrogate—Peter M. Vosburgh.

1849.

Judge—F. P. Stevens.
Sheriff—T. A. Hopkins.
Clerk—Moses Bristol.
Attorney—B. H. Austin.
Treasurer—C. Metz.
Surrogate—Peter M. Vosburgh.

1850.

Judge—F. P. Stevens.
Sheriff—Leroy Farnham.
Clerk—Wells Brooks.
Attorney—B. H. Austin.
Treasurer—C. Metz.
Surrogate—Peter M. Vosburgh.

1851.

Judge—F. P. Stevens.
Sheriff—L. Farnham.
Clerk—Wells Brooks.
Attorney—C. H. S. Williams.
Treasurer—C. Metz, Jr.
Surrogate—P. M. Vosburgh.

1852.

Judge—Jesse Walker.
Sheriff—Leroy Farnham.
Clerk—Wells Brooks.
Attorney—C. H. S. Williams.
Treasurer—C. Metz, Jr.
Surrogate—Charles D. Norton.

1853.

Judge—James Sheldon.
Sheriff—Joseph Candee.
Clerk—William Andre.
Attorney—John L. Talcott.
Treasurer—Christian Metz, Jr.
Surrogate—Charles D. Norton.

1854.

Judge—James Sheldon.
Sheriff—Joseph Candee.
Clerk—William Andre.
Attorney—Albert Sawin.
Treasurer—James D. Warren.
Surrogate—Charles D. Norton.

1855.

Judge—James Sheldon.
Sheriff—Joseph Candee.
Clerk—William Andre.
Attorney—Albert Sawin.
Treasurer—James D. Warren.
Surrogate—Charles D. Norton.

1856.

Judge—James Sheldon.
Sheriff—Orrin Lockwood.
Clerk—P. M. Vosburgh.
Attorney—Albert Sawin.
Treasurer J. D. Warren.
Surrogate—Abram Thorn.

---

* Hitherto County Treasurers were appointed by the Board of Supervisors.

1857.

Judge—James Sheldon.
Sheriff—Orrin Lockwood.
Clerk—P. M. Vosburgh.
Attorney—J. M. Humphrey.
Treasurer—J. D. Warren.
Surrogate—Abram Thorn.

1858.

Judge—James Sheldon.
Sheriff—Orrin Lockwood.
Clerk—P. M. Vosburgh.
Attorney—J. M. Humphrey.
Treasurer—L. B. Smith.
Surrogate—Abram Thorn.

1859.

Judge—James Sheldon.
Sheriff—G. A. Scroggs.
Clerk—O. J. Greene.
Attorney—J. M. Humphrey.
Treasurer—L. B. Smith.
Surrogate—Abram Thorn.

1860.

Judge—James Sheldon.
Sheriff—G. A. Scroggs.
Clerk—O. J. Greene.
Attorney—F. J. Fithian.
Treasurer—L. B. Smith.
Surrogate—Charles C. Severance.

1861.

Judge—James Sheldon.
Sheriff—G. A. Scroggs.
Clerk—O. J. Greene.
Attorney—F. J. Fithian.
Treasurer—Norman B. McNeal.
Surrogate—C. C. Severance.

1862.

Judge—James Sheldon.
Sheriff—R. H. Best.
Clerk—C. R. Durkee.
Attorney—F. J. Fithian.
Treasurer—N. B. McNeal.
Surrogate—C. C. Severance.

1863.

Judge—James Sheldon.
Sheriff—R. H. Best.
Clerk—C. R. Durkee.
Attorney—C. C. Torrance.
Treasurer—N. B. McNeal.
Surrogate—C. C. Severance.

1864.

Judge—James Sheldon.
Sheriff—R. H. Best.
Clerk—C. R. Durkee.
Attorney—C. C. Torrance.
Treasurer—Francis C. Brunck.
Surrogate—Jonathan Hascall.

1865.

Judge—Stephen Lockwood.
Sheriff—O. J. Eggert.
Clerk—L. P. Dayton.
Attorney—C. C. Torrance.
Treasurer—Francis C. Brunck.
Surrogate—Jonathan Hascall.

1866.

Judge—Stephen Lockwood.
Sheriff—O. J. Eggert.
Clerk—L. P. Dayton.
Attorney—L. K. Bass.
Treasurer—Francis C. Brunck.
Surrogate—Jonathan Hascall.

1867.

Judge—Stephen Lockwood.
Sheriff—O. J. Eggert.
Clerk—L. P. Dayton.
Attorney—L. K. Bass.
Treasurer—C. R. Durkee.
Surrogate—Jonathan Hascall.

1868.

Judge—Stephen Lockwood.
Sheriff—Charles Darcy.
Clerk—John H. Andrus.
Attorney—Lyman K. Bass.
Treasurer—C. R. Durkee.
Surrogate—Horatio Seymour.

1869.

Judge—R. L. Burrows.
Sheriff—Charles Darcy.
Clerk—John H. Andrus.
Attorney—L. K. Bass.
Treasurer—C. R. Durkee.
Surrogate—Horatio Seymour.

1870.

Judge—R. L. Burrows.
Sheriff—Charles Darcy.
Clerk—John H. Andrus.
Attorney—L. K. Bass.
Treasurer—William B. Sirret.
Surrogate—Horatio Seymour.

1871.

Judge—R. L. Burrows.
Sheriff—Grover Cleveland.
Clerk—J. H. Fisher.
Attorney—L. K. Bass.
Treasurer—W. B. Sirret.
Surrogate—Horatio Seymour.

1872.

Judge—R. L. Burrows.
Sheriff—Grover Cleveland.
Clerk—James H. Fisher.
Attorney—Benjamin H. Williams.
Treasurer—W. B. Sirret.
Surrogate—Z. Ferris.

1873.

Judge—Albert Haight.
Sheriff—Grover Cleveland.
Clerk—J. H. Fisher.
Attorney—B. H. Williams.
Treasurer—W. B. Sirret.
Surrogate—Z. Ferris.

1874.

Judge—Albert Haight.
Sheriff—John B. Weber.
Clerk—George L. Remington.
Attorney—B. H. Williams.
Treasurer—W. B. Sirret.
Surrogate—Z. Ferris.

1875.

Judge—Albert Haight.
Sheriff—John B. Weber.
Clerk—G. L. Remington.
Attorney—Daniel N. Lockwood.
Treasurer—W. B. Sirret.
Surrogate—Z. Ferris.

1876.

Judge—Albert Haight.
Session Justices—George W. Nichols, Frederick Gundlach.
Sheriff—John B. Weber.
Clerk—G. L. Remington.
Attorney—D. N. Lockwood.
Treasurer—W. B. Sirret.
Surrogate—Z. Ferris.
Coroners—J. C. Almendinger, Epenetus H. Davis, William Bacon, Watson H. Curtis.
School Commissioners—1st Dist., A. McCullen Ball; 2d Dist., George W. Holmes; 3d Dist., Mark Whiting.

SUPERVISORS.

WARDS. THE CITY.

First—James Manaher, John Norris.
Second—John M. Comstock, E. R. Saxton.
Third—E. W. Evans, W. W. Buffum.
Fourth—C. F. Mensch, Eug. Bertrand, Jr.
Fifth—Peter F. Lawson, Louis Fritz.
Sixth—Michael Loebig, Sebastian Elser.
Seventh—J. P. Braner, George Baer.
Eighth—Timothy Lyons, James Nunan.
Ninth—Frederick Busch, Earl D. Berry.
Tenth—Amos B. Tanner, Louis P. Beyer.
Eleventh—D. Gazlay, Thomas Prowett.
Twelfth—Peter Glor, Jr., Leonard Eley.
Thirteenth—Edward Corriston.

THE TOWNS.

Alden—L. W. Cornwell.
Amherst—John Schoelles.
Aurora—Lyman Cornwell.
Brant—W. W. Hammond.
Boston—A. K. Woodward.
Clarence—John Krauss.
Collins—William A. Johnson.
Cheektowaga—P. Winspear.
Colden—Richard E. Bowen.
Concord—Henry Blackmer.
Evans—David C. Oatman.
Eden—J. H. Lord.
Elma—William Winspear.
East Hamburgh—Frank M. Thorn.
Grand Island—C. Spohr.
Hamburgh—H. W. White.
Holland—Homer Morey.
Lancaster—N. B. Gatchell.
Marilla—Russel D. Smith.
North Collins—James Matthews.
Newstead—W. T. Magoffin.
Sardinia—Addison Wheelock.
West Seneca—Victor Irr.
Tonawanda—Philip Wendell.
Wales—Charles N. Brayton.

ERIE COUNTY PENITENTIARY.

Commissioners—W. Harrington, Henry Atwood, Frederick Miller.
Superintendent—William Weston.
Deputy Superintendent—David Huff.
Physician—H. L. Atwood, M. D.

Keeper of County Almshouse—Charles A. Loeberick.
Physician—J. J. Walsh, M. D.

EIGHTY YEARS IN CONGRESS.

The following table will show the representation of Western New York and Erie county from the Fifth to the Forty-fourth Congress, inclusive. In the First, Second, Third and Fourth Congresses, the county was in a District which was not numbered, but embraced the region then known as Albany, Herkimer, Montgomery, Onondaga, Ontario, Otsego, and Tioga counties. In 1797 the counties of Cayuga, Onondaga, Ontario, Steuben and Tioga, were constituted the Tenth Congressional District of New York, and from that time the representatives were:

1797-9. Hezekiah L. Hosmer, 5th Congress.
1799-1801. Wm. Cooper, 6th Congress.
1801-3. Thomas Morris, 7th Congress.
In 1802 Cayuga, Genesee, Ontario and Steuben counties were constituted the 16th Congressional District, and the representatives were:
1803-5. Oliver Phelps, 8th Congress.
1805-7. Silas Halsey, 9th Congress.
1807-9. John Harris, 10th Congress.
In 1808 Allegany, Cattaraugus, Chautauqua, Genesee, Niagara and Ontario were constituted the 15th Congressional District, and was represented by:
1809-11. Gen. Peter B. Porter, 11th Congress.

1811-13. Gen. Peter B. Porter, 12th Congress.
In 1812 the territory which now embraces Allegany, Chautauqua, Cattaraugus, Erie, Genesee, Livingston, Monroe, Niagara and Ontario counties was made the 21st Congressional District, with two representives, and they were:
1813-15. Samuel M. Hopkins, Nathaniel Howell, 13th Congress.
1815-17. Micah Brooks, Peter B. Porter, 14th Congress.
Gen. Porter resigned in 1816 and Archibald S. Clarke was elected to fill vacancy.
1817-19. Benjamin Ellicott, John C. Spencer, 15th Congress.
1819-21. Nathaniel Allen, Albert H. Tracy, 16th Congress.
1821-23. Wm. B. Rochester, Albert H. Tracy, 17th Congress.
Erie county was erected in 1821, and in 1822 Chautauqua, Erie and Niagara were constituted the 30th Congressional District, with one representative, and the members have been:
1823-25. Albert H. Tracy, 18th Congress.
1825-27. Daniel G. Garnsey, 19th Congress.
1827-29. Daniel G. Garnsey, 20th Congress.
1829-31. Ebenezer F. Norton, 21st Congress.
1831-33. Bates Cook, 22d Congress.
In 1832 Erie county was made the 32d Congressional District, and has been represented by:
1833-35. Millard Fillmore, 23d Congress.
1835-37. Thomas C. Love, 24th Congress.
1837-39. Millard Fillmore, 25th Congress.
1839-41. Millard Fillmore, 26th Congress.
1841-43. Millard Fillmore, 27th Congress.
1843-45. Wm. A. Moseley, 28th Congress.
1845-47. Wm. A. Moseley, 29th Congress.
1847-49. Nathan K. Hall, 30th Congress.
1849-51. E. G. Spaulding, 31st Congress.
1851-53. Solomon G. Haven, 32d Congress.
1853-55. Solomon G. Haven, 33d Congress.
1855-57. Solomon G. Haven, 34th Congress.
1857-59. Israel T. Hatch, 35th Congress.
1859-61. E. G. Spaulding, 36th Congress.
1861-63. E. G. Spaulding, 37th Congress.
In 1862 Erie county was made the 30th District.
1863-65. John Ganson, 38th Congress.
1865-67. James M. Humphrey, 39th Congress.
1867-69. James M. Humphrey, 40th Congress.
1869-71. David S. Bennett, 41st Congress.
1871-73. William Williams, 42d Congress.
1873-75. Lyman K. Bass, 43d Congress.
In 1873 it was made the 32d District.
1875-77. Lyman K. Bass, 44th Congress.

THE SENATE.

Until the adoption of the Constitution of 1821 the State was divided into the Eastern, Middle, Southern and Western Senatorial Districts, with a number of senators in each, there being ten allotted to the Western District. The first senator hailing from what may be called the western part of the State, was Vincent Matthews, of Elmira, then in Tioga county, who was one of the ten from the Western District, and a member from 1791 to 1803. Then followed Lemuel Chipman from Wayne county, 1802 to 1805; Alexander Rea, Genesee county, 1808 to 1811; Archibald S. Clarke, Cattaraugus, 1813 to 1816; Jediah Prendergrast, Chautauqua, 1815 to 1818; Isaac Wilson, 1818 to 1821. Oliver Forward was the first and only senator from Buffalo under the old Constitution, and he served but the fraction of a term during 1821-22.

Under the Constitution of 1821 the State was divided into eight Senatorial Districts, each of which was entitled to four senators, one being elected each year; term of office four years. The Eighth District embraced the counties of Allegany, Cattaraugus, Chautauqua, Erie, Genesee, Livingston, Monroe, Niagara and Steuben, and the senators were:

1823. Timothy H. Porter, David Eason, Heman J. Redfield, Joseph Spencer.
1824. John Bowman (vice Spencer deceased), James McCall.
1825. Samuel Wilkeson.
1826. Ethan B. Allen.
1827. Charles H. Carroll.
1828. Timothy H. Porter.
1829. George H. Boughton (vice Carroll resigned), Moses Hayden.
1830. Albert H. Tracy.
1831. Philo C. Fuller (vice Hayden deceased), Trumbull Cary.
1832. John Birdsall.
1833. John Griffin.
1834. A. H. Tracy.
1835. Chancey J. Fox (vice Birdsall resigned), Isaac Lacy.
1836. Chancey J. Fox.
1837. Samuel Works.
1838. William A. Mosely.
1839. Henry Hawkins.
1840. Abram Dixon.
1841. Samuel Works.
1842. Gideon Hard.
1843. Harvey Putnam.

1844. Fred. F. Backus.
1845. Carlos Emmons.
1846. Gideon Hard.
1847. Francis H. Ruggles.

Under the Constitution of 1846 the State was divided into thirty-two districts, each of which being entitled to one senator, and all were elected biennially, each odd year. The county of Erie constituted the Thirty-first District, and has been represented by:

1848-9. John T. Bush.
1850-1. George R. Babcock.
1852-3. George R. Babcock.
1854-5. James O. Putnam.
1856-7. James Wadsworth.
1858. James Wadsworth.
1859. Erastus S. Prosser.
1860-1. E. S. Prosser.
1862-3. John Ganson.
1864-5. James M. Humphrey.
1866-7. David S. Bennett.
1868-9. Asher P. Nichols.
1870-1. Loran L. Lewis.
1872-3. Loran L. Lewis.
1874. John Ganson.
1875. A. P. Laning.
1876. Sherman S. Rogers.

THE ASSEMBLY.

Under the first Constitution the Assembly Districts were large, each embracing several counties, and the counties composed of large sections of the sparsely populated portions of the State. Several members were chosen from each district, and all on a general ticket. Erie county had no immediate representation until the formation of Niagara county in 1808, of which Erie formed a part. Niagara, Cattaraugus and Chautauqua constituted a district, and the representatives thereafter were:

1809. Archibald S. Clarke.
1810. Archibald S. Clarke.
1811. Archibald S. Clarke.
1812. Ebenezer Walden.
1813. Jonas Williams.
1814. Jonas Williams.
1815. Joseph McClure.

In 1815 the district was allowed two members thereafter.

1816. Daniel McCleary, Elias Osborne.
1817. Jediah Prendergast, Richard Smith.
1818. Robert Fleming, Isaac Phelps.
1819. Isaac Phelps, Philo Orton.
1820. Elial T. Foot, Oliver Forward.
1821. Wm. Hotchkiss, Jediah Prendergast.
1822. Thos. B. Campbell, David Eason.

The Constitution of 1821 fixed the number of Assemblymen at 128, permanently. Erie county was created the same year from a portion of Niagara and made a separate district, with one member, and the representatives have been:

1823. Ebenezer F. Norton.
1824. Samuel Wilkeson.
1825. Calvin Fillmore.
1826. Reuben B. Heacock.

In 1826 the district was allotted an additional member thereafter.

1827. David Burt, Oziel Smith.
1828. David Burt, Peter B. Porter.
1829. David Burt, Millard Fillmore.
1830. Millard Fillmore, Edmund Hull.
1831. Millard Fillmore, Nathaniel Knight.
1832. Horace Clark, Wm. Mills.
1833. Horace Clark, Wm. Mills.
1834. Joseph Clary, Carlos Emmons.
1835. Wm. A. Mosely, Ralph Plumb.
1836. George P. Barker, Wells Brooks.

Hereafter another member is apportioned to Erie county.

1837. Benjamin A. Bivins, S. S. Case, David Sheldon.
1838. Lewis F. Allen, Asa Warren, Cyrenus Wilbur.
1839. J. A. Barker, Truman Cary, Henry Johnson.
1840. S. C. Hawley, Stephen Osborn, Aaron Salisbury.
1841. C. Emmons, S. C. Hawley, S. Osborn.
1842. Wm. A. Bird, B. H. Colgrove, S. S. Case.
1843. George R. Babcock, Wells Brooks, J. M. Ketchum.
1844. Daniel Lee, Elisha Smith, Amos Wright.
1845. J. T. Bush, Truman Dewey, Daniel Lee.
1846. J. T. Bush, N. K. Hall, James Wood.

Henceforth Erie is given a fourth member.

1847. O. J. Green, John D. Howe, Horatio Shumway, Wm. H. Pratt.
1848. E. G. Spaulding, Henry Slade, I. E. Irish, C. C. Severance.
1849. Benoni Thompson, Aug. Raynor, Marcus McNeal, Luther Buxton.
1850. Orlando Allen, Elijah Ford, Ira E. Irish, Joseph Candee.
1851. Orlando Allen, William A. Bird, Henry Atwood, C. C. Severance.
1852. I. T. Hatch, Jasper B. Youngs, Aaron Riley, Joseph Bennett.
1853. A. M. Clapp, Wm. T. Bush, Israel N. Ely, Nelson Welch.
1854. W. W. Weed, Rolland Germain, Chas. A. Sill, E. N. Hatch.
1855. W. W. Weed, Daniel Devening, Jr., L. D. Corey, S. W. Goddard.
1856. John G. Deshler, D. Devening, Jr., Jno. Clark, Benjamin Maltby.
1857. A. J. Tiffany, G. D. W. Clinton, Horace Boies, S. C. Adams.
1858. A. P. Laning, A. J. McNett, John T. Wheelock, Amos Avery.

1859. Daniel Bowen, H. B. Miller, John S. King, Wilson Rogers.
1860. O. Allen, H. B. Miller, Hiram Newell, J. H. Plumb.
1861. S.V. R. Watson, V. M. Rice, B. H. Long, Z. Ferris.
1862. J. W. Murphy, H. Seymour. E. P. Goslin, J. A. Case.
1863. J. W. Murphy, H. Seymour, T. A. Hopkins, A. G. Conger.
1864. W. W. Stanard, F. P. Stevens, T. A. Hopkins, Seth Fenner.
1865. W. W. Stanard. Harmon S. Cutting, J. G. Langner, E. W. Godfrey.
1866. Wm. Williams, J. J. L. C. Jewett, John G. Langner, Levi Potter.
After this period Erie county is allowed five members.
1867. C. W. Hinson, Wm. Williams, R. L. Burrows, Alpheus Prince, J. H. Plumb.
1868. G. J. Bamler, Richard Flach, L. P. Dayton, A. Prince, James Rider.
1869. G. J. Bamler, P. H. Bender, J. A. Case, C. B. Rich, A. C. Calkins.
1870. G. J. Bamler, Jas. Franklin, A. H. Blossom, H. B. Ransom, Lyman Oatman.
1871. Geo. Chambers, J. Howell, F. A. Alberger, H. B. Ransom. J. M. Wiley.
1872. Geo. Chambers, G. Baltz, Franklin A. Alberger, Whitford Harrington, J. M. Wiley.
1873. John O'Brian, Geo. Baltz, F. A. Alberger, John Nice, R. B. Foot.
1874. Pat. Hanrahan, Joseph W. Smith, F. A. Alberger, John Nice, R. B. Foot.
1875. Pat. Hanrahan, W. W. Lawson, E. Gallagher, H. B. Ransom, W. A. Johnson.
1876. Daniel Cruice. W. W. Lawson, E. Gallagher, B. Chaffee, C. F. Tabor.

ERIE COUNTY BAR.

CITY.

Adams, S. Carey.
Allen, Jas. A.
Austin, B. H.
Avery, T. G.
Babcock, Geo. R.
Bacon, E. R.
Baker, Lyman M.
Ball, B. T.
Barton, Hiram.
Barton, O. F.
Bartholomew, A.
Bass, Lyman K.
Bath, Thos. E.
Beckwith, Chas.
Beecher, J. C.
Benedict, Willis J.
Bissell, W. S.
Blanchard, A. A.
Bowen, Dennis.
Box, Henry W.
Bradley, Chester B.
Brunck, S. U.
Bryant, Wm. C.
Burrows, R. L.
Butler, Jay S.
Carman, L.
Clark, D. F.
Cleveland, G.
Clinton, Geo. W.
Clinton, Geo.
Clinton, Spencer.
Coe, S. C.
Cook, Josiah.
Copeland, D. S.
Copeland, J. D.
Corlette, Thos.
Cothran, Geo. W.
Cottle, O. O.
Crandall, De Forest.
Cutting, H. S.
Cutting, Thos.
Cutler, W. H.
Cutter, Ammi.
Daniels, Charles.
Davis, Thaddeus C.
Day, David F.
Day, Hiram C.
De Witt, O. C.
Donihee, W. B.
Dorsheimer, Wm.
Douglass, S. J.
Douw, P. J.
Eeles, J. H.
Fairchild, J. L.
Farrington, B. L.
Fillmore, M. P.
Finkenstaedt, F. L.
Fischer, Geo. W.
Fisher, James H.
Fitch, Wm. C.
Fitzgerald, H. D.
Folsom, Benj.
Ford, Elijah.
Ford, Jas. E.
Fullerton, Jas. C.
Gardner, John T.
Germain, C. B.
Gibbs, Jas. S.
Goodyear, C. W.
Gould, S. O.
Graves, John C.
Greene, H. B.
Greene, John B.
Greene, Wm. H.
Griswold, E, A.
Gurney, W. H.
Haight, Albert.
Hamlin, C. W.
Hawkins, O. F.
Hawkins, Wm. M.
Hawks, E. C.
Hennig, Herman.
Henry, Louis.
Hibbard, Geo. B.
Hickman, A. W.
Hinson, C. W.
Holmes, Thos. C.
Hopkins, Nelson K.
Hopkins, R. W.
Houghton, A. A.
Howard, A. A.
Hudson, J. T.
Huetter, Carl.
Humphrey, J. M.
Humphreys, Geo.
Hubbell, F. H.
Hubbell, John.
Hubbell, M. S.
Ingelhart, F. M.
Jackson, D. J.
Johnson, U. S.
Jones, Wm. L.
Kennedy, J. H.
Kingston, Geo. L.
Lang, Joseph.
Laning, A. P.
Lansing, Livingston.
Lewis, L. L.
Locke, F. D.
Lockwood, D. N.
Lockwood, S.
Loomis, F. M.
Lyman, C. M.
Lyon, Wm. W.
McMillan, D. H.
McNeal, N. B.
March, F. R.
Marshall, C. D.
Marshall, O. H.
Marvin, Geo. L.
Marvin, Le Grand.
Matteson. P. A.
Michael, Edward.
Millburn, J. G.
Miller, Warren F.
Miller, Wm. F.
Moore, M. B.
Morey, Norris.
Morse, F. R.
Muldoon, J. G.
Nash, Daniel D.
Nichols, A. P.
Norris, John.
Palmer, E. W.
Park, C. H.
Parker, Llewellyn.
Parker, P. G.
Parker, W. T.

Pattison, A. E.
Pattison, E. C.
Perkins, E. B.
Perkins, F. R.
Perkins, L. P.
Phelps, Geo. E.
Plumley, E. J.
Porter, S. B.
Potter, Geo. S.
Putnam, Jas. O.
Quimby, Geo. T.
Read, A. L.
Rice, A. G.
Robbins, E. C.
Rogers, S. S.
Romer, J. L.
Rowley, W. W.
Saunders, P. D. K.
Saunders, R.
Schelling, R. F.
Scroggs, G. A.
Seaver, J. V.
Shearer, J. H.
Sheehan, M. H.
Sheldon, James.
Shepard, C. C.
Sherman, R. F.
Sibley, J. C.
Sicard, G. J.
Sidway, Jonathan.
Sizer, Thos. J.
Slosson, F. N.
Smith, Jas. M.
Smith, Lyman B.
Smith, W. G. L.
Spaulding, E. G.
Sprague, E. Carlton.
Squier, H. R.
Stevens, Robt. H.
Strong, Geo. A.
Strong, Jas. C.
Strong, John C.
Tabor, C. F.
Talcott, J. L.
Tanner, Alonzo.
Thayer, Edwin.
Thomas, C. J.
Titus, B. C.
Tyler, John.
Vedder, E. B.
Veile, Sheldon T.
Wadsworth, Geo.
Walker, J. L.
Wardwell, Geo. S.
Warren, Wm. T.
Welch, S. M., Jr.
Welch, T. F.
Wenz, James.
Wheeler, C. B.
White, Truman C.
Whitney, M. A.
Wierling, W. J.
Willett, Jas. M.
Williams, B. H.
Wilson, R. P.
Wing, Geo.
Winship, James.
Woodworth, W. N.

TOWNS.

Akron—Tabor, Russ. C.
Alden—Ewell, Joseph E.
Aurora—Johnson, W. C., Shearer, Joseph.
Farnum—Hammond, W. W.
Gowanda—Allen, H. F., Torrance, C. C.
Hamburgh—Calkins, A. C., Thorne, Abram.
Lancaster—Romer, J. L., Tabor, C. F.
Springville—Severance, C. C., Stanbro, A. M.
Tonawanda—Benedict, Willis J., Bush, W. T., Young, B. T.
Williamsville—Eggert, A. W.

PUBLIC SCHOOLS.

List of the Principals of the Normal, Central and District Schools of the city of Buffalo:

Normal—H. B. Buckham, A. M.
Central—Ray T. Spencer, A. M.

DISTRICT SCHOOLS.

No. 1—A. Z. Barrows.
No. 2—W. L. French.
No. 3—D. W. Blanchard.
No. 4—J. W. Barker.
No. 5—E. L. Chamberlayne.
No. 6—Byron F. Pratt.
No. 7—F. D. Love.
No. 8—Samuel Slade.
No. 9—Mrs. S. C. Claraluna.
No. 10—E. E. Fish.
No. 11—Mrs. H. F. Fullerton.
No. 12—W. C. Pomeroy.
No. 13—W. H. Meads.
No. 14—Jacob Berry.
No. 15—William C. Feagles.
No. 16—Henry F. Fullerton.
No. 17—Emily J. Hawkins.
No. 18—Charles W. Colyer.
No. 19—George H. Stowits.
No. 20—James A. Roberts.
No. 21—Mary H. Caughey.
No. 22—Ezra Welch.
No. 23—Mrs. Anna H. Pollard.
No. 24—O. G. Nichols.
No. 25—Frank S. Fosdick.
No. 26—J. C. Bump.
No. 27—David Farnsworth.
No. 28—Kate Wilson.
No. 29—Mrs. M. L. Sage.
No. 30—Mrs. Jennie W. Dyson.
No. 31—James F. Crooker.
No. 32—N. G. Benedict.
No. 33—O. S. Throop.
No. 34—E. F. Cook.
No. 35—H. H. Rogers,
No. 36—A. B. Ellsworth.

The prevailing style of the school buildings belonging to the department is shown by the illustrations on the four following pages.

BUFFALO STATE NORMAL SCHOOL AND COLLEGE.

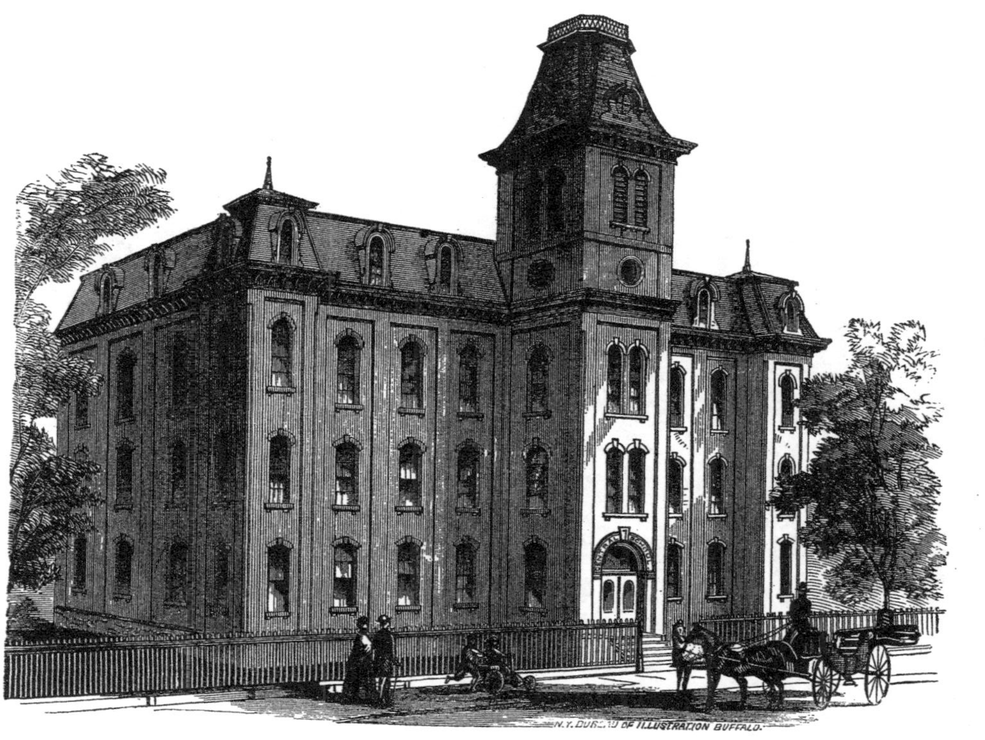

BUFFALO CENTRAL SCHOOL.

PUBLIC SCHOOL No. 6.

PUBLIC SCHOOL No. 14.

WORLD'S DISPENSARY,

At Nos. 80, 82, 84 and 86 West Seneca Street, cor. of Terrace,

BUFFALO, N. Y.

Established for the cure of all **Chronic** (or lingering) **Diseases of either Sex,** particularly those of a **Delicate, Obscure, Complicated** or **Obstinate Character,** also for the skillful performance of all **Surgical Operations,** and as a headquarters for **Dr. Pierce's Family Medicines,** is the largest establishment of its kind in the world. It is organized with an eminent corps of Physicians and Surgeons, each devoting his whole time and attention to some particular branch of practice, by which the greatest skill is attained, while R. V. Pierce, M. D., is the Physician and Surgeon-in-chief, and is consulted in all important cases. Thousands of cases are annually treated, and each has the advantage of an educated and eminent **Council of Physicians.**

AN IMPORTANT ENTERPRISE.

We learn that Dr R. V. Pierce, proprietor of the "World's Dispensary," in this city. has perfected the purchase of a large lot of land, on which he proposes to erect a large hotel for the accommodation of his numerous patients, coming hither from all points of the compass. The land purchased by the enterprising Doctor is 234 feet front on Prospect Avenue, running through to Fargo Avenue, 332 feet; also an adjoining lot extending from the above to Connecticut Street. It is in the midst of our extensive system of public parks, fronts the old and beautiful Prospect Park, is but a short distance from the "Circle" in one direction, and the "Lake Front" in the other. The site selected is a fine one, being both beautiful and healthful; is one of the highest portions of our city, easily accessible, yet sufficiently retired to secure quiet, and commands a pleasant view of the lake and river, as well as of the surrounding city and country. We understand that it is the intention of Dr. Pierce to erect a hotel at the cost of at least two hundred thousand dollars, where those who come to enjoy the benefit of his treatment may find all desired accommodations under one roof, instead of being scattered over the city, as at present. We are further given to understand that our architects will be invited to submit plans for the proposed structure without delay.—*Buffalo Express.*

DR, PIERCE'S FAMILY MEDICINES,

If you would patronize Medicines, scientifically prepared by a skilled Physician and Chemist, use **Dr. Pierce's Family Medicines.** Golden Medical Discovery is nutritious, tonic, alterative, or blood cleansing, and an unequaled cough remedy; Pleasant, Purgative Pellets, scarcely larger than mustard seed, constitute an agreeable and reliable physic; Favorite Perscription, a remedy for debilitated females; Extract of Smart-Weed, a magical remedy for pain, bowel complaints, and an unequaled liniment for both human and horse flesh; while his Dr. Sage's Catarrh Remedy is known the world over as the greatest specific for Catarrh and "Cold in the Head" ever given to the public,

R. V. PIERCE, M. D.,

Proprietor, BUFFALO, N. Y.

BROEZEL'S HOTEL.

JOHN BROEZEL, Prop.

This House is entirely New, and newly furnished.

Corner Seneca and Wells Streets, BUFFALO, N. Y.

The Proprietor has fitted up his new Hotel with all the most improved and modern facilities. Being only two minutes walk from the Railroad Depots, makes it the most desirable and convenient Hotel in the city. The charges are moderate, and treatment courteous.

FIRE AND MARINE INSURANCE.

ÆTNA
INSURANCE COMPANY,

OF HARTFORD, Conn.

INCORPORATED 1819.
CHARTER PERPETUAL.

L. J. HENDEE, President
J. GOODNOW, Secretary.

PAID UP CAPITAL, $3,000,000.

(Three Millions of Dollars.)

ASSETS JANUARY 1st, 1876, ... $6,792,649.98

LIABILITIES—Claims not due, and unadjusted, ... **$246,385.50**

Losses Paid in 56 Years, ... $44,000.000

The undersigned would solicit from the citizens of Buffalo and vicinity, a continuance of their confidence and patronage in the above sound and reliable company.

☞ All Losses promptly adjusted and paid at this office.

E. P. DORR, Agent.

Office in ÆTNA BUILDINGS, first floor, corner Lloyd and Prime streets.

www.ingramcontent.com/pod-product-compliance
Lightning Source LLC
LaVergne TN
LVHW011222110826
845150LV00006B/1512

* 9 7 8 1 4 2 5 5 1 5 6 4 5 *